T0323482

RISK GOVERNANCE

Biases, blind spots and bonuses (or incentives more broadly) have led to numerous risk management disasters. Risk governance is a potential solution to these problems yet is not always as effective as we would like it to be. One reason for that is the current dearth of risk governance expertise.

This book seeks to address this issue, providing:

- Understanding of the fundamental forces that cause disasters: the biases, blind spots and bonuses. This understanding is drawn from the disciplines of economics/finance and psychology;
- Explanation of the structures of risk governance and common challenges experienced in their use e.g. board risk committee, risk/compliance function, assurance function, risk appetite statement, risk disclosures;
- Thorough investigation of risk culture and its importance in risk governance, including the assessment of risk culture;
- Understanding of the mechanisms of executive compensation and how they link to risk management – one of the most difficult challenges confronting both risk and remuneration committees;
- Explanation of the risk management process (based on international standards ISO31000), including practical guidance on risk communication, analysis and treatment;
- Guidance on the management of strategic risk, emphasising the importance of scenario analysis;
- Application of these principles to cyber risk, climate risk – two pervasive risks affecting almost every organisation;
- Numerous case studies and examples drawn from various industries around the world; and
- Discussion of what has been learned about risk governance from the COVID-19 experience.

The book is an essential guide for postgraduate students; participants in professional education programs in governance and risk management; directors; senior executives; risk, compliance and assurance professionals as well as conduct and prudential regulators worldwide.

Elizabeth Sheedy is a professor and risk governance expert based in the Department of Applied Finance of Macquarie Business School. She teaches courses in the Master of Applied Finance and Global MBA programs.

Routledge Contemporary Corporate Governance

Series Editor: Thomas Clarke, *Professor of Corporate Governance, University of Technology Sydney, Australia.*

Editorial Board: Professor Bernard Taylor, *Executive Director of the Centre for Board Effectiveness, Henley Management College, UK*

Dr David Wheeler, Erivan K Haub *Professor of Business and Sustainability, Schulich School of Business, York University, Canada*

Professor Esther Solomon, *Graduate School of Business, Fordham University, New York, US*

Professor Jean-Francois Chanlat, *CREPA, Director of Executive MBA, Université Paris IX Dauphine, France*

The *Routledge Contemporary Corporate Governance* Series aims to provide an authoritative, thought-provoking and well-balanced series of textbooks in the rapidly emerging field of corporate governance. The corporate governance literature traditionally has been scattered in the finance, economics, accounting, law and management literature. However the international controversy now associated with corporate governance has focused considerable attention on this subject and raised its profile immeasurably. Government, financial institutions, corporations and academics have become deeply involved in tackling the dilemmas of corporate governance due to widespread public concerns.

The *Routledge Contemporary Corporate Governance* Series will make a significant impact in this emerging field: defining and illuminating problems; going beyond the official emphasis on regulation and procedures to understand the behaviour of executives, boards, and corporations; analysing the wider impact and relationships involved in corporate governance. Issues that will be covered in this series include:

- Exploring the impact of the globalisation of corporate governance
- Assessing ongoing contest between shareholder/stakeholder values
- Examining how corporate governance values determine corporate objectives
- Analysing how financial interests have overwhelmed corporate governance
- Investigating the discourse of corporate governance
- Considering the imperative of sustainability in corporate governance
- Addressing the contemporary crises in corporate governance and how they might be resolved.

The Rule of Culture
Corporate and State Governance in China and East Asia
Hong Hai

Risk Governance
Biases, Blind Spots and Bonuses
Elizabeth Sheedy

For more information about this series, please visit www.routledge.com/Routledge-Contemporary-Corporate-Governance/book-series/RCCG

RISK GOVERNANCE

Biases, Blind Spots and Bonuses

Elizabeth Sheedy

Routledge
Taylor & Francis Group

LONDON AND NEW YORK

First published 2021
by Routledge
2 Park Square, Milton Park, Abingdon, Oxon OX14 4RN

and by Routledge
605 Third Avenue, New York, NY 10158

Routledge is an imprint of the Taylor & Francis Group, an informa business

© 2021 Elizabeth Sheedy

British Library Cataloguing-in-Publication Data
A catalogue record for this book is available from the British Library

Library of Congress Cataloging-in-Publication Data
Names: Sheedy, Elizabeth, author.
Title: Risk governance : biases, blind spots and bonuses / Elizabeth
   Sheedy.
Description: Abingdon, Oxon ; New York, NY : Routledge, 2021. |
   Series: Routledge contemporary corporate governance | Includes
   bibliographical references and index.
Identifiers: LCCN 2020055596 (print) | LCCN 2020055597 (ebook)
Subjects: LCSH: Risk management. | Corporate governance. |
   Sustainability.
Classification: LCC HD61 .S442 2021 (print) | LCC HD61 (ebook) |
   DDC 658.15/5—dc23
LC record available at https://lccn.loc.gov/2020055596
LC ebook record available at https://lccn.loc.gov/2020055597

ISBN: 978-0-367-64266-2 (hbk)
ISBN: 978-0-367-64265-5 (pbk)
ISBN: 978-1-003-12373-6 (ebk)

Typeset in Bembo
by Apex CoVantage, LLC

Access the Support Material: www.routledge.com/9780367642655

To my parents, Ruth and Graham.

CONTENTS

FIGURES

TABLES

BIOGRAPHY

Professor Elizabeth Sheedy is a risk governance expert based in the Department of Applied Finance of Macquarie Business School. Since 2012 her research focus has been risk governance, culture and remuneration in financial institutions.

Elizabeth uses a range of research methods to build understanding of behaviour in financial services including: surveys, experiments, interviews as well as the econometric methods traditionally used by finance scholars. She has collaborated with scholars in other disciplines, including organisational psychology and experimental economics. This multi-methods, multi-disciplinary approach has produced a number of ground-breaking findings in the field, including development of the Macquarie University Risk Culture Scale. This psychometrically validated survey instrument has been found to predict a range of behaviours important in this industry.

The quality and relevance of Elizabeth's work has been enhanced through industry collaboration. She has received funding or in-kind support from the Australia and New Zealand Institute for Insurance and Finance (ANZIIF), Australian Prudential Regulation Authority (APRA), the Australian Securities and Investment Commission (ASIC), the Centre for International Finance and Regulation (CIFR), the Financial Institutions' Remuneration Group, the Financial Services Council (FSC), the Financial Services Institute (FINSIA), the Governance Risk and Compliance Institute, Insurance Council of Australia (ICA), the Institute of Internal Auditors of Australia, Mercer Australia, RSA Archer and 17 separate financial institutions.

This work has enabled Elizabeth to contribute to the policy debate on financial services misconduct, remuneration practices, enhancing financial services culture/conduct and related issues. She is a popular speaker at industry conferences and a regular media commentator.

FOREWORD

Risk is synonymous with business enterprise. In this authoritative work Professor Elizabeth Sheedy demonstrates the conceptual and historical basis of risk governance. The structures and processes for the effective governance of risk are outlined. An evidence-based understanding of risk culture is presented, together with the tools to assess risk. Issues of performance measurement, reward and accountability are examined to the extent that they may encourage excessive risk. How a better understanding of risk may be communicated is explored. The measurement of risk utilising quantitative models is fully analysed. Adaptive responses to risk are investigated, and the multiple ways of managing risk clearly set out.

The importance of a clear risk management framework is established with effective monitoring and review. The complex causes of risk governance failure are empirically examined with signal examples of risk governance failure analysed. Beyond particular instances of risk, the possibilities of strategic risk now being encountered are faced including cyber risk, pandemics and climate change. Impending generalised risks such as these present the greatest challenge to business and to all existing business operations and strategies. These strategic risks require the greatest resilience and the most intelligent and far-sighted response. As a leading international authority in the field Professor Sheedy guides the reader with expert knowledge through the minefield of risk governance.

Professor Thomas Clarke
Editor
Routledge Contemporary Corporate Governance

PREFACE

A book on risk, written during a pandemic, is inevitably a product of its time. But this book is also a product of everything I've learned and experienced in the last 40 years of professional life. I first entered the 'risk management industry' in the early 1980s, working in the treasury of CSR Limited. At the time, CSR was one of Australia's largest diversified listed companies with significant operations in the resources sector as well as sugar refining and the manufacture of building materials. What we called risk management back then amounted to making economic forecasts of what exchange rates and commodity prices would do and then choosing whether to hedge the company's massive natural exposures – or not, with forward contracts. I quickly learned that I had very limited ability to predict these rates – it was a fool's game and no way to manage risk.

From there I went on to a banking career which likewise centred around derivative contracts. We were expert at 'engineering' options, swaps, forward contracts in various configurations, to address the risk management requirements of corporate and institutional clients. Like my early days at CSR, this approach to risk management was very much focused on only one type of risk – market risk – and tended to ignore the vast range of risk treatments available. While considered cutting-edge at the time, it was a blinkered, siloed way of thinking about risk, very different from what is now considered best practice.

In 1993, I had the opportunity to start my academic career at Macquarie University in Sydney. At that time, the Master of Applied Finance was rapidly growing under the visionary leadership of Professor Bill Norton. It was the post-graduate program of choice for professionals wanting to learn about the newly deregulated financial markets and enter the rapidly growing financial services industry. So successful was this program that at various times it was offered not only in Sydney but also in Beijing, Brisbane, Hong Kong, Melbourne, Perth, Shanghai, Singapore and Tokyo. It was a remarkable opportunity to educate a generation of finance professionals in the region, taught by academics with industry experience.

At the same time I started my PhD, focused on quantitative assessment of market risk under the expert supervision of Rob Trevor. This formative experience gave me a solid appreciation for quantitative methods and their value for guiding risk management decisions. Quantitative analysis remains fundamental for understanding risk and evaluating the treatment options.

Having said that, risk governance is very much more than just quantitative risk analysis; it is the ultimate multi-disciplinary challenge. In my home discipline of economics/finance we tend to emphasise the role of incentives in driving behaviour and to highlight principal agent conflicts. Understanding of risk has now been transformed by the contribution of psychologists and the so-called behavioural biases. My thinking has been strongly influenced by the discipline of organisational psychology and I owe a particular debt to Barbara Griffin for teaching me so much, especially about culture. Our ground-breaking work in the area of risk culture is one of the things I'm most proud of in my research career.

This book is first a book for post-graduate students. After 27 years teaching in the Master of Applied Finance and 2 years teaching in the Global MBA program at Macquarie Business School, I owe my students an enormous debt. They have often challenged me with their searching questions, drawn from current industry experience. They help keep me informed of 'what's happening in the real world'. Speaking honestly, very few students come into a course on risk full of anticipation. They expect something rather technical, worthy and dull. This has inspired me to find ways of making a complex and technical topic interesting and understandable, and occasionally I've succeeded. I hope this book will provide the resource my students need and hopefully those studying in many other programs worldwide.

Second this book is for those serving in risk governance roles. We have learned a great deal about how to do risk governance better in the last 30 years. It is still, however, a very young profession. Many people in risk governance roles, whether as executives or as non-executive directors, are not as well trained as they could be. In my opinion this has contributed to some of the governance problems that have occurred. It's not sensible to think anyone could do a two-day training course on risk governance and learn enough to be effective. I hope that this book will provide a primer for professionals who find themselves in risk governance roles. While this small volume cannot cover every aspect of risk governance, I've provided many suggestions for further reading for those who need to dig deeper.

Apart from those people already mentioned there are others who have given me wonderful professional support, mentoring, opportunities and inspiration in my professional life. Special thanks to (in alphabetical order): Carol Alexander, Richard Allan, Margaret Beardow, Anne Cooper, Phil Dolan, Jay Hennock, Kevin Jameson, Sheelagh McCracken, Ralph McKay, Jonathan Rourke, Tom Smith, Lucy Taksa.

I also need to acknowledge a few insightful minds who have helped shape my thinking about risk governance: Elizabeth Arzadon, Frank Ashe, Tony Carlton, Michael Grimwade, Paul Kennedy, Pat McConnell, Roger Miles and Mike Power. It has been an honour – and mostly a pleasure – to know them all personally.

PART A
Foundations of risk governance

1

EMERGENCE OF RISK GOVERNANCE

The 2010 Deepwater Horizon incident[1] conjures images of environmental catastrophe as well as the tragic loss of 11 lives. An oil rig operating 66 km off the Louisiana coast, the Deepwater Horizon ignited and exploded after a leak of methane gas. This caused the largest ever accidental oil spill, threatening species from whale sharks to sea grass. For BP, the operator of the oil rig, the incident was also disastrous as it faced billions of dollars in fines and reputational damage.

The Dieselgate scandal engulfed Volkswagen and its subsidiaries[2] when a 'defeat device' was discovered in 2015 for deceiving US regulators. It created the false impression that the diesel vehicles complied with strict environmental standards for protecting the health of the population, crucial for those with chronic respiratory conditions. Volkswagen subsequently spent billions on vehicle rectification and fines.

In 2019, Australia's oldest bank, Westpac, was accused of 23 million breaches of anti-money laundering laws, ignoring transactions likely to be associated with child exploitation.[3] If proven, the allegations will also result in significant fines and reputational damage.

Three different scandals, all in the last decade but in different parts of the world and involving different industries. All three failures arguably could have been prevented by better governance. All three resulted in changes in the executive team, the board or both. In the Westpac case, for example, the CEO, the chairman and the chair of the board risk committee all stepped down in the weeks following the news, accepting accountability for serious failures of risk management. Importantly, the push for resignations came from the shareholder community, through institutional shareholders and proxy advisors.

These examples illustrate a worldwide phenomenon: that directors and senior executives are ultimately held responsible for risk management within their organisations. It is no longer possible to hide behind excuses of ignorance or group decision making. Directors are expected to own the organisation's risk choices, take responsibility for the risk management framework, challenge the executive in relation to risk issues and ensure that a risk culture is established. In other words, risk governance is an expected norm of modern organisations.

Some directors are outraged by what they see as unrealistic expectations or inappropriate intrusion into areas that should be the remit of the executive. But many if not most shareholders see these risk governance tasks as reasonable. From the perspective of the shareholder, often holding shares in anticipation of retirement, directors are well paid and enjoy high status for exercising independent oversight on their behalf. Directors who feel unable or unwilling to take on these responsibilities are free to leave the field; plenty of others are ready to replace them.

So how did risk governance evolve? What are the forces and societal trends that led us to this point? I will argue that risk governance can be explained by three main forces:

- An increasingly litigious and regulated society that led to the development of risk management as a discipline and profession, as organisations defended themselves against reputational damage, legal costs and fines;
- The understanding that humans are prone to poor risk management through a range of biases and blind spots;
- Incentive conflicts that cause managers, acting out of self-interest, to pay insufficient attention to longer-term risk issues that are important to most other stakeholders.

Table 1.1 highlights some of the important risk governance milestones that have both stimulated and signalled change.

1.1 Risk management and regulation

'The risk management of everything' was a term coined by accounting scholar, Professor Mike Power, documenting an explosion of interest in risk management in the late twentieth century.[4] As Power sorted through his collection of *Accountancy* magazines to prepare for a cull, he observed a change in the focus of articles. Early editions contained many articles that discussed the audit model and how it should address the risks in client business models. Over time, however, there was increasing commentary on risks to the auditor arising from the audit process, that is, the legal and reputational risks to professional partnerships that might arise from a material misstatement of results.

This focus on legal and reputational risks is not unique to audit professionals but arguably extends across all industries and business structures. The issue of occupational health and safety is a case in point, with relevant legislation and regulation emerging in developed economies from the early 1970s.[5] Safety regulations have been a fundamental cause of improved safety outcomes with fewer

TABLE 1.1 Milestones in Risk Management

1960s	• Consumer movement emerges following cases such as the ***Ford Pinto***.
1970s	• Occupational health and safety regulations proliferate.
	• Black and Scholes publish landmark paper on option theory in 1972,[6] contributing to growing use of derivatives, risk transfer mechanisms, for treating financial risk.
1980	• ***3 Mile Island*** incident in 1979 is a catalyst for concern about man-made disasters[7] and the inevitability of accidents.
	• Zohar publishes first paper on safety climate,[8] focusing on management commitment as a prerequisite.
1984	• ***Bhopal gas tragedy*** kills and injures thousands,[9] raising issues of corporate negligence and employee sabotage.
	• Perrow publishes 'Normal Accidents',[10] arguing that accidents are unavoidable in complex technological systems.
1986	• ***Chernobyl nuclear accident*** highlights numerous causal factors including flawed reactor design and poor safety culture.[11]
	• ***Space Shuttle Challenger*** disaster underscores problems in NASA's organisational culture and decision making processes.[12]
	• Institute for Risk Management, one of the first associations for risk professionals, is established in the UK.[13]
1987	• ***Black Monday October 19, 1987*** – share markets in many countries fall by more than 20% in one day. This event emphasised the evolving interconnectedness of financial markets and the need for central bank intervention.[14]
1988	• Basel Accord I announced – international regulations relating to bank capital, highlight the importance of equity capital as the last line of defence against risk.
1992	• Bankers Trust publishes 'The Risk Management Revolution', promoting the quantification of risk and the use of these risk measurements for business decisions such as determining capital needs, pricing and allocation of resources.[15]
1994	• JP Morgan publishes Value-at-Risk (VaR) methodology on the internet, influencing capital management and regulation worldwide. VaR is a measure of potential losses from speculative trading positions, at a specified confidence level. This is another milestone in the quantification of risk.
1995	• ***Barings collapse*** – arguably the most famous rogue-trader case. Nick Leeson's losses from unauthorised and concealed derivatives trades amounted to US$1.3 billion due to governance failures.[16] Internal controls, such as segregation of duties, were not present. Managers and directors provided inadequate oversight.
	• First risk management standards (AS/NZS4360) published in Australia and New Zealand.
1996	• Bernstein publishes 'Against the Gods',[17] arguing that the notion of controlling risk is one of the central ideas that distinguishes modern times from the distant past.

(Continued)

TABLE 1.1 (Continued)

	• *Asian banking crisis* starts with a range of contributing factors including rapid expansion, crony capitalism and fixed exchange rates. Many firms had too much debt. When the bubble burst, defaults exploded especially in Thailand, Indonesia and Malaysia, and a number of banks failed. Poor governance (protection for minority shareholders), allowing managerial expropriation, is cited as a contributing factor.[18]
1998	• Russian bond crisis brings down the hedge fund *Long–Term Capital Management (LTCM)*. The case illustrates the consequences of simplistic, flawed risk models to guide business decisions.[19]
1999	• Turnbull report, revised in 2005, introduces risk assessment and internal controls to corporate governance for UK listed companies.
2001	• *9/11 catastrophe* illustrates how terrorists can exploit behavioural biases (dread risks) to their advantage; brings greater focus on geopolitical risks. Dread risks are risks that produce disproportionate fear and induce sub–optimal responses. After 9/11 many people reduced air travel in favour of car travel, causing many additional and needless road deaths. Air travel remains one of the safest modes of transport given the vanishingly small probability of terrorist attack.[20]
	• *Enron bankruptcy* underscores many risk governance issues including failure of the board to understand the risks of the business, failure of auditors to uncover managerial fraud, preventing the flow of accurate information to investors.[21]
2002	• Sarbanes–Oxley Act responds to governance failures at Enron. The Act aimed to enhance the quality of financial disclosures by addressing audit quality, the quality of internal controls and impose greater responsibilities on directors serving on the audit committee. It also included enhanced whistle–blower protections and the possibility of clawback of bonuses following fraud.
	• *SARS epidemic* focuses attention on risk of infectious disease and relevant risk management practices e.g. scenario planning, business continuity planning.[22]
	• Kahneman, a pioneer in the field of behavioural biases, wins Nobel Memorial Prize in Economic Sciences for work completed in the late twentieth century.
2003	• *NAB foreign exchange option scandal*. Rogue traders caused losses of $360 million. This case was one of the first to explicitly identify culture as an underlying cause, contributing to the failure of controls in a financial institution.[23]
2004	• COSO Enterprise Risk Management (ERM) framework launched.[24] COSO defined ERM as 'a process, effected by an entity's board of directors, management and other personnel, applied in strategy setting and across the enterprise, designed to identify potential events that may affect the entity, and manage risk to be within its risk appetite, to provide reasonable assurance regarding the achievement of entity objectives'.

	• Basel II published with expanded use of internal quantitative risk models for banks in the regulation of capital for risk mitigation purposes.
2007	• OECD revises corporate governance principles, extending the responsibilities of directors in relation to risk management.[25]
	• Taleb publishes 'The Black Swan'[26] describing biases associated with low probability events. During the global financial crisis Taleb becomes one of the most strident critics of quantitative risk models.
	• *Global Financial Crisis* begins as the sub-prime mortgage market deteriorates.[27] A US housing boom, driven by securitisation and loose lending to high-risk borrowers, comes to an end when these borrowers start defaulting.
2008	• *Lehman Brothers bankruptcy* results from risky assets (financing housing and sub-prime mortgages) and excessive reliance on short-term debt; the legacy of infamous CEO Dick Fuld.[28] Many other financial institutions share the same fate or are bailed out or taken over by rivals.
2009	• International risk management standards (ISO31000) released.
2010	• *BP Deepwater Horizon* disaster. Accident analysis[29] highlights that many warning signals were missed. Poor safety culture was an underlying cause of the incident.
	• Basel Committee for Banking Supervision endorses 'Three Lines of Defence' and issues new governance principles for banks with greater emphasis on risk.
2011	• *Fukushima nuclear disaster* caused by earthquake and tsunami. Case points to governance failures; leaders failed to respond to new scientific information, well before the earthquake, about the possibility of a large tsunami wave that could affect the site.[30]
	• Kahneman publishes 'Thinking Fast and Slow' – a book for the general reader that surveys research on behavioural biases.[31]
2012	• *Bankruptcy of Eastman Kodak* heightens interest in strategic risk management, especially the effects of technological disruption.
	• *JPMorgan London Whale* incident[32] provides an example of failed risk management processes, with overconfidence as an underlying theme. A group of traders took large, speculative positions in complex derivative securities, resulting in over US$6 billion of trading losses.
	• *LIBOR-rigging* comes to light,[33] that is, the manipulation of the London Interbank Offered Rate (LIBOR) by unscrupulous traders and managers in some of the largest banks around the world. Case focuses attention on 'conduct risk' – the risk of harm to customers or competitive markets from the conduct of financial institutions or their staff.
2013	• *Salz Review of Barclays* released.[34] Details misconduct including alleged mis-selling of products to customers; manipulation of LIBOR and failure to comply with government sanctions. Criticises the board, incentive schemes and culture.
	• Financial Stability Board releases 'Thematic Review on Risk Governance'.[35] Finds evidence of improved governance at financial institutions post-crisis but more work needed in risk culture.

(Continued)

TABLE 1.1 (Continued)

2016	• **Bank of Bangladesh** case highlights cyber risk, with losses of around US$100 million. Fraudulent instructions were issued by security hackers through the SWIFT network to illegally transfer funds from an account belonging to Bangladesh Bank with the Federal Reserve Bank of New York.[36] Perpetrators, suspected to be linked to the government of North Korea, may have been assisted by insiders at Bangladesh Bank.
	• First executive accountability regulations take effect for UK banks[37]
	• **Wells Fargo scandal**[38] underscores concerns about conduct risk and incentive schemes. The firm admitted that employees had opened as many as 2 million accounts without customer authorization over a five-year period, motivated by a cross-selling incentive scheme.
2018	• International Risk Management Standard ISO31000 updated.
	• **Commonwealth Bank of Australia (CBA) Prudential Inquiry**[39] released and Australia's Royal Commission into financial services misconduct announced. The CBA accused of mis-selling of margin loans to retail customers, misconduct by financial advisers; fees for no service in financial advice; use of an outdated definition of heart attack in insurance products; anti-money laundering (AML) breaches and mis-selling of credit card insurance. Report highlights failures of executive accountability and culture of complacency.
2019	• **Climate risk** concerns escalate in a disastrous year for severe weather events including floods, fires, cyclones across all continents.[40]
2020	• **Coronavirus** pandemic highlights problems in preparing for low-frequency events with ambiguous consequences. Death, illness and economic calamity are the consequences.

deaths and serious injuries on a per worker basis. In the UK, fatalities at work have declined from 2.9 per 100,000 workers in 1974 to 0.4 per 100,000 workers in 2012–13, adjusted for economic and occupational changes.

This remarkable achievement occurred because organisations, fearing fines and other sanctions, as well as reputational damage, have changed their workplace practices. Developed economies have experienced a proliferation of laws and regulations designed to protect consumers, as well as employees. The consumer rights movement, championed by Ralph Nader in the 1960s and 1970s, was also a catalyst for new legislation. Campaigns for consumer safety were given ample ammunition following the Ford Pinto case.[41] The Pinto had serious design flaws making the vehicle likely to ignite following a rear-end collision. Internal Ford documents showed that the company considered making design changes to correct this flaw but rejected the change to preserve the vehicle's stylish appearance and reduce costs. Many were outraged that the $11 cost of the change per vehicle was considered too high, given the potential for serious injury and even death of passengers.

The reason that safety regulations are often so effective is that they transfer risk from the worker or consumer to the shareholder. In the past, consumers could incur serious physical harm from dangerous products with little or no compensation, but now the producers of these products – and ultimately their shareholders – must pay compensation and/or regulatory fines. Not surprisingly, shareholders are keen to reduce these costs as well as the consequent reputational damage. In the regulated world, reducing the risk of dangerous products is good for shareholders as much as it is good for consumers. Risk management frameworks and controls soon followed in the corporate world.

1.2 Biases and blind spots

The notorious 1979 Three Mile Island accident in a nuclear reactor sparked debate about the nature of industrial accidents. According to the World Nuclear Association website,[42] a minor malfunction in a cooling circuit caused the temperature in the coolant to rise. In about a second, the reactor automatically shut down, but a relief valve failed to close. Instrumentation did not show this, so operators were unable to diagnose or respond properly; the core suffered severe damage as a result. Some radioactive gases were released into the atmosphere. Root cause analysis revealed deficiencies in control room instrumentation and emergency response training.

The incident was a catalyst for debate about the nature of industrial accidents and whether they are preventable. Perrow's 'normal accident' theory[43] asserts that incidents of this kind are inevitable in tightly coupled, complex systems. In such systems, each part is linked to many other parts, so failure at one point in the system can quickly affect other parts, making intervention difficult. But the alternative to this pessimistic view is to consider, rather, that warning signs are almost always apparent prior to a large-scale accident, so better management can reduce their likelihood.

As explained by Hopkins,[44] although the exact sequence of events at Three Mile Island was unique, there had been previous warnings because crucial aspects of the event sequence had occurred previously. In an incident 17 months earlier, company investigators recognised the possibility of repetition and proposed 9 preventative recommendations. Senior management failed to act on these recommendations and so an important learning opportunity was missed. Rather than supporting the case that nuclear accidents are inevitable, the Three Mile Island incident prompts questions about why warning signs are so often missed. Why do managers do such a poor job at handling risk?

The answers are complex, but one very important element is the existence of behavioural biases and blind spots. Research by psychologists in the late twentieth century demonstrated that humans exhibit a number of flaws in the way they respond to information about risk. Analysis of risk requires considerable mental effort, with consideration of both the likelihood of particular events occurring and the potential impact of these events. As humans have many claims on their attention and only limited resources, we often rely on intuition, simple heuristics or rules of thumb.

As explained by Nobel prize-winner Daniel Kahneman,[45] the human brain operates in two different modes. System 1 is automatic and intuitive, requiring relatively little effort. This is the system we use when driving on an empty expressway or adding 1+1. System 2 is much more analytical and careful, requiring concentration. This is the system we use when doing a reverse park in a busy street or doing a complex calculation with pencil and paper. Thinking about risk typically requires System 2 but we too often rely on System 1, especially when we're tired and depleted, and this is when mistakes commonly occur.

An example of this is the *availability heuristic*, which helps explain why humans generally do a poor job of addressing risks with relatively low probability. Availability bias is arguably one of the leading causes of risk management failure. When people think about the likelihood of an adverse event, like a pandemic or severe storm, their concept of likelihood is shaped by the ease with which they can recall similar events occurring. The more frequently an event occurs, the more likely that salient examples will come to mind. If people have not had any recent, impactful experience of such an occurrence, they are prone to underestimate the risk. Underestimation leads to undermanagement.

The 2020 COVID-19 pandemic provides an excellent example of this phenomenon. Mercifully, pandemics are not everyday events, but there were three pandemics during the twentieth century (Spanish flu of 1918, Asian flu of 1957 and the Hong Kong flu of 1968). More recently, the avian flu scare of the early 2000s raised many concerns about the risks of another global pandemic. In May 2006, the European Actuarial Consultative Group[46] suggested that the probability of a pandemic in the following 10 years was more than 50%. In his well-circulated TED talk of 2015, watched by millions, Bill Gates[47] urged the world to prepare for the inevitable.

Despite these warnings, many organisations and governments were caught flat-footed by the pandemic, referring to it as a 'black swan' event. The term 'black swan' comes about because, before coming to Australia, Europeans thought all swans were white. Much as we now say 'pigs will fly', Europeans in the early eighteenth century used to say 'swans are black'. In other words, something completely at odds with empirical experience and therefore unpredictable. But as mentioned previously, the occurrence of a pandemic was highly predictable based on past experience, more a question of 'when' rather than 'if'. The term 'black swan' seems inappropriate and more indicative of management failure due to availability bias.

Consider the Global Risk Report, produced each year by the World Economic Forum. The 2020 Global Risk Report[48] reports on a survey conducted in September and October 2019 of the Forum's network of business, government and other leaders. For the first time in the report's fifteen-year history, the top five global risks by likelihood were considered to be environmental: extreme weather, climate action failure, natural disasters, biodiversity loss and human-made environmental disasters. Three of these, climate change failure, extreme weather and biodiversity loss, also appeared in the top five global risks by impact, joined by water crises (clearly related to the environment) and weapons of mass destruction. Notably, the risk of pandemic, arguably the greatest risk that eventuated in 2020, was not high on the agenda of the experts surveyed in late 2019.

According to the availability bias, this is not surprising since infectious diseases and pandemics did not occur in the years immediately leading up to the survey; pandemic risk was not top of mind. The risk of pandemic or infectious diseases was, however, considered a 'top 5' global risk by impact in the reports published in each of 2007, 2008 and 2015, using survey data from 2007, 2007 and 2014. The 2006 and 2007 surveys are likely to have been influenced by the avian flu scares at that time, while the 2014 survey was conducted in the context of the Ebola crisis. Clearly our thinking about risk depends on recent experience, meaning that important risks are often underestimated and undermanaged.

Availability bias is likely to be related to other human biases: overconfidence and optimism. Optimism bias[49] is the tendency to think that while adverse events may happen to others, we are immune. It helps explain the planning fallacy,[50] whereby people tend to underestimate how long projects will take to complete and how much they will cost. This is because they ignore or underestimate risk; that is, they underestimate the possibility of problems they will encounter along the way, which will both create delays and add to costs.

Overconfidence in ability is reflected in the fact that 90% of people consider themselves to be above-average drivers. The implication is that people may be overconfident in their ability to manage a bad outcome, just as an expert driver may be better able to handle poor road conditions. The consequence of misplaced confidence is that individuals do not do enough to prevent or avoid the bad outcomes.

Many people are also overconfident in their knowledge – they know less than they believe they know. This problem can be demonstrated with trivia tests where respondents are asked to specify a range such that they are 90% confident that the correct answer lies within it. For example, if asked for the year of birth

TABLE 1.2 Overconfidence Test

	Low Guess	High Guess
1. How old was Martin Luther King when he died?		
2. How long, in kilometres, is the Nile River?		
3. How many countries are there in OPEC?		
4. How many books are there in the Old Testament of the Bible?		
5. What is the diameter of the moon in kilometres?		
6. What is the weight of an empty Boeing 747 in kilograms?		
7. In what year was Wolfgang Amadeus Mozart born?		
8. How long, in days, is the gestation period (from conception to birth) of an Asian elephant?		
9. What is the air distance, in kilometres, from London to Singapore?		
10. How deep is the deepest known point in the ocean in kilometres?		

of Queen Elizabeth II, a respondent might give the range 1900–1950. (The correct answer is 1926.)

The following questions, adapted from Russo and Schoemaker[51] illustrate the concept. Solutions may be found at the end of the chapter. Complete the test in Table 1.2 to gauge how overconfident you are.

Once you have completed the table, check the solutions in Table 1.3, at the end of this chapter, and identify all those cases where the solution lay within the range you gave. Since the range was defined with 90% confidence, the solution should be within your range in 9 of the 10 cases. Most people end up with a score between 4 and 7. Too often, people set the range much too narrowly, demonstrating overconfidence in their knowledge. The exercise demonstrates that people are too often surprised by unexpected outcomes. Adverse outcomes come along much more often than people expect, so they are often unprepared for them.

1.3 Timing and incentives

No discussion of risk can occur without considering the time dimension and incentives. In risk analysis we invariably consider a range of possible future states of the world, with different outcomes, some less favourable than others. Treating those risks often involves taking steps now to change those future states or make some states of the world more or less likely. For example, the management at Ford considered but rejected changes to the design of the Pinto to reduce the likelihood of future car fires. In this example, like many others, there is a short-term cost to avoid a future problem, just as investors must give up consumption now in order to obtain a long-term benefit.

In the field of finance, the lowliest undergraduate should understand the 'time value of money' – the fact that a dollar in the future is valued less than a dollar today. But people routinely discount future outcomes far more than can be explained by standard economic models; they engage in 'hyperbolic discounting'.[52] A psychologist[53] would say that this temporal discounting occurs because we feel less connected to our future selves than to our current selves; the present is more salient than the future and dominates our thinking. The bias to overemphasise the short-term, at the expense of the future, could even be considered another outworking of the availability bias. It is sometimes referred to as myopia bias and explains why many people have difficulty incurring short-term costs for long-term gain.

A primary consideration in governance is how to manage incentive conflicts between stakeholder groups, especially owners (shareholders) and managers. Owners appoint managers to act in their interests, but there is a danger that managers will act out of self-interest to the detriment of the owners. Examples include shirking duties, empire building, taking excessive perquisites and entrenchment. But an often-neglected conflict is in the different attitudes that stakeholder groups have to time and risk.

Managerial short-termism, relative to the interests of other stakeholder groups, is one of the largest impediments to risk management, as illustrated by many of the risk management case studies. Managers tend to be unduly focused on short-term performance, to the detriment of longer-term outcomes that concern shareholders. Skimping now on measures to eliminate a possible future disaster means that short-term performance is boosted, resulting in higher status and maybe even a cash bonus. The long-term benefit is heavily discounted by the manager because a) the benefit exists in the future and b) the extent of the benefit is uncertain and c) he or she may not even be around to share in those benefits should they emerge. Short-term thinking or managerial myopia obstructs effective risk management that would be a benefit to many stakeholders, especially to those shareholders with a long-term focus. The rise of pension funds, managing retirement savings for the aging of populations of the developed world, means that a significant portion of shareholders do care about long-term outcomes.

The discount rate that we apply when thinking about future outcomes depends on how certain the future outcomes are. The greater the uncertainty regarding future outcomes, the larger the discount rate that is used; this is down to risk aversion. Discount rates increase when there are 'known unknowns' – situations where we have a good sense of the range of possible outcomes and their probability, like a bet on a roulette wheel. An even larger discount applies to the case where the outcomes are ambiguous – the 'unknown unknowns'. In these cases we don't have a clear idea of what all the possible outcomes are, or their probabilities, so temporal discounting is even greater. This is known as ambiguity aversion.

During 2018, the Australian Royal Commission into Misconduct in Banking, Financial Services and Superannuation[54] examined numerous cases that illustrate this phenomenon. One case involved the sale of credit card insurance to customers for whom the product was clearly unsuitable. Under the terms and conditions, customers who were unemployed or students were ineligible ever to claim on the insurance. Despite this, some bankers promoted the product to these groups, in some cases even lying to prospective customers about the possibility of claiming. The bankers were able to boost short-term profits – and their own status and remuneration – despite the risk that at some point in the future customers would realise the product was unsuitable and complain. This might then cause regulators to become involved and impose penalties, creating reputational damage both to their organisations and themselves as individuals.

We can explain this behaviour with managerial short-termism. For the bankers it's likely that longer-term considerations lack salience, especially considering that many customers are disengaged from financial services and lack financial literacy; they rarely complain or change their financial institution. In addition, regulators are sometimes slow to act and penalties range from severe to immaterial. Given all of the uncertainties surrounding the long-term outcomes and the possibility that the banker may have moved elsewhere by the time these outcomes emerge, it's easy to see how managerial myopia contributes to such scandals. Indeed, the Commissioner concluded as follows:

> One simple, but telling, observation informs those inquiries. *All the conduct identified and criticised in this report was conduct that provided a financial benefit to the individuals and entities concerned.* If there are exceptions, they are immaterial. For individuals, the conduct resulted in being paid more. For entities, the conduct resulted in greater profit.
>
> *Financial Services Royal Commission 2018, p. 301, emphasis added*

This example is notable for three things: the long time delay in adverse consequences, ambiguity about the exact nature of these adverse consequences and short-term managerial incentives. This combination of issues, relevant to many risks, notably climate risk, means that managers are prone to heavily discount the future. Short-term focus creates a chronic tendency to undermanage these risks with their ambiguous but potentially serious long-term consequences.

1.4 Financial institutions as risk governance catalysts

The previous sections have argued that risk governance can be explained by:

- An increasingly litigious and regulated society;
- The understanding that humans are prone to poor risk management through a range of biases and blind spots;
- Incentive conflicts that cause managers to pay insufficient attention to longer-term risk issues.

These issues are writ large in the financial services industry, and therefore the industry has often been at the forefront of developments in risk management and governance. As Table 1.1 shows, many of the most notorious risk cases involve financial institutions and markets e.g. the 1987 stock market crash, Barings, Asian banking crisis, LTCM, NAB foreign exchange options scandal, Lehman Brothers, JP Morgan, Barclays and the broader LIBOR-rigging scandal, Wells Fargo and Commonwealth Bank of Australia. Over and again, financial institutions fall foul of behavioural biases such as overconfidence; poorly designed incentives cause excessive risk-taking and misconduct.

It is therefore not surprising that the financial services industry is one of the most highly regulated. A failed bank has disastrous consequences for its depositors, many of whom are unable to make sophisticated risk assessments. In addition, the failure of one bank can cause repercussions for other financial institutions due to the interconnectedness of the global financial system. Multiple failures can threaten the stability of the entire global economy, as was illustrated in the crisis of 2007–09.

Another reason for the risk focus in financial institutions is the fact that they play a key role in the transference of risk. Many individuals and organisations manage their risks by taking out insurance contracts. Insurance companies are willing to assume these risks for a fee, relying on techniques such as risk pooling. Financial institutions are also active in the market for derivatives, which are also contracts for transferring risks between parties. These activities have allowed financial institutions to build up expertise in understanding and quantifying risks, expertise that exploded with the rapid uptake of derivatives markets.

International regulations from the Basel Committee on Banking Supervision focus on capital adequacy, that is the proportion of equity capital relative to the size and riskiness of total assets. Insolvency occurs when the value of assets falls below the value of debts, such that it is no longer possible to meet obligations to creditors. The greater the reliance on equity capital, as opposed to debt capital, the greater the capacity of the bank to withstand unexpected events and continue operating. Equity capital is considered the last line of defence against insolvency, so regulations dictate the minimum acceptable ratio of equity capital to total assets.

From the 1990s financial institutions developed quantitative risk models with J. P. Morgan and Bankers' Trust being trailblazers (see Table 1.1 for detail). The so-called Risk Management Revolution, built on the skills developed for pricing derivative contracts, created quantitative risk measurements for determining capital needs, as well as for pricing and allocation of resources. The quantitative risk models were even incorporated into the Basel II regulatory capital requirements, although subject to regulatory scrutiny and disclosure requirements. By the 2000s, banks were not only quantifying risk from their loan portfolios (credit risk) and their trading portfolios (market risk) but they were also quantifying operational risks such as fraud and execution errors.

But as early as 1998, there were some misgivings about risk quantification. The LTCM case illustrated the perils of flawed risk models. These misgivings only grew during the crisis of the mid-2000s when numerous financial institutions were found to have inadequate capital. In some cases the quantitative models had understated the true risk, causing institutions to have insufficient capital buffers.

One of the biggest problems associated with quantitative models of any sort is that they can encourage uncritical acceptance of the signals produced by the model. You may have come across the 'Death by GPS' phenomenon whereby people have become lost, leading to injury and even death, when using a GPS.[55] In remote locations people can be overly reliant on the satnav, rather than paying attention to road signs, barriers and the terrain itself. This kind of uncritical acceptance of models is a failure of common sense. In an ideal world, people use quantitative models and satnav systems as a decision tool. Using a model critically, with an awareness of its underlying assumptions and the 'terrain' being traversed, is the key to success. Discarding quantitative risk models altogether is not an appealing alternative, given the tendency for poor risk decision making due to the behavioural biases. The ideal is to use models that encourage thoughtful engagement, that invoke System 2 thinking and encourage the users to combine judgement with the quantitative tools.

The crisis of the mid-2000s stimulated soul searching not just about the uncritical use of models. It revealed a malaise in the governance of financial institutions. The US inquiry[56] into the financial crisis concluded that 'dramatic failures of corporate governance and risk management at many systemically important financial institutions were a key cause of this crisis. . . . Too many of these institutions acted recklessly, taking on too much risk, with too little capital, and with too much dependence on short-term funding'.

This finding was a catalyst for significant governance reforms and enhanced regulatory requirements for financial institutions in relation to risk governance. The work of the Basel Committee and the Financial Stability Board (see Table 1.1) was a guide for national reforms in many jurisdictions. The case for governance reform was further strengthened by the post-crisis scandals involving LIBOR-rigging, Barclays, J. P. Morgan, Wells Fargo and the Commonwealth Bank of Australia (see Table 1.1). Many of the financial institutions had weathered the earlier crisis, only to find themselves embroiled in conduct scandals that suggested risk governance was far from adequate. Arguably the earlier success may have contributed to a sense of complacency and overconfidence that undermined risk governance structures.

The decade of the 2010s also saw a new risk emerge as significant for the industry: cyber risk, as illustrated by the 2016 Bank of Bangladesh cyber-heist. Once again, the rigour and managerial oversight applied to financial risk management had not consistently flowed through to non-financial risks. In an attempt to address failures in the management of operational, compliance and conduct risks, new regulations with regard to executive accountability were implemented for UK banks in 2016.

Financial services has often been the petri dish for experiments in risk governance and related regulation. But the trends observed in this industry often flow through to others; risk governance reforms have now extended much more broadly. In 2015 the OECD produced new governance principles for all industries and jurisdictions, incorporating learning from the crisis. Specifically, the OECD further clarified director responsibilities for reviewing and guiding risk management procedures and for ensuring the integrity of risk management systems.[57] Numerous countries have now adopted risk governance principles into listing requirements and national governance codes.

According to the OECD,[58] the most rapid uptake in risk governance occurred after the financial crisis as practices developed in the finance industry spread more broadly. As of 2019, 87% of jurisdictions now have either laws, regulations or codes relating to the board's responsibilities in risk management. Of all jurisdictions, 90% require or recommend an enterprise-wide internal control and risk management system. More than half (57%) of jurisdictions now mandate either a separate risk committee or that the audit committee must address risk management.

1.5 Conclusion

One of the strongest imperatives driving the risk governance agenda is the realisation that risk management is not an activity that comes naturally to humans. There is a range of behavioural biases and blind spots that regularly impede our ability to succeed in this domain, despite its obvious importance. The incentive conflicts that are inherent in many large organisations are also problematic for risk management. Managerial short-termism is fundamentally at odds with the longer-term interests of most shareholders and other stakeholders. Numerous cases mentioned in this chapter provide evidence for this.

Risk governance reforms are designed to resolve or at least mitigate these problems. Can risk governance achieve this challenging objective?

TABLE 1.3 Solutions

Solutions to Overconfidence Quiz	
1. How old was Martin Luther King when he died?	39
2. How long, in kilometres, is the Nile River?	6,650 km
3. How many countries are there in OPEC?	15 (as of 2020)
4. How many books are there in the Old Testament of the Bible?	39
5. What is the diameter of the moon in kilometres?	3,474 km
6. What is the weight of an empty Boeing 747 in kilograms?	183,500 kg
7. In what year was Wolfgang Amadeus Mozart born?	1756
8. How long, in days, is the gestation period (from conception to birth) of an Asian elephant?	617
9. What is the air distance, in kilometres, from London to Singapore?	10,880 km
10. How deep is the deepest known point in the ocean in kilometres?	10.9 km

Notes

1 Allen, Katie. (2016, September 12). Everyone loses out when corporate governance falls by the wayside, *The Guardian*. Available at www.theguardian.com/business/2016/sep/11/corporate-governance-deepwater-horizon-shareholders
2 Elson, Charles M., Ferrere, Craig, & Goossen, Nicholas J. (2015, November 25). The bug at Volkswagen: Lessons in co-determination, ownership, and board structure. *Journal of Applied Corporate Finance*, 27(4). Available at SSRN: https://ssrn.com/abstract=2737544
3 Frost, J., & Eyres, J. (2019, November 26). Westpac CEO, Chairman to step down, *Australian Financial Review*.
4 Power, M. (2004). *The risk management of everything: Rethinking the politics of uncertainty*. Demos.
5 Esbester, M. (2014). *The health and safety at work act, 40 years on*. Available at www.historyandpolicy.org/opinion-articles/articles/the-health-and-safety-at-work-act-40-years-on
6 Black, F., & Scholes, M. (1973). The pricing of options and corporate liabilities. *Journal of Political Economy*, 81(3), 637–654.
7 Hopkins, A. (2001). Was three mile island a 'normal accident'? *Journal of Contingencies and Crisis Management*, 9(2), 65–72.
8 Zohar, D. (1980). Safety climate in industrial organizations: Theoretical and applied implications. *Journal of Applied Psychology*, 65(1), 96.
9 Mishra, P., Samarth, R., Pathak, N., Jain, S., Banerjee, S., & Maudar, K. (2009). Bhopal gas tragedy: Review of clinical and experimental findings after 25 years. *International Journal of Occupational Medicine and Environmental Health*, 22(3), 193–202.
10 Perrow, C. (1984). *Normal accidents: Living with high risk technologies-Updated edition*. Princeton University Press.
11 International Nuclear Safety Advisory Group. INSAG-7 The Chernobyl accident: Updating INSAG-1. Accessed from www-pub.iaea.org/MTCD/publications/PDF/Pub913e_web.pdf
12 Esser, J. K., & Lindoerfer, J. S. (1989). Groupthink and the space shuttle Challenger accident: Toward a quantitative case analysis. *Journal of Behavioral Decision Making*, 2(3), 167–177.
13 www.theirm.org/
14 Bernhardt, D., & Eckblad, M. (2013). Stock market crash of 1987. *Federal Reserve History*. Available at https://www.federalreservehistory.org/essays/stock-market-crash-of-1987
15 Guill, G. D. (2016). Bankers trust and the birth of modern risk management. *Journal of Applied Corporate Finance*, 28(1), 19–29.
16 Hogan, W. P. (1997). Corporate governance: Lessons from Barings. *Abacus*, 33(1), 26–48.
17 Bernstein, P. (1996). *Against the gods: The remarkable story of risk*. John Wiley & Sons
18 Johnson, S., Boone, P., Breach, A., & Friedman, E. (2000). Corporate governance in the Asian financial crisis. *Journal of Financial Economics*, 58(1–2), 141–186.
19 Jorion, P. (2000). Risk management lessons from long-term capital management. *European Financial Management*, 6(3), 277–300.
20 Gigerenzer, G. (2006). Out of the frying pan into the fire: Behavioral reactions to terrorist attacks. *Risk Analysis: An International Journal*, 26(2), 347–351.
21 Vinten, G. (2002). The corporate governance lessons of Enron. *Corporate Governance: The International Journal of Business in Society*, 2(4), 4–9.
22 Tan, W. J., & Enderwick, P. (2006). Managing threats in the global era: The impact and response to SARS. *Thunderbird International Business Review*, 48(4), 515–536.
23 Australian Prudential Regulation Authority. (2004). *Report into irregular option trading activity at the National Australia Bank*.
24 COSO is the Committee of Sponsoring Organisations, established in 1985, to address the issue of fraudulent financial reporting. The ERM framework is available at: www.coso.org/Pages/erm-integratedframework.aspx
25 OECD. (2004). *Principles of corporate governance*. Available at www.oecd.org/corporate/ca/corporategovernanceprinciples/31557724.pdf

26 Taleb, N. (2007). *The black swan: The impact of the highly improbable.* Random House.
27 Brunnermeier, M. K. (2009). Deciphering the liquidity and credit crunch 2007–2008. *Journal of Economic Perspectives, 23*(1), 77–100.
28 Wiggins, Rosalind, Piontek, Thomas, & Metrick, Andrew. (2014, October 1). The Lehman Brothers bankruptcy A: Overview. Yale Program on Financial Stability Case Study 2014–3A-V1. Available at SSRN: https://ssrn.com/abstract=2588531 or http://dx.doi.org/10.2139/ssrn.2588531
29 National Commission on the BP Deepwater Horizon Oil Spill and Offshore Drilling. Report to the President. Available at www.govinfo.gov/content/pkg/GPO-OILCOM-MISSION/pdf/GPO-OILCOMMISSION.pdf
30 World Nuclear Association report into the Fukushima Daiichi accident. Available at www.world-nuclear.org/information-library/safety-and-security/safety-of-plants/fukushima-daiichi-accident.aspx
31 Kahneman, D. (2011). *Thinking, fast and slow.* Macmillan.
32 McConnell, P. J. (2014). Dissecting the JPMorgan whale: A post-mortem. *Journal of Operational Risk, 9*(2).
33 McConnell, P. (2013). Systemic operational risk: The LIBOR manipulation scandal. *Journal of Operational Risk, 8*(3), 59–99.
34 Salz. (2013). *Salz review: An independent review of Barclays' business practices.* Available at https://online.wsj.com/public/resources/documents/SalzReview04032013.pdf
35 Financial Stability Board. (2013). *Thematic review on risk governance.* Available at www.fsb.org/wp-content/uploads/r_130212.pdf
36 KPMG. (2016). *Bangladesh hack highlights increasing sophistication of attacks.* Available at https://assets.kpmg/content/dam/kpmg/xx/pdf/2016/08/swift-it.pdf
37 Allen, T. (2018). Strengthening the link between seniority and accountability: The senior managers and certification regime. *Bank of England Quarterly Bulletin, 58*(3), 1–10.
38 Tayan, B. (2019, January 8). The Wells Fargo cross-selling scandal. *Rock Center for Corporate Governance at Stanford University Closer Look Series: Topics, Issues and Controversies in Corporate Governance No. CGRP-62 Version, 2,* Stanford University Graduate School of Business Research Paper No. 17–1, Available at SSRN: https://ssrn.com/abstract=2879102
39 Australian Prudential Regulation Autority. (2018). *Prudential inquiry into the Commonwealth Bank of Australia.* Available at www.apra.gov.au/sites/default/files/CBA-Prudential-Inquiry_Final-Report_30042018.pdf
40 Christian Aid. (2019). *Counting the cost: 2019 a year of climate breakdown.* Available at www.christianaid.org.uk/sites/default/files/2019-12/Counting-the-cost-2019-report-embargoed-27Dec19.pdf
41 Leggett, C. (1999). The Ford Pinto case: The valuation of life as it applies to the negligence-efficiency argument. *Law and Valuation,* Spring. Available at https://users.wfu.edu/palmitar/Law&Valuation/Papers/1999/Leggett-pinto.html
42 World Nuclear Association. (2020). *Three mile island accident.* Available at www.world-nuclear.org/information-library/safety-and-security/safety-of-plants/three-mile-island-accident.aspx
43 Perrow, C. (1982). The president's commission and the normal accident. In D. Sils, C. Wolf, & V. Shelanski (Eds.), *Accident at three mile island: The human dimensions* (pp. 173–184). Westview, Boulder.
44 Hopkins, A. (2001). Was three mile island a 'normal accident'? *Journal of Contingencies and Crisis Management, 9*(2), 65–72.
45 Kahneman, D. (2011). *Thinking, fast and slow.* Macmillan.
46 European Actuarial Consultative Group. (2006). *Actuarial reflections on pandemic risk and its consequences.* Available at https://actuary.eu/documents/pandemics_web.pdf
47 Gates, W. (2015). The next outbreak: we're not ready. *TED Talk.* Available at www.ted.com/talks/bill_gates_the_next_outbreak_we_re_not_ready?language=en
48 World Economic Forum. *Global Risk Report 2020.* Available at www3.weforum.org/docs/WEF_Global_Risk_Report_2020.pdf

49 See discussion of optimism in Chapter 24 of Kahneman, D. (2011). *Thinking, fast and slow*. Macmillan and also in Chapter 4 of Meyer, R., & Kunreuther, H. (2017). *The ostrich paradox: Why we underprepare for disasters*. Wharton School Press.

50 See discussion of the planning fallacy in Chapter 23 of Kahneman, D. (2011). *Thinking, fast and slow*. Macmillan.

51 Russo, J. E., Schoemaker, P. J., & Russo, E. J. (1989). *Decision traps: Ten barriers to brilliant decision-making and how to overcome them*. New York, NY: Doubleday/Currency.

52 See discussion of myopia bias in Chapter 2 of Meyer, R., & Kunreuther, H. (2017). *The ostrich paradox: Why we underprepare for disasters*. Wharton School Press.

53 Bartels, D. M., & Rips, L. J. (2010). Psychological connectedness and intertemporal choice. *Journal of Experimental Psychology: General, 139*, 49–69.

54 Financial Services Royal Commission. *2018, Interim Report*, Volume 1. Available at https://financialservices.royalcommission.gov.au/Pages/reports.aspx#interim

55 The Guardian. (2016). *Death by GPS*. Available at www.theguardian.com/technology/2016/jun/25/gps-horror-stories-driving-satnav-greg-milner

56 The Financial Crisis Inquiry Report: Final Report of the National Commission on the Causes of the Financial and Economic Crisis in the United States. Available at https://fraser.stlouisfed.org/title/financial-crisis-inquiry-report-5034

57 OECD. *Principles for corporate governance*, Section VI, available at www.oecd.org/corporate/principles-corporate-governance/

58 OECD. (2019). *Corporate governance factbook*. Available at www.oecd.org/corporate/corporate-governance-factbook.htm

2

STRUCTURES OF RISK GOVERNANCE

Chapter 1 explored the trends that have led to risk governance: regulation, behavioural biases and incentive conflicts. Behavioural biases and incentive conflicts are powerful forces that help explain why so many organisations struggle to manage risk effectively. Regulation has gone some way to tempering these forces but arguably is not sufficient on its own. The continued appearance of risk management failures across multiple regulated industries demonstrates this.

Psychologists such as Kahneman have argued that behavioural biases are fundamentally difficult to address. Over millennia our brains may evolve to better handle risk, but this is clearly not a short-term solution. One of the reasons behavioural biases are difficult to resolve is that they come from our flawed intuition, our lazy yet quick 'System 1' thinking that is prone to decision errors. These biases are very difficult to observe in oneself, especially when incentives act to support the biases.

Risk governance is a potential solution to these problems. Risk governance is the system of rules and relationships in an organisation that support decisions and oversight relating to risk. One crucial principle of risk governance is the involvement of multiple individuals or teams who are independent of one another. A second, independent pair of eyes is much more likely to identify decision errors that may be the result of biases, incentive conflicts or a combination of both. The risk governance system also slows down the decision-making process. While this can be frustrating, the benefit is that it creates more space for System 2 thinking – thinking that is deliberate, analytical and less error-prone.

This chapter examines the formal structural elements that are useful for effective risk governance, such as board committees, specialist risk functions and the like. It will explain what is known in the academic literature about the efficacy of these structures, and it will also discuss some of the challenges that have emerged in the implementation, including finding suitable directors to serve on risk committees.

2.1 Defining risk and risk management

Before proceeding, it's important to clearly define what is meant by risk and risk management. Under international risk management standards, risk is defined as *'the effect of uncertainty on objectives'*.[1] Notice that this definition differs from statistical definitions of risk such as range or variance,[2] which focus on the range of outcomes and variation around the expected outcome respectively. Here the business or organisational context is paramount for guiding our thinking.

BOX 2.1 WHY RISK DEFINITIONS MATTER

Assume you are flying in an aeroplane at 2,000 metres when all the engines fail. You are offered a parachute and given a choice. Option 1 is to jump with the parachute; option 2 is to jump without the parachute. Which option is most risky?

The answer depends on your definition! If you select Option 1 and jump with the parachute, then that is very risky under statistical definitions. You could make a perfect landing and walk away unscathed. You might twist your ankle or break a leg on landing. Or the parachute might be faulty in which case you will die. So, we have a wide range of alternative outcomes, signifying lots of risk under the traditional statistical definitions. But if you select Option 2 and jump without the parachute, then you will certainly die. Under the statistical definitions, this is a low risk alternative, even though it's clearly undesirable.

What if we switch definitions? Assuming that our objective is to survive, then Option 1 is the only possible solution because it provides a path to survival, despite the uncertainties involved. It is low risk in the sense that it maximises the chances of achieving objectives. This example shows why defining risk in terms of objectives makes sense.

Risk management refers to activities that direct and control an organisation in terms of risk, including the identification, analysis, treatment and monitoring of risk. Most importantly, risk management does not necessarily mean eliminating risk; it is not always or even typically a defensive activity. Indeed, risk-taking is essential and even desirable in many business contexts, especially when the risks are understood and where the expected return for bearing risk is acceptable. Under international risk management standards, ISO31000,[3] the goal of risk management is the creation and protection of value. Done properly, risk management can encourage rather than suppress innovation; it supports the achievement of objectives.

In a start-up, for example, the objective might be to get a new product to market in a given timeframe. The biggest risk might be running out of funds before this can be achieved. In this context risk management would likely focus on trying to identify the possible problems that might stand in the way of getting the new product to market, then finding ways to reduce their likelihood and mitigate their impact. For example, it might involve setting up contingency plans for raising more funds if certain adverse events occur. But the risk management focus is on achieving a successful launch, not on preventing it from occurring. In other words, risk management should be an enabler for success, not a drag on performance.

2.2 The role of the board of directors

Scholars of governance identify four fundamental board responsibilities:[4] formulating strategy, policy making, supervising executive activities and providing accountability to shareholders and other relevant stakeholders. Risk is relevant to all these activities as explained in the following sections.

2.2.1 Risk appetite and strategy

Strategic direction and risk appetite are fundamentally linked, such that it is impossible to discuss one without the other. Indeed, risk appetite can be defined as the degree of risk an organisation is prepared to accept in the pursuit of its strategic objectives and business plan. The definition of risk, the effect of uncertainty on objectives, highlights the strategic importance of risk. Strategy and risk appetite should therefore be developed concurrently, with one informing the other. In practice this task is often an iterative process, with both the executive and directors contributing. But ultimately both strategy and risk appetite must be approved by the board of directors.

2.2.2 Risk framework and policy

Turning strategy and risk appetite into reality relies on policy making. The board must approve the risk management framework established by executives, including all policies relating to risk. Relatedly, the board has ultimate responsibility for the organisation's compliance with external laws and regulations. Therefore, the board must ensure that systems and processes are in place and adequately resourced to identify, analyse, treat and monitor all material risks and support compliance. The board must also ensure that controls and other mitigants are present and effective and that systems for oversight and assurance are present and effective.

2.2.3 Supervising the executive

Supervision in relation to risk is vital yet highly problematic. This is partly because of the behavioural biases that plague risk management, including overconfidence and groupthink. Another challenge relates to the fact that many risks are not apparent in the short term; adverse consequences of operating plans may only become apparent in the long term. Some risks, like climate risk and cyber risk, are evolving over time, with significant ambiguity relating to both timing and impact. Add to this the fact that many risk management strategies, like purchasing insurance or investing in controls, produce short-term costs with benefits experienced only in the long-term. In a world where executives are often rewarded based on short-term performance, there is an inherent bias for executives to understate risk and underinvest in risk treatment. Clearly this can be harmful to shareholders and other stakeholders. Directors have sought to address these issues through a variety of means, including implementation of the 'three lines model' [Section 2.7] and modifying performance measurement and reward systems.

2.2.4 Risk accountability

> 'Success has many fathers while failure is an orphan'[5]

Following from the previous sections, risk accountability has proven to be one of the most significant challenges for boards. When an organisation fails to meet its objectives, executives often hide behind ignorance and group decision-making processes, despite the disastrous consequences experienced by shareholders, customers, employees and society more broadly. Too often there are no negative consequences, such as loss of incentives, for executives who fail to deliver on their accountabilities.

Another common strategy employed by executives is to blame failure on 'black swan events', implying that failure was caused by some entirely unpredictable and unforeseeable event. But in many cases this is far from true. For example, a serious world-wide pandemic was predicted by many experts in the early 2000s and 2010s, yet many claimed to be surprised by the COVID-19 pandemic.[6] Arguably it is the job of senior executives, especially in large organisations, to consider a wide range of possible future challenges and to be prepared for them. Surprisingly few firms listed pandemics as a concern in their market risk disclosures prior to 2020.

2.3 Board risk committee

A board risk committee is essential in risk governance, although in some organisations one board committee oversees risk in combination with audit and compliance. In either case, the board risk committee acts as an advisory committee to the main board. It allows a subset of directors to have a greater risk focus, reducing the burden on the board as a whole. Risk issues are discussed in detail within the committee before going to the main board.

The work of the committee means that the full board can have focused and informed board discussions on risk-related matters. This squarely places risk on the board agenda and helps ensure that adequate board time is allocated to risk issues. Importantly the full board retains ultimate accountability for the organisation's principal risks and for the overall effectiveness of risk management.

Risk committees should be comprised of independent directors and certainly chaired by an independent director, since the committee must be in a position to challenge the executive where necessary. Careful thought must be given to ensuring that the committee has an appropriate balance of skills, cognitive diversity and relevant expertise to discharge its duties, with the support of external expert advice as necessary. The committee should provide an environment that encourages constructive debate when performing its work.

The Risk Coalition[7] proposes a number of other principles for the board risk committee:

- **'Risk strategy and risk appetite**. The board risk committee should provide the board with advice on the continued appropriateness of the board-set risk strategy and risk appetite in light of the organisation's stated purpose, values, risk culture expectations, corporate strategy and strategic objectives.
- **Principal risks and continued viability**. The board risk committee should assess and advise the board on the organisation's principal and emerging risks and how these may affect the likely achievement of the organisation's strategic objectives and continued viability of its business model.
- **Risk management and internal control systems**. The board risk committee should monitor and periodically advise the board on the overall effectiveness of the organisation's risk management and internal control systems.
- **Risk information and reporting**. The board risk committee should assess and advise the board on the quality and appropriateness of the organisation's risk information and reporting.
- **Risk culture and remuneration**. The board risk committee should consider and periodically report to the board as to whether the organisation's purpose, values and board-approved risk culture expectations are appropriately embedded in the organisation's risk strategy and risk appetite, and are reflected in observed behaviours and decisions.
- **Chief risk officer and risk function independence and objectivity**. The board risk committee should safeguard the independence and objectivity, and oversee the performance, of the chief risk officer and the second line risk function'.

One of the most difficult challenges for many boards is to find suitably qualified directors to serve on the risk committee. Since the risk profession is young, there is a lack of experienced senior risk executives ready to take on board roles. For this reason, a tailored continuing professional education program for board risk committee members is essential. The attributes of a good risk director include:

- Knowledge of the organisation and its risks, likely gained through experience in the industry or other similar organisations;
- Expertise in risk management, including the ability to interpret risk reports that may have a statistical or quantitative element;
- Independent mindset, willing to challenge/question assumptions.

2.4 Risk in the executive – chief risk officer

An effective system of risk governance requires a strong voice for risk in the executive. In financial institutions and many other large organisations this voice takes the form of a Chief Risk Officer (CRO). The CRO, supported by the risk function, is not responsible for risk-taking per se – that is the responsibility of the business units themselves. Rather the CRO is accountable for ensuring that there is robust, independent oversight and challenge of risk-taking activities across the organisation.

The CRO – or most senior risk officer – should have status and authority in the organisation and this is best achieved by ensuring that (s)he has a place on the most senior executive committee. In many organisations, remuneration is an important signal of status, so careful thought should be given to remuneration relativities within the executive team.

Since an effective CRO might be unpopular with other members of the executive, (s)he should have direct access to the board to discuss concerns that may arise. For further protection, removal of the CRO must be approved by the chair of the board risk committee. It's essential that the CRO be independent of any business unit and revenue-generating responsibility and have a direct reporting line to the chief executive officer.

In smaller organisations, it may not be possible to have a dedicated CRO. Sometimes the role of CRO and chief financial officer are combined, but this creates a situation where risks within the finance function may not be adequately scrutinised. Another possible model is to assign responsibility for specific risks to various members of the executive team.

The accountabilities of the CRO[8] typically relate to the following issues:

- Risk reporting. CRO provides assurance to the board risk committee that the reporting of risks by the relevant executives is complete and accurate;
- Corporate strategy and objectives. In discussion of corporate strategy and business planning at the executive, the CRO ensures appropriate consideration of risk;
- Risk function independence and effectiveness. The CRO is responsible for the independence and effectiveness of the risk function. If risk work

is co-sourced or outsourced, the CRO remains responsible for all work performed.

2.5 Risk management function

The risk management function supports the CRO in delivering independent risk oversight and challenge of risk-taking activities across the organisation. The risk management function is independent of all revenue-generating responsibilities and led by the CRO or equivalent. Its scope should be unrestricted, including consideration of any aspect of the organisation and to relevant third-party providers.

A central risk function is important to ensure that all risks – and interactions between risks– are captured and considered. The independent and objective viewpoint is necessary due to the various biases and incentives that cause risk to be under-reported and under-treated in many cases. The risk management function is therefore a crucial support to assist the board in fulfilling its risk management responsibilities and ensuring that risks remain within appetite.

An effective risk management function should identify and challenge System 1 thinking; thinking that is lazy and error-prone. By asking the right questions and stimulating debate, the risk management function can help businesses engage System 2 thinking about risk – thinking that is more deliberate, reflective and analytical. Advanced communication skills are needed to guide business leaders, helping them appreciate the benefits of engaging and even partnering with the risk function.

Some organisations have adopted a risk governance model where the risk function has a 'sign-off' or approval role.[9] Ownership of risk still exists in the relevant business unit, but before making decisions, the risk function's approval must be sought and given. Proposals sent to the executive by the business must include independent input from the risk function. The advantage of this approach is that it raises the status of the risk function and ensures that risk is considered at an early stage in the development of new business proposals.

Many risk functions aim to act as partners to the business. A business partnership[10] exists between the risk function and builds risk capability across the business, providing education and advice, e.g. how can we find a cost-effective control to enable us to pursue an attractive opportunity? Genuine benefits are most likely to be provided when the professionals within the risk function are qualified and experienced in the risk discipline, as well as the business domain itself. This is something that many organisations have struggled to achieve, so ongoing education opportunities for risk professionals are valuable.

The risk function may provide expert advice and support to the organisation for the quantitative modelling of risk and for stress-tests and scenario analysis. Where this happens, it's important to ensure that business units maintain ownership of models and risk analysis. This would include responsibility for crucial modelling assumptions and for presenting the analysis to the executive.

Risk experts residing in the risk management function will lead the development of the risk management framework, subject to approval by the board of directors. This would include developing risk strategy and appetite documents, risk policies, procedures and training materials. The function will support business units in implementing this framework and producing useful risk reports. It will also monitor the effective operation of the framework and report on its findings and recommendations.

Since the risk function is responsible for monitoring the effectiveness of the risk framework, this should also encompass risk culture. The risk function should monitor, assess and report on risk culture, both to the executive and the board risk committee. See Chapter 3 for detailed discussion of risk culture and methods for assessing it.

The risk function plays a special role during periods of innovation and change. When there are changes in either the internal or external environment, the risk function should support the organisation to adapt accordingly. This was particularly evident during the COVID-19 crisis when many organisations were forced to quickly adapt to ensure public safety.

2.6 Compliance function

The compliance function and the risk management function are distinct, although it's common for the compliance function to report to the CRO and for risk and compliance functions to be closely aligned. Another common approach is to combine the compliance and legal functions under the General Counsel.

Compliance refers to conformity both with external laws and regulations and internal policies. The two types of compliance are related because some internal policies are designed to ensure that the organisation complies with external laws and regulations. As discussed in Section 2.7, compliance with policy is the responsibility of line management, and the compliance function should have an advisory focus.

One of the most important roles of the compliance function is to identify changing legal and regulatory requirements that may impact on the organisation. The compliance function educates managers about changing external requirements and will also assist line management in the interpretation of laws and regulations. This helps the organisation determine what is acceptable behaviour, hence the appropriate internal controls, given the organisation's risk appetite in relation to legal/regulatory risk. Not surprisingly, compliance functions tend to employ many staff with legal training and can employ large teams in organisations operating within highly regulated industries.

In addition to its advisory role, the compliance function should monitor compliance with laws, regulations and policies. It should provide independent reporting on the extent to which compliance is occurring within the organisation. Within a well-functioning compliance framework you would expect to see both an up-to-date register of obligations and a register of breaches (incidents of non-compliance with obligations). The latter is helpful for understanding why breaches are occurring and adapting practices accordingly. In order to reduce the possibility of retaliation against whistle-blowers, many firms establish a confidential reporting hotline. A final element in the framework is to consider procedures for corrective action in the event of non-compliance, including reporting to regulators and consequence management.[11]

Many organisations use attestations, recorded in the compliance system along with the relevant registers, to help provide assurance of compliance. Staff and executives are required to 'attest' or formally declare that they have complied with relevant obligations or controls. Attestations serve to remind staff of their obligations and are useful for promoting accountability. They further provide comfort to senior executives and the board that the organisation is complying with its obligations.

Both the risk and compliance functions must have appropriate status, independence, resources and access to the board in order to be effective.

2.7 Assurance

Despite the presence of a CRO, a risk management function and a compliance function, risk management failures still occur. Lehman Brothers, for example, failed in 2008, despite having all these risk governance structures. Scandals at the Commonwealth Bank of Australia occurred despite having a highly paid CRO and an apparently well-resourced risk function (see Chapter 12).

There are many reasons why risk governance may be ineffective, including lack of expertise and resourcing in the risk function. The culture of the organisation may compromise the effectiveness of the risk management framework, causing other priorities, such as generation of short-term profits, to override risk management considerations. The risk function itself may be affected by the same biases and incentives that are an impediment to risk management more generally, causing risk staff to understate and under-treat risk.

A system of assurance and review is therefore desirable to independently assess the effectiveness of the risk governance system and to recommend improvements. This role is normally filled by the Internal Audit function, which is ideally placed to ensure that controls are operating effectively and to observe everyday business practices that shed light on the functioning of the risk governance system. Internal Audit is therefore a vital source of intelligence for the Board, reporting to the audit committee. Similar to the CRO, the Chief Audit Executive (CAE) needs certain protections to maintain independence. CAE removal should require the approval of the chair of the audit committee.

The internal audit function aims to help protect the assets, reputation and sustainability of the organisation by providing independent assurance to both the board audit and risk committees. This assurance relates to the adequacy and effectiveness of the organisation's governance, risk management and internal control systems, including the effectiveness of the risk function itself. The internal audit function should provide insight on key risks, control weaknesses and audit findings. It should also provide a periodic assessment of the quality of risk reporting.

In some organisations the Internal Audit function is outsourced or co-sourced. Where this occurs, internal audit's work should be subject to the same quality assurance work as the in-house functions.

In many risk governance scandals, including the Commonwealth Bank of Australia, internal audit reports were ignored. This suggests that more must be done to ensure that internal audit can be effective in discharging its responsibilities. Both the UK and Australian professional bodies have risen to this challenge, with detailed guidance along these lines. Most recently the Institute of Internal Auditors in Australia has proposed six principles for improving the effectiveness of internal audit in the context of financial institutions:[12]

1   Position internal audit for success
2   Ensure adequate resourcing and seniority
3   Provide assurance, which adds value
4   Employ methods and tools appropriate for the task
5   Report to influence positive change
6   Adopt appropriate methodologies for auditing risk culture. Internal audit should provide an alternate perspective of risk culture, challenging as necessary.

2.8 Three lines model (aka three lines of defence)

With the emergence of specialist risk, compliance and assurance functions comes a danger. Employees and managers in other business units may consider that risk management is the job of the experts and can safely be left in their capable hands. Unfortunately, this approach has proven to be highly problematic since the specialists rarely, if ever, have adequate understanding of the business environment. Only those on the business front line understand how risks are evolving over time and how their practices might be contributing to those risks. In addition, no organisation has sufficient risk/compliance experts to take on all the risk management duties.

The 'three lines of defence' system of risk governance was first adopted by the internal audit profession in the 1990s.[13] It provides a potential solution by giving primary responsibility for risk management to the business itself. That is, the business unit is the first line of defence, with risk/compliance functions being the second line and internal audit being the third line. This approach has been widely adopted, with financial institutions being among the first.[14] While the functional separation of risk management duties is a sound principle, the term 'defence' is an unfortunate choice, inconsistent with current thinking about risk management as an enabler for success. In this book, therefore, the terminology 'three lines model' (or 3LM) is used. The model is summarized in Figure 2.1.

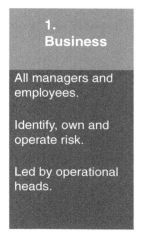

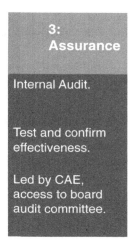

1. Business	2: Risk and Compliance	3: Assurance
All managers and employees.	Risk and compliance specialists.	Internal Audit.
Identify, own and operate risk.	Guide, challenge, support, approve.	Test and confirm effectiveness.
Led by operational heads.	Led by CRO, access to board risk committee.	Led by CAE, access to board audit committee.

FIGURE 2.1 Three Lines Model (a.k.a. Three Lines of Defence)

The role of the first line is to own and manage risks, including implementing controls and ensuring compliance. Every business must identify, assess, control, mitigate and report on risks; every manager must lead the development of policies and procedures to ensure that objectives are met; every employee has a role to play in risk management. Employees are expected to comply with risk procedures and policies but should go beyond 'mere compliance'. Ideally all employees have a commitment to helping the organisation meet its objectives, so this would involve raising any concerns they have, in a constructive fashion, about business practices, emerging risks and even the risk policies themselves.

Under the 3LM, it is often said that 'everyone is a risk manager', and certainly every employee has a role to play in the risk management process. The clear message is that the business cannot abrogate risk management responsibility to the specialists. In practice, however, many firms experience difficulty implementing the 3LM. Probably the greatest difficulty is in getting the first line to truly take responsibility for risk. People have busy jobs, with multiple performance objectives that often seem to be conflicting. A person working in sales, for example, might be focused primarily on short-term sales targets. Motivating someone in sales to engage with the risk management process can be challenging, especially when compliance with risk policy sometimes means that it's necessary to reject profitable transactions. There will be a tendency for people in front-line roles to view risk management as something for the risk experts. They might choose to do the bare minimum for the sake of compliance but no more.

The 2013 UK Parliamentary Committee on Banking Standards[15] criticised the 3LM for creating a misplaced sense of security, for blurring responsibilities and for diluting the accountability of the first line. It reported that implementation of 3LM might create the illusion that risk management was in hand, when in reality many participants in the system were simply engaging in a box-ticking exercise. Staff in the second and third line lacked the status to challenge front-line staff effectively. In other words, the 3LM can be more about form than substance.

Ultimately the success of the 3LM, like all risk structures, relies on the existence of a favourable risk culture, as explained in Chapter 3.

2.9 Executive compensation

Executive compensation has long been considered an important element of corporate governance. Traditionally the focus has been to try to align the incentives of executives with shareholders, thus encouraging executives to focus their efforts on achieving shareholder goals. Variable remuneration – or cash bonuses – paid on the achievement of short-term profit targets or share-price targets, have been a popular choice. The financial crisis in the early 2000s demonstrated that this approach can work against risk management. Too often short-term profits are produced at the expense of longer-term adverse consequences, jeopardising organisational objectives.

More recently organisations and their regulators have explored ways of linking executive compensation to the achievement of long-term objectives, consistent with risk governance. This topic is explored in Chapter 4.

2.10 Risk disclosures

In many jurisdictions risk disclosure is considered a crucial element of corporate governance. The 2015 OECD principles[16] state that

> Users of financial information and market participants need information on reasonably foreseeable material risks that may include: risks that are specific to the industry or the geographical areas in which the company operates; dependence on commodities; financial market risks including interest rate or currency risk; risk related to derivatives and off-balance sheet transactions; business conduct risks; and risks related to the environment.

The principles go on to also recommend disclosures regarding the system for monitoring and managing risk.

Both in prospectuses and annual reports there is a tendency for organisations to under-disclose risk. For example prior to the COVID-19 pandemic, surprisingly few (i.e. less than 21%) US firms mentioned pandemic-related terms in their mandatory risk disclosures.[17] Given the general awareness that, for at least the past decade, pandemics have been identified as a significant global risk, it seems that this number should have been higher.

Under-disclosure could be explained by various biases and incentives, including the perception that greater disclosure of risk might discourage some investors. There is evidence that firms with stronger governance (i.e. more independent directors) tend to provide more meaningful risk disclosure.[18] There is also some emerging evidence that greater risk disclosure is associated with higher firm value.[19]

2.11 Evidence for risk governance

Does risk governance work? This is an obvious and important question to ask – but much more difficult to answer, especially as risk governance is a relatively new phenomenon. One of the difficulties in answering it is that the benefits of risk governance are observed only in the long-term. If an organisation experiences an adverse outcome, to what extent is that down to poor governance or just bad luck? And to what extent might the adverse outcome simply reflect a valid choice to take high risk?

Much of the evaluation of risk governance that has occurred to date has focused on the outcomes of financial institutions at the time of the financial crisis that started in 2007. The ability of organisations to withstand the crisis is a good test of risk governance since we can assume that all financial institutions would aim, at the very least, to remain solvent. Another reason that evaluations covering this time period make sense is that risk governance had not yet become a regulatory standard in the financial services industry. We are able to observe the experience of firms with significantly different risk governance practices.

Ellul and Yerramilli[20] were among the first to test whether risk governance explains the varying experiences of US banks in the crisis. They constructed an index designed to measure the strength and independence of the risk management function, using the following proxies: the presence of a CRO, whether the CRO is an executive of the bank, whether the CRO is among the five highest paid executives, the ratio of the CRO's total compensation to the CEO's total compensation, the board's risk committee experience and how active the board's risk committee is.

They first examined the characteristics of firms that implemented risk governance, finding that risk governance was associated with greater risk-taking (lower capital ratios, larger derivatives trading operations, CEO compensation contracts that induce risk-taking). This is consistent with the principle that if you want to drive a fast car, you need good brakes. They also found that firms with better corporate governance generally (more independent boards, less entrenched management) were also more likely to implement risk governance. During the crisis period, US banks with stronger risk governance had better outcomes measured by lower nonperforming loans and higher share price.

Aebi, Sabato and Schmid's[21] findings relate specifically to the role of the CRO. They further support the benefits of risk governance in a sample of US banks, finding that where the CRO had direct access to the board of directors, the firm had higher (i.e. less negative) stock returns and higher return on equity during the crisis. This suggests that CROs can potentially play a role in restraining excessive risk-taking.

Magee, Schilling and Sheedy[22] similarly explored risk governance, this time in an international sample of insurance companies. The index of risk governance included the existence of a chief risk officer on the executive committee, risk committee characteristics and board industry experience. During the crisis period of 2008–09, firms with a higher *RGI* generally had lower likelihood of insolvency. Interestingly, during non-crisis years, risk governance did not have a risk-reducing effect but was positively associated with shareholder returns, risk-adjusted performance measures and Tobin's Q.[23] This suggests that risk governance can be a business enabler during the good times, while still providing protection during the bad times.

The latter study also documented the expansion of risk governance practices post-crisis. Insurance companies typically upgraded their risk governance following a negative shock, especially in countries that were well regulated and had weaker shareholder rights. In the financial services sector, firms now have little choice but to implement risk governance due to regulatory pressure. And this raises questions as to whether risk governance will be as effective in firms that implement it as a requirement as opposed to a free choice. Where risk governance is not implemented by choice, there is a danger that the structures are undermined by an unfavourable risk culture. This issue is explored in Chapter 3.

Notes

1 International Standards ISO31000: Risk Management, 2018. Available at www.iso.org/iso-31000-risk-management.html
2 Variance is defined as the expected value of the squared deviation of all outcomes from the mean. Range is defined as the difference between the highest and the lowest outcomes.
3 International Standards ISO31000: Risk Management, 2018. Available at www.iso.org/iso-31000-risk-management.html
4 Tricker, B. (2015). *Corporate governance: Principles, policies and practices* (3rd ed.). Oxford University Press, Figure 2.6.
5 This saying was popularized by President John F. Kennedy but coined by the Italian diplomat – and son-in-law of Mussolini – Count Caleazzo Ciano (1903–44).
6 Bill Gates' Ted Talk from 2015 'The next outbreak: we're not ready'. Available at www.ted.com/talks/bill_gates_the_next_outbreak_we_re_not_ready?language=en
7 This guidance was provided in the context of UK financial institutions but is arguably relevant to many contexts. See The Risk Coalition. *Raising the bar: Principles-based guidance for board risk committees and risk functions in the UK Financial Services sector*. Available at https://riskcoalition.org.uk/the-guidance
8 This guidance was provided in the context of UK financial institutions but is arguably relevant to many contexts. See The Risk Coalition. *Raising the bar: Principles-based guidance for board risk committees and risk functions in the UK Financial Services sector*. Available at https://riskcoalition.org.uk/the-guidance
9 See Macquarie Group for example. Information about their risk management philosophy may be found at www.macquarie.com/au/en/about/company/risk-management.html
10 Kaplan, R. S., & Mikes, A. (2016). Risk management: The revealing hand. *Journal of Applied Corporate Finance, 28*(1), 8–18.
11 Coglianese, Cary, & Nash, Jennifer. (2020, May 7). Compliance management systems: Do they make a difference? In D. Daniel Sokol & Benjamin van Rooij (Eds.), *Cambridge handbook of compliance*. Cambridge University Press, Forthcoming; U of Penn, Inst for Law & Econ Research Paper No. 20–35. Available at SSRN: https://ssrn.com/abstract=3598264

12 Institute of Internal Auditors Australia 'Internal Audit Better Practice Guide for Financial Services in Australia' www.iia.org.au/technical-resources/publications/internal-audit-better-practice-guide-for-financial-services-in-australia

13 Institute of Internal Auditors. *The three lines of defense in effective risk management and control.* Available at https://global.theiia.org/standards-guidance/recommended-guidance/Pages/The-Three-Lines-of-Defense-in-Effective-Risk-Management-and-Control.aspx

14 The Basel Committee for Banking Supervision adopted three lines of defense in 2010, see *Consultation paper: Sound practices for the management and supervision of operational risk.* Available at www.bis.org/publ/bcbs183.pdf

15 See paragraph 143, Volume II, Final Report of the Parliamentary Commission on Banking Standards, 2013. Available at www.parliament.uk/documents/banking-commission/Banking-final-report-vol-ii.pdf

16 OECD. (2015). *G20/OECD principles of corporate governance.* Available at www.oecd.org/corporate/principles-corporate-governance/#:~:text=%E2%80%8CThe%20G20%2FOECD%20Principles%20of,sustainable%20growth%20and%20financial%20stability

17 Loughran, T., & McDonald, B. (2020). *Management disclosure of risk factors and COVID-19.* Available at SSRN 3575157.

18 Elshandidy, T., & Neri, L. (2015). Corporate governance, risk disclosure practices, and market liquidity: Comparative evidence from the UK and Italy. *Corporate Governance: An International Review*, 23(4), 331–356.

19 Düsterhöft, Maximilian, Schiemann, Frank, & Walther, Thomas. (2020, September 14). *Let's talk about risk! The firm value effect of risk disclosure for European energy utilities.* Available at SSRN: https://ssrn.com/abstract=3692372 or http://dx.doi.org/10.2139/ssrn.3692372

20 Ellul, A., & Yerramilli, V. (2013). Stronger risk controls, lower risk: Evidence from US bank holding companies. *The Journal of Finance*, 68(5), 1757–1803.

21 Aebi, V., Sabato, G., & Schmid, M. (2012). Risk management, corporate governance, and bank performance in the financial crisis. *Journal of Banking & Finance*, 36(12), 3213–3226.

22 Magee, S., Schilling, C., & Sheedy, E. (2019). Risk governance in the insurance sector—determinants and consequences in an international sample. *Journal of Risk and Insurance*, 86(2), 381–413.

23 Named after the economist James Tobin, the Q ratio is calculated as the market value of the firm's assets divided by the book value of the firm's assets, where the market value of the firm's assets is computed as the difference between the book value of total assets and the book value of equity plus the market value of equity. It is used as a proxy for firm value for listed firms.

Further reading and resources

Institute of Internal Auditors. (2017). *International standards for professional practice of internal auditing.* Available at https://iia.org.au/sf_docs/default-source/quality/ippf-standards-2017.pdf?sfvrsn=2

Institute of Internal Auditors Australia. (2020). *Internal audit better practice guide for financial services in Australia.* Available at www.iia.org.au/technical-resources/publications/internal-audit-better-practice-guide-for-financial-services-in-australia

The Risk Coalition. (2019). *Raising the bar: Principles-based guidance for board risk committees and risk functions in the UK financial services sector.* Available at https://riskcoalition.org.uk/the-guidance

3

ASSESSING AND EMBEDDING RISK CULTURE

'Human behaviour and culture significantly influence all aspects of risk management at each level and stage'.

ISO31000 (2018)

Chapter 2 explored the structures of risk governance such as board committees, the risk framework and the three lines model. Some evidence exists to suggest that these structures can help to produce better risk management behaviour (e.g. reporting concerns, implementing appropriate controls) and ultimately better risk outcomes (organisation is resilient and achieves its objectives). But many of the risk cases illustrate that structures alone are not sufficient, and they can be undermined by cultural problems. As shown in Chapter 12, the culture at the Commonwealth Bank of Australia contributed to not just one, but multiple scandals from 2010–18.

Unfortunately, it is quite common for organisational culture to undermine risk structures, causing them to be ineffective. This is particularly common in regulated industries where organisations adopt risk governance structures as a requirement rather than of their own accord. Crucial elements such as the second and third line may not be well-resourced if they are seen as a regulatory requirement rather than as value-adding. Under-resourcing may mean that risk experts and assurance staff cannot be effective in their roles, and/or their reports and recommendations may be ignored. If the true priority of the organisation is short-term profits rather than long-term resilience, then violations of the risk policies by top profit earners may not be taken seriously; this will encourage others to violate the policy and the risk structures will become ineffective.

This author first became aware of concerns that organisational culture was undermining risk governance in the early 2000s. Culture was fingered as an underlying cause of the National Australia Bank foreign exchange option trading scandal at that time.[1] Soon after, the term 'risk culture' was extensively used in discussion of the financial crisis of 2007–09. A report on reforming the financial services industry was produced in 2009 by the Institute of International Finance (a global association of the financial services industry), noting that 'A robust and pervasive risk culture throughout the firm is essential. This risk culture should be embedded in the way the firm operates and cover all areas and activities'.[2]

The term 'risk culture' has led to some misunderstanding, with some mistakenly seeing risk culture as distinct from the broader organisational culture. This chapter provides an evidence-based understanding of what risk culture is and how to assess it. It links risk culture to risk management maturity and paints a picture of maturity that organisations can aspire to. It also explores the role of leaders, including directors, in building that culture, while acknowledging the challenge of culture change.

3.1 Risk culture/climate versus organisational culture

There is a great deal of confusion about risk culture and how it relates to organisational culture. To complicate matters still further, the term 'climate' is sometimes used in place of 'culture'. This section attempts to clear the fog, with considerable guidance from the work of Ehrhart, Schneider and Macey.[3]

As shown in Table 3.1, the two concepts of culture and climate come from different theoretical roots; they have developed simultaneously but largely siloed, in different parts of the academic literature. At times, the two different schools of thought have been critical of one another, although they share much in common and lately there is greater appreciation of their complementary perspectives. Both concepts are concerned with, for example, the context in which people work, the role of leaders and leadership in creating that context and the relationship between culture/climate and organisational effectiveness.

The methods of investigation also tend to differ, with culture being more associated with qualitative methods and climate with quantitative methods. Having said that, there is some methodological overlap with anthropologists sometimes using surveys and psychologists sometimes using observations and interviews.

A significant difference lies in the depth of analysis. Scholars of culture are interested in the deep layers of culture, involving values and underlying assumptions that are difficult to observe. The more superficial layers of culture – behaviour, processes, even office layout and styles of dress – are seen as artefacts or symptoms of the underlying values. The iceberg metaphor is often invoked to describe the different layers of culture. Values and assumptions are hidden below the surface while behaviours and processes are more obvious, lying above the surface. The literature on organisational climate takes instead a more pragmatic approach, focusing much more heavily on that which is easily observable i.e. behaviour.

TABLE 3.1 Culture versus Climate Concepts

	Culture	Climate
Theoretical roots and methodology	Anthropology, usually based on case studies and qualitative methods (observation, interviews)	Organisational Psychology, with surveys as the 'go-to' method
Depth	Seeking to investigate all levels (values and assumptions as well as behaviour and practices)	Focus on more observable levels i.e. behaviour and practices
Malleability	Seen as very stable, since it relates to deeply held values and assumptions	Seen as more malleable
Strategic Focus	No strategic focus	Focusing on a strategic goal e.g. safety climate, service climate, innovation climate, risk climate
Typical Definition	A system of shared assumptions, values, and beliefs, which governs how people behave in organisations	Shared perceptions among employees of the relative priority given to [safety/service/risk management etc], including perceptions of the [safety/ service/risk]-related practices and behaviours that are expected, valued and supported
Underlying Logic	Assumptions and values drive the behaviour	People learn how to behave by observing both policies and practices and sharing their perceptions with one another

Arguably the biggest difference in the two approaches lies in the presence – or not – of strategic focus. Strategic focus is a feature of recent organisational climate research, with vast literatures emerging since the 1980s on both safety climate and service climate and to a lesser extent on ethical climate, innovation climate and others. Alignment of policies, practices and rewards is a crucial factor, so that employees gain a clear understanding of what is expected of them. So rather than values driving behaviour, as in the culture approach, employees infer the values of the organisation from the practices and events they observe.

Consider the example of safety climate, as illustrated in Figure 3.1, which was an important forerunner of risk climate. Suppose that an employee observes a set of safety policies and formal statements of leaders claiming that safety is the highest priority of the organisation. She considers that information, but she also observes that employees who are highly productive but sometimes violate the safety policies are more likely to enjoy high status or get promoted. From this she might infer that the true priority of the organisation is productivity and not

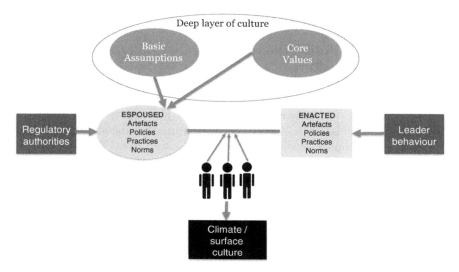

FIGURE 3.1   Culture versus Climate

safety as claimed. She might perceive that the espoused focus on safety is mere whitewashing, designed to satisfy regulators. These perceptions are shared among staff through verbal and non-verbal communication, and over time groups come to form common beliefs about what really matters. In contrast, an organisation with a favourable safety climate has alignment between the espoused policies/ structures and the enacted practices, so employees develop a clear and shared perception that safety is a high priority.

The focused climate approach has proven to be enormously effective for predicting outcomes of interest, and this is one of the reasons why it is so useful for practitioners. If you care about safety outcomes, such as lower injury rates, then logically you should focus attention on the aspects of the organisational environment that are most relevant for predicting them. The concept of safety climate was introduced by Zohar in 1980,[4] stimulated by some of the major industrial accidents of the 1970s such as Three Mile Island. Forty years later, there can be no doubt that favourable safety climate predicts safety behaviour, such as compliance with safety policies and reporting of safety events. Safe behaviour in turn predicts lower rates of accidents.

In 2010, Zohar wrote an important article reflecting on some of the most important learnings from 30 years of research on safety climate.[5] He highlighted that *relative* priority is important for safety climate – and presumably other focused organisational climates. For safety to be seen as the true priority of the organisation, it must prevail over other competing priorities such as productivity. The true priorities of the organisation are most clearly seen when competing priorities, such as safety and productivity, butt up against each other. For example, if the group is behind on its production targets and the manager subtly hints that safety rules can be ignored for now, employees understand that productivity is the true priority. In other words, they infer values from workplace practices. What is enacted is seen as more useful information than what is espoused in formal policy statements.

Our research team based at Macquarie Business School has demonstrated that the same logic applies to risk management. People understand how to behave in relation to risk management by observing not just policies but also behaviour in their workplaces. In 2017 we conducted an experimental study,[6] inviting finance professionals into our behaviour laboratory in the financial district in Sydney. During a twenty-minute session, we created a business simulation designed to reflect aspects of a real-world financial institution. Participants were asked to evaluate a series of transactions, of which around 30% were inconsistent with risk limits imposed by the hypothetical employer. A compliant participant should therefore reject all such transactions, despite the fact that more transactions boosted their payments. We compared compliance rates between two hypothetical workplace environments: profit-focused and risk-focused.

Participants were given descriptive text regarding the hypothetical workplace environment at the start of the experiment and repeated as regular intervals. As shown in Table 3.2, information was provided about observed behaviour in the workplace. As expected, the priming information about behaviour had a significant impact on actual compliance behaviour of the participants. This suggests that employees adapt their behaviour to match the practices they observe in their workplace.

TABLE 3.2 Workplace Climates

Profit-focused Climate	*Risk-focused Climate*
In your workplace compliance with risk policy seems to have a low priority compared with meeting **profit** targets. Non-compliance is common. Your manager rarely mentions the risk policy but talks often about the need to **meet budget**. He is always giving you motivational messages to encourage you to boost **profits**. You notice that colleagues who breach policy are excused if they are top performers. The risk policies are often criticised by staff because they can interfere with meeting **profit** targets; risk managers have low status compared with people who have **great profit figures**.	In your workplace non-compliance with **risk policy is taken very seriously** and is extremely rare. Breaches are not excused or tolerated, even if they produce high profits. Your manager is an excellent role model of risk management behaviour and talks frequently about the **need to comply with risk policy**, even when the team is behind on profit targets. It is clear from what colleagues do and say that compliance with risk policy is regarded as essential for the firm to survive and prosper. **Risk managers are highly respected** because they are seen as adding value to the organisation.

What then can we say about 'risk culture'? The concept of 'risk culture', with its strategic focus on risk management, really comes from the organisational climate tradition, despite the use of the word 'culture'. The term 'risk climate' is arguably more accurate; but consistent with industry usage, the term 'risk culture' is used hereafter in this book.

Risk culture is concerned with how managers and employees understand and prioritise their risk management duties relative to competing priorities such as short-term profits. Because risk culture emerges from observation of practices and interactions between staff, it is not necessarily consistent throughout a large organisation. Culture is a characteristic of a group, where members of the group know and interact with one another. It is much harder for consistent risk culture to develop across very large organisations, because the work practices and managerial approaches can differ between business units. We observed this phenomenon in our study of large commercial banks in 2014/15.[7] Employees within the same business unit generally 'agreed[8]' with one another's perceptions, but in a number of cases business units deviated from one another.

3.2 Risk culture and risk management maturity

To better understand risk culture it is helpful to consider how organisations typically evolve in their approach to risk management. This risk management maturity model, illustrated in Figure 3.2, has been adapted from similar models in the field of safety.[9]

Many organisations start at Level 5 where risk is not on the agenda at all but rather the focus is elsewhere (growth, short-term profits etc). Biases such as over-confidence may cause leaders to ignore risk issues. As explained in Chapter 1, risk management is not something that comes naturally to most humans. Early risk management initiatives are typically reactive (Level 4); attention is given to risk only when something disastrous happens or the regulator requires it. Often a major problem, scandal or regulatory intervention is the catalyst for implementing a system of risk governance.[10]

Level 3, calculative, is the stage at which organisations implement the structures of risk governance as described in Chapter 2. This would involve ensuring the firm has directors and executives able to fulfil risk governance duties, whether through recruiting or training. The board would review its strategy to consider risk appetite and/or risk criteria; the organisation would establish a risk framework with appropriate policies, systems and processes. At Level 3 we would expect to see formal statements from leaders about the importance of risk management.

Introducing risk governance, like any program of change in organisations, is never straightforward. As resources are allocated to risk, they must inevitably be taken from elsewhere. Changes to business practices are met with suspicion and doubt. Since the benefits of risk management are most clearly seen in the long term, these short-term disruptions are particularly problematic. For this reason,

FIGURE 3.2 Risk Management Maturity

many organisations become stuck at Level 3 as leaders struggle to communicate the value of handling risk in a more structured way. Indeed, many of the leaders may themselves doubt the value of risk governance if it is imposed by regulators. If risk governance has been implemented following a disastrous event, then memories of that event will fade over time and it's easy for the old habits of overconfidence to be re-established. At this stage, risk management practices are typically seen as a handbrake on progress rather than an enabler for success. This means that the risk structures are not fully effective because they are continually undermined by resistance in pockets of the organisation.

Returning to the prior discussion in Section 3.1, what we typically observe at this point is a gap between what is espoused and what is enacted in relation to risk management. On the one hand, policies and formal communications suggest that risk governance is established, but everyday implementation is poor and risk policies are not consistently applied. This could be because the risk/

compliance/assurance functions aren't adequately resourced, or their reports tend to be ignored. Employees may sense a type of 'wilful blindness' in the leaders and managers who, perhaps subtly, give the impression that they do not want too much information about risk issues and incidents. Such information would mean that they would need to do something to resolve the issues, and this might reduce short-term profits. The more leaders display a desire for ignorance, the fewer issues will be reported and resolved.

In this situation, staff form the view that risk is not a priority and compliance with risk policies suffers, causing a downward spiral in risk management effectiveness. This pattern has played out in numerous risk scandals and can be described as an 'avoidance' pattern; the CBA case in Chapter 12 provides an excellent example. The research conducted by our team at Macquarie University identified avoidance, in relation to risk management, as an important predictor of poor risk outcomes. The avoidance trap plays out as shown in Table 3.3.

In 2014–15 our team conducted a research project examining the risk culture of 7 of the world's largest commercial banks – three headquartered in Australia and four in Canada.[11] All 7 banks had implemented standard risk governance structures i.e. board risk committees with independent directors having relevant experience, high status CRO with access to the board, risk appetite statements etc. We assessed the risk culture of each bank using employee surveys, finding that perceptions of avoidance were the single biggest predictor of poor risk management behaviours such as non-compliance.

Interestingly, we observed significantly higher levels of avoidance in the Australian samples relative to the Canadian. We were surprised by this outcome given the apparent similarity in Australian and Canadian regulatory environments and banking markets. We considered it possible that the less favourable ratings by Australian employees may not reflect a 'true' cultural difference but rather could result from a survey response bias (i.e. Australians may be less concerned than their Canadian peers about responding in a socially desirable manner). If a true country difference exists, one would expect that this might be reflected in subsequent risk outcomes, and this proved to be the case. In the years following that study there were multiple misconduct scandals in the Australian context, leading ultimately to the Royal Commission into Misconduct in the Banking, Financial Services and Superannuation Industry in 2018. The scandals embroiled all the major Australian banks, including those that participated in the study, while similar misconduct scandals rarely occurred in Canadian banks. It was a powerful demonstration of the avoidance effect and its consequences.

The higher levels of risk management maturity differ from Level 3 in that there is a reduced gap between the espoused risk governance and what is enacted; the avoidance pattern becomes less and less common. At Level 2 (proactive) the organisation is increasingly living out the practices of risk governance, learning from risk events, raising and resolving issues rather than allowing them to be swept under the carpet. In a proactive risk culture, one would expect to see line 1 displaying accountability for risk. All staff in the organisation would

TABLE 3.3 The Avoidance Trap in Risk Management

Employees Observe . . .	So employees Believe . . .	Then employees Behave . . .
• Reward and status flow to people who generate high short-term profits (or other key objectives), even if risk outcomes are bad or even if they have violated risk policies. • Leaders and managers foster 'deliberate ignorance', preferring not to know too much about risk problems as that would necessitate action and the resolution of issues that might dampen profits. • Risk/compliance functions are under-resourced, staff in those functions have low status. • Managers and opinion leaders talk about risk/compliance in a disparaging or perfunctory way, whereas profit targets are often highlighted as important. • Warning signals and red flags are ignored. • There is a 'tick the box' mentality when it comes to risk/compliance matters.	• Risk and compliance are not an important priority. • Leaders don't want to hear about or address risk issues.	• Employees focus their attention on priorities other than risk e.g. short term profits. • Compliance with risk policy drops. • Gaming behaviour becomes common e.g. faking adherence to policy. • Risk events don't get reported or discussed, so issues don't get solved.

understand that they have a role to play in the risk management process and would take that role seriously i.e. thoughtful engagement as opposed to 'mere compliance'. Risk management would not be seen as just something for the risk experts. Risk events would be constructively analysed to improve business practices. There would be regular discussion and consideration of risk in all key decision making and rapid escalation of risk incidents, issues and concerns. Information about risk issues would flow easily through the organisation to the people who need it for decision making.

As will be explained in Chapter 4, accountability is a crucial element in risk management, that is, the system of rewards and sanctions broadly defined. Accountability works because people, being social creatures, are concerned about their reputation and status. Having clear individual accountability when things go awry means that the mechanisms of shame and humiliation are invoked. In order to avoid possible future shame, accountable managers work hard to manage risk. They pay attention to red flags, they actively seek out information about risk and they promptly resolve issues that may eventually lead to serious adverse outcomes.

As these proactive risk management practices take root, a virtuous cycle emerges. As more of the risk management behaviour is practiced, the behaviour becomes contagious since people learn how to behave by watching what goes on around them. The organisation starts to see the benefits of risk management, that is, the organisation is taking the right amount of the right risks and is achieving its objectives. Risk management is seen as adding value to the organisation rather than a drag on performance; it's viewed as an enabler for success.

At Level 1 (generative), risk management is embedded into the organisational culture as the best way of doing business.[12] Risk management is no longer regulator-driven but self-generated. There is no meaningful gap between statements of commitment to risk management and reality on the ground. There is a danger that an organisation at this stage may become overconfident in its risk management capacity, but hubris must be avoided. One would instead observe commitment to continuous improvement of the risk management framework. This could also be thought of as 'chronic unease' regarding risk. An example of this might be participation in benchmarking with both peer firms and firms from outside the industry in order to learn and improve. The incident reporting system would be comprehensive (i.e. captures all risk events) and this information would be analysed and used for organisational learning. The risk management system would be regularly audited and follow-up timely/thorough.

3.3 Measuring risk culture

Measuring risk culture presents significant challenges since it has to do with perceptions of behavioural norms (or alternatively values and assumptions). Despite this challenge, it's important for senior leaders to understand the risk culture of the organisation and how this might be impacting on the success of the overall risk framework. There are several methods available for assessing risk culture, all with advantages and disadvantages. Leaders should consider utilising a mixture of methods.

3.3.1 Observation and interviews

Observations and interviews are excellent ways to gain deep insights into culture. Through these methods it's possible to learn not only what behaviour is occurring but also the perceptions and reasons underlying the behaviour. This methodology is resource intensive as it requires observers or interviewers with appropriate skills, skills that are not typically taught in the standard business curriculum.

This expertise would normally be developed or taught in the Faculty of Arts, within the disciplines of anthropology and ethnography.[13] The core ethnographic method is participant-observation, where the observer spends lengthy periods of time among the observed and participates in their practices to develop a deep understanding of culture within a particular community. Interviews and focus groups may also be used, but observation is considered fundamental because what people say they do is often different from what they actually do. Long-term fieldwork can uncover these discrepancies.

As this method is time-consuming and requires a high level of skill, it works best for evaluating the culture in small business units or teams. As noted previously, risk culture in a large organisation cannot be assumed to be homogeneous. Evaluating the risk culture throughout a large organisation at a single point in time would be extremely difficult and expensive using this methodology.

Despite the challenges, some of these practices are starting to be incorporated into risk governance, especially in large European financial institutions.[14] Internal audit is ideally placed to observe everyday business practices and informal communications that shed light on the actual, as opposed to the desired, risk culture. As internal audit teams go about their normal work, rotating around the various business units, they can provide a vital source of intelligence for the board with regard to risk culture. Table 3.4 lists a set of behavioural flags relating to risk culture, grouped around the four risk culture factors of avoidance, manager, proactive and valued identified by Sheedy, Griffin and Barbour.[15]

This model identifies four dimensions of risk culture:

1 Proactive is a group of favourable behavioural norms that are associated with effective risk management by employees
2 Manager/leader is another set of norms that specifically related to the risk management behaviour of managers and leaders, who play a fundamental role in the development of risk culture
3 The valued dimension refers to risk management being genuinely valued by the organisation, and seen as an enabler for success, as opposed to being begrudgingly implemented at regulator behest.

TABLE 3.4 Behavioural Flags for Risk Culture Assessment

Proactive (desirable)

- Business units (line 1) display accountability for managing the risks of their business.
- Communication about risk management is regular/normal.
- Staff are proactive about raising their risk management concerns
- Discussions about risk issues are constructive and focused on problem-solving rather than blaming/shaming.
- Risk events are reported promptly; under-reporting and recurring issues are rare.
- Past risk events and near misses are analysed and information used to adjust business practices where appropriate.
- Risk reporting is meaningful to the users and guides business decisions.
- Staff consistently comply with policies.
- Non-financial risks (operational, compliance, conduct) are managed as actively and systematically as financial risks.
- Staff understand their role in the risk management framework and what behaviours are expected of them in relation to risk management (i.e. compliance with policy, plus raising issues/concerns).
- Risk is generally within appetite (i.e. we take the right amount of the right risks). Exceptions to this are dealt with promptly.

Avoidance (undesirable)

- Employees perceive that managers/leaders don't want to hear bad news; raising issues is a waste of effort.
- Employees perceive that top performers can get away with non-compliance.
- Risk/compliance/internal audit budgets are under undue pressure; there is a lack of investment in systems, high-quality people resources and their professional development.
- There is a sense of complacency, perhaps due to past strong performance.
- There is an undue focus on short-term profits and self-interest (e.g. immediate bonuses).
- When the business is under pressure (e.g. sales/profits low, costs blow out), risk management is de-prioritised.
- Risk issues remain unresolved for lengthy periods of time.
- Breaches are not reported promptly to regulators.
- There is a lack of clarity about what is considered acceptable/desirable behaviour.
- There is a lack of clarity about accountabilities.
- There is a lack of challenge/discussion about business practices or evidence of groupthink, perhaps due to an unduly dominating manager or a lack of cognitive diversity.
- There is resistance to the assessment of risk culture.
- Risk reports are unread or ignored.
- Poor behaviour is justified with diffusion of responsibility ('Everyone does it'); euphemistic language downplays the seriousness of the misconduct.

(Continued)

Table 3.4 (Continued)

Avoidance (continued)

- Gaming behaviour is apparent (e.g. manipulation of accountabilities, working to 'appear good' rather than actually do the right thing).
- Risk/compliance/internal audit people or policies are mocked or disparaged.
- There is a 'tick box' approach to addressing internal audit findings, rather than putting in place appropriate actions to address the findings.
- Budgets and performance targets are overly ambitious and/ or workloads are excessive, creating inherent conflict with risk management objectives.

Valued (desirable)

- Risk management, compliance and internal audit staff are respected by the business.
- There is a sense of 'chronic unease' regarding risk management (i.e. we can always do better).
- Staff are thoughtfully engaged with the risk management process/ framework, as opposed to 'mere compliance'.
- Risk management is seen as an enabler, rather than a barrier, for achieving business objectives.

Leaders and Managers (desirable)

- Leaders and managers have a good understanding of the business environment, the risks that are present, and how they may be changing
- Managers and opinion leaders in the business are good role models of risk management behaviour, e.g. reporting and resolving risk issues, complying with policies.
- People who speak up about risk issues/concerns are valued by managers, their concerns are taken seriously and managers respond to their concerns appropriately.
- Leaders and managers regularly communicate about risk management, in both formal and informal ways.
- When non-compliance occurs or when employees display lack of accountability for their risk obligations, there are direct and proportional consequences in performance reviews, rewards, promotions, etc.

4   The avoidance dimension has been found to be one of the most important for predicting poor risk and control outcomes, such as misconduct and non-compliance with policy. Some risk culture models omit this crucial dimension, and many organisations are not sufficiently focused on identifying the issues that might work against risk management. Avoidance is not just a lack of the proactive culture dimension, it is indicative of the fact that other strategic priorities are undermining the risk culture, usually undue focus on short-term profits or cost reduction. In other words, there is a conflict between risk and other priorities that remains unresolved, so low levels of avoidance are preferred e.g. Employees perceive that top performers can get away with non-compliance with risk policy.

RBS, a major British bank, has created a behavioural risk team within internal audit. It is comprised of professionals from organisational psychology, behavioural science, anthropology and other disciplines. The team conducts reviews in specific parts of the business using a range of methods. This would include examination of documents such as policies, processes, performance measures, meeting agendas/minutes, organisational charts and plans. Team members attend meetings and observe employees working at their tasks, noting the group dynamics and interactions. Confidential conversations and focus groups are used to gain an understanding of the behaviours observed.

De Nederlandsche Bank, the Dutch Central Bank, has also adopted observational practices in its supervision of the behaviour and culture of financial institutions. Their approach focuses on observation of boards, including group dynamics, decision-making processes and communication.[16]

One of the common concerns regarding observation is the possibility that the presence of the observer will change the dynamics. The observer effect – or reactivity – tends to diminish over time as participants become habituated to the presence of the observer.[17] Most people find it difficult to maintain unnatural behaviour for long periods of time. Reactivity can be reduced if the observer blends in by, for example, wearing similar clothing to those being observed. Reactivity will be heightened if participants think that the observer is looking for socially unacceptable or deviant behaviour.

Another problem with these qualitative methods is the inherent subjectivity of interpretation. The observer interacts with those being observed, making it difficult to be entirely neutral. Two different observers might draw different conclusions, depending on their backgrounds and biases. In addition, it is difficult to make objective comparisons between different business units or between the same business unit at different points in time. Michael Patton, in his excellent guide to qualitative methods, provides some excellent guidance to enhance neutrality.[18]

3.3.2 Risk culture surveys

Risk culture surveys may not offer the same depth of insight as observation/interviews, but they do offer significant advantages. Provided that survey instruments are used with demonstrated reliability and validity, they allow for more objective assessment of risk culture. It is possible to compare scores between business units and across times, testing for statistical significance. They are also very efficient; data can be gathered from large samples at relatively low cost. The final advantage of surveys is that depending on the methodology, they can offer anonymity, something that is never possible with interviews or observations. Arguably you can obtain the most candid responses from participants if they are confident in confidentiality.

Home-grown surveys can be used for a range of useful information-gathering purposes. When assessing culture with a survey, however, it's essential to use a scientifically valid survey instrument. To create an analogy, if you were testing the intelligence of job applicants as part of a selection decision, it's unlikely you would create your own IQ test; rather you would use an IQ test that has been through a rigorous validation process. It is important to be sure that any survey instrument measures what it purports to measure, otherwise poor decisions may ensue. In the case of risk culture, an invalid instrument may provide a false sense of comfort that all is well, and opportunities for management to intervene may be missed.

Creating a valid risk culture assessment survey, sometimes called a scale, is a task involving specialist psychometric expertise, skills in writing effective survey questions that minimise biases, as well as expertise in the field of risk governance. Proving validity takes a number of years with testing in multiple samples, applying the established protocols of survey design and validation. Independent peer review should also be applied before relying on any survey instrument. Figure 3.3 depicts the typical steps taken in survey validation.[19]

Research[20] in the field of risk culture suggests that it is a multi-dimensional concept with at least four unique factors or components that influence behaviour in different ways. An example of an evidence-based four-factor risk culture model is presented in Section 3.3.1. Each one of these components typically requires 3–6 survey items for reliable measurement. This suggests that short surveys with less than 10 survey items may not cover the full range of the construct with adequate reliability. For example, the risk culture scale we developed at Macquarie University has 18 items across the 4 factors: avoidance, proactive, manager and valued.

For all these reasons, most organisations will generally not have sufficient resources to create a valid and reliable risk culture survey in-house. Those organisations

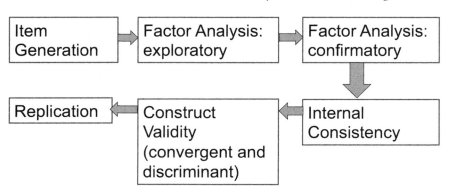

FIGURE 3.3 Process for Developing Scientifically Valid Survey Instruments

wishing to utilise survey methods should consider outsourcing or using a validated survey instrument under license. An in-house survey may be a 'cheaper' option but ultimately poor value for money and a waste of resources.

It is common for consulting firms to provide 'free' surveys as part of consulting engagements. Users should consider whether such surveys have adequate independence and evidence of peer-reviewed validity or rather, are part of a sales strategy for the consultant. There are benefits in using a survey that is independent of associated consulting services. Before and after surveys, checking for results in control teams that did not receive the intervention, can then be used to determine whether the consulting service had any meaningful effect.

The manner in which a survey is implemented is also very important for obtaining meaningful results. There is evidence that faking behaviour is an issue in high-stakes surveys, such as self-report personality tests administered as part of a selection process.[21] For example, Griffin and Wilson (2012)[22] conducted personality tests on prospective students seeking admission into medical school. When the tests were repeated on the same people after admission into medical school, the test scores were significantly worse on the criteria of relevance to selection. This suggests that respondents adapted their survey responses to enhance their chances of success.

The lesson here is that faking behaviour is significantly increased if there are significant consequences flowing from the test scores, such as a selection decision or remuneration adjustments. If risk culture scores become a key performance indicator for managers, with consequences for promotion or remuneration, then one would expect that they will find ways to enhance the scores. There is anecdotal evidence that this occurs, with managers coaching their staff in how they ought to respond. Similarly, if risk culture questions are included in the staff engagement survey – and engagement is a high-stakes key performance indicator – then the risk culture results may be contaminated.

Relatedly, anonymity is an important principle in survey methodology. It has been known for many years that anonymity is one of the most important conditions for producing candid responses,[23] but surprisingly, this principle is often not applied. Many surveys of staff are invitational, meaning that each employee receives a unique link to the survey. Consequently staff perceive, correctly or otherwise, that their responses will be tracked. Reporting test scores for small teams or requiring responses to demographic questions are other practices that reduce participant willingness to provide honest responses.

So some important tips for implementing surveys are as follows:

- Surveys should be anonymous (everyone gets the same link) not invitational (everyone gets a unique link). This helps employees feel safe to give honest responses;
- Do not report results for small teams, say less than 10 responses. Again, this helps employees feel safe to answer honestly;
- Ensure that the results will not feed into promotion or reward decisions; the aim should be solely to understand more about culture and help managers do a better job.

Some questions to consider when appointing a survey provider:

1   What evidence exists that the survey instrument has been developed using sound psychometric principles? Ask for both exploratory and confirmatory factor analysis and evidence of solid underlying theory.
2   What is the expertise of those who developed the survey? Look for advanced academic qualifications as well as experience, as this is a highly technical field.
3   What evidence exists for predictive validity? Does the survey predict behaviours and/or other outcomes that you care about? Be sceptical of evidence that relies only on a few case studies with vague outcomes and lack of any controls.
4   Has the scale been through a process of independent peer review? Are you relying only on the word of the developer that this scale measures what it purports to measure?
5   How will the survey be implemented? Is the survey invitational or anonymous? Will results be reported for teams where there are fewer than 10 responses? Are you confident that participants feel psychologically safe to give honest answers?
6   Does the provider have any biases that could influence the results? For example is the provider hoping for a consulting engagement following the survey? Is the provider likely to feel pressure to report what the organisation wants to hear in order to maintain an ongoing business relationship?

3.3.3 Other data sources

Big data analytics offer an intriguing opportunity to assess organisational culture, subject to ethical and privacy concerns. At present it is difficult to find independent evidence to support claims of validity for such measures, although a number of vendors provide services of this kind.

The basic idea is to extract large amounts of text, say from employee emails, transcripts of exit interviews with departing employees, company reports, meeting agendas/minutes or social media posts. The text can then be analysed using tools such as Leximancer and NVivo. These software programs are useful for analysing any kind of unstructured text.

The main challenge is to find useful sources of text. Analysing a company's annual report, for example, is useful for understanding the espoused culture of the organisation but is unlikely to shed much light on the actual culture. If employees know that their emails are being monitored, then they are unlikely to say anything in the emails that is contrary to the espoused culture. Observer effects are a potential issue whenever anonymity is lacking and those being observed have reason to restrain their behaviour.

One promising area is the use of crowdsourced employee review platforms such as Glassdoor. These are useful because they are anonymous, so employees feel free to express their honest opinion. Some evidence of validity has already emerged. Firms experiencing improvements in crowdsourced employee ratings go on to exhibit higher sales, profits, earnings and share returns, relative to firms with declines.[24] Firms with lower levels of job satisfaction (as measured by employees) and lower levels of 'culture and values' are more likely to be subjected to SEC fraud enforcement actions and securities class action lawsuits.[25]

Since the employee review platforms are available to all members of the public, they provide a unique opportunity for regulators and other external stakeholders to gain insights into the culture of organisations of interest. It is important, however, to consider the potential for this source of data to be contaminated, especially if the sample size is small. In the case of consumer review sites, there is evidence that merchants, upon realising the benefits of favourable customer reviews, have paid people to provide positive reviews. In addition, some have tried to prevent unfavourable reviews through gag clauses and threats of various kinds.[26]

In addition to this kind of big-data text analytics, there are some other sources of data that are potentially useful for gaining insights in risk culture.

- Analysis of data related to performance reviews, reward and consequence management (e.g. variation in manager ratings, suitability of consequences where misconduct identified, etc.). Are risk/compliance outcomes receiving appropriate consequences?
- Analysis of data from staff (e.g. exit interviews, staff turnover, use of confidential hotlines etc.);
- Analysis of data related to customer outcomes (e.g. number/nature of complaints, time taken to resolve complaints, customer turnover etc.);
- Analysis of risk/issue reporting and the reasons for under-reporting and repeat/recurring issues;
- Analysis of data related to risk management effectiveness e.g. risk appetite breaches, control failures, regulatory breaches;
- Root cause analysis of major risk events.

3.4 Building risk culture

Embedding risk culture is an immense leadership challenge, especially when, as is often the case, risk management has historically been a low priority. Cultural change programs fail at least as often as they succeed,[27] and this is usually down to a combination of employee resistance and lack of management support.

The first step is to establish the risk structures as explained in Chapter 2: risk, compliance and assurance functions; board risk committee; a risk framework with appropriate systems, policies and processes. These structures, along with formal statements from leaders expressing commitment to risk management, take organisations to Levels 4/3 of risk management maturity (as illustrated in Figure 3.2). But reaching the upper levels is much more difficult and time-consuming, because it involves winning the battle for hearts and minds.

The ultimate goal is for members of the organisation to see risk management as fundamental for success, not a brake on success. To achieve that it will be necessary to communicate how risk management is helping the organisation to achieve its goals.

3.4.1 Guidance for boards

Non-executive directors often struggle to understand how they can play a part in influencing the culture of the organisations they oversee. But director behaviour is vital for embedding risk culture in the following respects:

- Strategic risk management. The board has ultimate responsibility for strategy and the management of risks to that strategy. The way the board discharges this responsibility has ramifications throughout the organisation and sets the tone for how the executive will approach risk. Effective management of strategic risk models the management of other risks for the rest of the organisation;
- Challenge and constructive debate. A chief executive needs critical friends with diverse perspectives. True (cognitive) diversity is not just about gender and race, although they may be indicative of diversity of experience. Cognitive diversity is about the capacity to consider problems in new ways and has been shown to be useful for reducing behavioural biases such as the illusion of control.[28] Constructing a board with cognitive diversity is counterintuitive as most humans have a natural inclination to surround themselves with yes-men and women, people who see the world as they do;
- Time and capability. Following from the previous point, non-executive directors will struggle to deliver challenging and constructive debate when they lack the time and capability. Directors who take on too many board roles and boards/committees that meet too infrequently cannot be as effective;
- Demanding accountability of the executive. Establishing clear and specific accountabilities and avoiding joint accountabilities is essential. Hiding behind ignorance and group or joint accountabilities is not acceptable. The board does not shirk its responsibility to impose such accountability and so executives who fail to deliver suffer meaningful consequences, both financial and reputational. This sends a clear and powerful message about accountability throughout the organisation;
- Culture assessment and response. The board should facilitate regular assessment of the risk culture, using the principles explained in Section 3.3. Where problems are apparent, the board should support and monitor executive initiatives to address them.

3.4.2 Speaking up and listening up

One of the most common challenges of building risk culture is to create an environment where a) employees speak up and b) managers listen. These elements are at the heart of risk management maturity.

If employees are failing to speak up about new and emerging risks, to question business practices or to report breaches and issues, it is important to understand why that might be. This question can be explored using survey methods as we did in a study of under-reporting in large Australian pension funds.[29] Reasons for under-reporting can range from the prosaic (the reporting mechanism is cumbersome to use) to fears of possible retribution from managers or team-members. Other reasons include: perception that the manager prefers not to hear about issues, doubts that anything will be done to fix the problem, excessive work pressure, lack of motivation/accountability for risk management, concern that reporting might hurt the chances of being rewarded. Having understood the underlying reasons for under-reporting, the organisation is much better placed to tackle those causes.

Fear is an important motivator and undoubtedly it can be a factor in preventing employees and managers from speaking up. In her book, The Fearless Organisation, Amy Edmondson explores the issue of psychological safety. This is a shared belief that the group/team will not embarrass, reject or punish someone for speaking up. Such a belief flourishes in an environment of trust and mutual respect. She explains how leaders can encourage open discussion so that mistakes are dealt with productively rather than being swept under the carpet. These recommendations are presented in Table 3.5.

TABLE 3.5 Building Psychological Safety (adapted from Edmondson)

Leadership Tasks	Examples
Setting the stage to create shared expectations and meaning.	• Emphasize the inevitability of 'issues' in complex organisations and the need for open discussion to resolve. • Clarify purpose i.e. the benefits of issue resolution for all stakeholders.
Inviting participation to create confidence that speaking up is welcome.	• Demonstrate humility, acknowledge gaps. • Ask good questions and model intense listening. • Create forums for input, including a system for confidential reports. • Provide guidelines for constructive debate/discussion.
Responding productively to create an orientation towards continuous learning.	• Express appreciation for speaking up, regardless of quality. Praise those who disagree constructively, even if you disagree. • Investigate and respond to issues raised within a reasonable time, keeping the person who raised the issue updated. • Destigmatise failure by looking forward, discussing solutions and offering help. • Sanction clear violations in a fair, consistent and transparent manner.

She encourages leaders to frame the work challenge appropriately, emphasising the extent of uncertainty and the need for interdependence. Leaders should acknowledge their fallibility and their reliance on team members to contribute their ideas. Leaders can also encourage multiple views and voices by demonstrating curiosity and asking lots of questions.

Notes

1 Australian Prudential Regulation Authority. (2004). *Report into irregular currency option trading at the National Australia Bank.*
2 Institute of International Finance. (2009). *Reform in the financial services industry: Strengthening practices for a more stable system.* Appendix A. III Risk Culture.
3 Ehrhart, M. G., Schneider, B., & Macey, W. H. (2013). *Organisational climate and culture: An introduction to theory, research, and practice.* Routledge.
4 Zohar, D. (1980). Safety climate in industrial organisations: Theoretical and applied implications. *Journal of applied psychology, 65*(1), 96.
5 Zohar, D. (2010). Thirty years of safety climate research: Reflections and future directions. *Accident Analysis & Prevention, 42*(5), 1517–1522.
6 Sheedy, E., Zhang, L., & Tam, K. C. H. (2019). Incentives and culture in risk compliance. *Journal of Banking & Finance, 107*, 105611.
7 Sheedy, E., & Griffin, B. (2018). Risk governance, structures, culture, and behavior: A view from the inside. *Corporate Governance: An International Review, 26*(1), 4–22.
8 A 'within-group agreement index' was calculated to assess the extent that respondents within the business unit groupings were consistent in their ratings of risk culture. An agreement index of .70 or greater is taken as evidence that employees in a particular unit rate culture consistently with one another. For more information see LeBreton, J. M., & Senter, J. L. (2007). Answers to 20 questions about interrater reliability and interrater agreement. *Organisational Research Methods, 11*, 815–852.
9 For more information on the translation of safety concepts to risk management and the development of this model, see Sheedy, E. A., & Jepsen, D. (2018, September 17). *Final report: Risk management maturity in large Australian superannuation funds.* Macquarie University Faculty of Business & Economics Research Paper. Available at SSRN: https://ssrn.com/abstract=3171833. An important source for understand how safety culture develops is Parker, D., Lawrie, M., & Hudson, P. (2006). A framework for understanding the development of organisational safety culture. *Safety Science, 44*(6), 551–562.
10 This pattern is demonstrated in the insurance industry by Magee, S., Schilling, C., & Sheedy, E. (2019). Risk governance in the insurance sector–determinants and consequences in an international sample. *Journal of Risk and Insurance, 86*(2), 381–413.
11 Sheedy, E., & Griffin, B. (2018). Risk governance, structures, culture, and behavior: A view from the inside. *Corporate Governance: An International Review, 26*(1), 4–22.
12 Kemp, M. H. D., & Patel, C. C. (2012). Entity-wide risk management for pension funds. *British Actuarial Journal, 17*(2), 331–394.
13 Howell. (2018). Ethnograpy. *Cambridge Encyclopedia of Anthropology.* Available at www.anthroencyclopedia.com/entry/ethnography
14 Engler, & Wood. (2020). How banks are using behavioral science to prevent scandals. *Harvard Business Review.* Available at https://hbr.org/2020/04/how-banks-are-using-behavioral-science-to-prevent-scandals
15 Sheedy, E. A., Griffin, B., & Barbour, J. P. (2017). A framework and measure for examining risk climate in financial institutions. *Journal of Business and Psychology, 32*(1), 101–116; McKinsey Working Papers on Risk (2010). Taking Control of Organisational Risk Culture.
16 De Nederlandsche Bank. (2015). *Supervision of behaviour and culture.* Available at www.dnb.nl/en/binaries/Book%20Supervision%20of%20Behaviour%20and%20Culture_tcm47-380398.pdf

17 Patton, M. Q. (2014). *Qualitative research & evaluation methods: Integrating theory and practice.* Sage publications, p. 410.

18 Patton, M. Q. (2014). *Qualitative research & evaluation methods: Integrating theory and practice.* Sage Publications, chapter 9.

19 Robert DeVellis. (2016). *Scale development: Theory and applications* (3rd ed.). Sage.

20 Sheedy, E. A., Griffin, B., & Barbour, J. P. (2017). A framework and measure for examining risk climate in financial institutions. *Journal of Business and Psychology, 32*(1), 101–116; McKinsey Working Papers on Risk (2010). Taking Control of Organisational Risk Culture.

21 Rosse, J. G., Stecher, M. D., Miller, J. L., & Levin, R. A. (1998). The impact of response distortion on preemployment personality testing and hiring decisions. *Journal of Applied Psychology, 83*(4), 634.

22 Griffin, B., & Wilson, I. G. (2012). Faking good: Self-enhancement in medical school applicants. *Medical Education, 46*(5), 485–490.

23 Klein, S. M., Maher, J. R., & Dunnington, R. A. (1967). Differences between identified and anonymous subjects in responding to an industrial opinion survey. *Journal of Applied Psychology, 51*(2), 152–160.

24 Green, T. C., Huang, R., Wen, Q., & Zhou, D. (2019). Crowdsourced employer reviews and stock returns. *Journal of Financial Economics, 134*(1), 236–251.

25 Ji, Yuan, Rozenbaum, Oded, & Welch, Kyle T. (2017, June 1). *Corporate culture and financial reporting risk: Looking through the glassdoor.* Available at SSRN: https://ssrn.com/abstract=2945745 or http://dx.doi.org/10.2139/ssrn.2945745

26 Ponte, L. M. (2016). Protecting brand image or gaming the system: Consumer gag contracts in an age of crowdsourced ratings and reviews. *William and Mary Business Law Review, 7,* 59.

27 McKinsey. (2015). *Changing change management.* Available at www.mckinsey.com/featured-insights/leadership/changing-change-management

28 Meissner, P., & Wulf, T. (2017). The effect of cognitive diversity on the illusion of control bias in strategic decisions: An experimental investigation. *European Management Journal, 35*(4), 430–439.

29 Sheedy, Elizabeth A., & Jepsen, Denise. (2018, September 17). *Final report: Risk management maturity in large Australian superannuation funds.* Macquarie University Faculty of Business & Economics Research Paper. Available at SSRN: https://ssrn.com/abstract=3171833 or http://dx.doi.org/10.2139/ssrn.3171833

Further reading and resources

De Nederlandsche Bank. (2015). *Supervision of behaviour and culture.* www.dnb.nl/en/binaries/Book%20Supervision%20of%20Behaviour%20and%20Culture_tcm47-380398.pdf

Edmondson, A. C. (2018). *The fearless organisation: Creating psychological safety in the workplace for learning, innovation, and growth.* John Wiley & Sons, especially Chapter 7

Gentile, M. C. (2010). *Giving voice to values: How to speak your mind when you know what's right.* Yale University Press.

Westpac Banking Corporation. (2020). *Re-assessment of the culture, governance and accountability remediation plan.* Available at www.westpac.com.au/content/dam/public/wbc/documents/pdf/aw/media/WBC_CGA_Reassessment.pdf

4

INCENTIVES AND ACCOUNTABILITY

Many risk management disasters have been caused by – or exacerbated by – poorly designed systems for measuring performance, remuneration and accountability. Performance measures can encourage short-term focus; the criteria designed to encourage risk compliance can often be gamed/faked. Executive accountability for risk is non-existent because executives claim ignorance or hide behind group decision-making processes. This chapter investigates our current knowledge in this area and discusses solutions such as deferrals and accountability regulations.

4.1 Accountability

Accountability is one of those buzzwords that is often thrown around but possibly not always well-understood. It is certainly not a new concept. In ancient Greece,[1] accountability was considered important for those in public office and procedures existed that gave the people a voice in judging performance. Plato argued that 'without accountability for our actions we would all behave unjustly'.

> Accountability refers to an implicit or explicit expectation that one's decisions or actions will be subject to evaluation by some salient audience(s) with the belief that there exists the potential for one to receive either rewards or sanctions based on this expected evaluation.
>
> *(Hall and Ferris, 2011)[2]*

Interest in accountability in governance intensified in the mid-2010s after the global financial crisis and the conduct scandals that came to light shortly afterward (see Chapter 1). While some firms incurred significant fines, members of the general public were dismayed by the fact that few senior executives suffered personal conse-quences. Instead, they hid behind ignorance and group decision-making processes, often claiming they were unaware of what was happening at lower levels. Many other corporate scandals, such as the recent destruction of the Juukan Gorge rock shelters by Rio Tinto, have raised questions about executive accountability.

BOX 4.1 RIO TINTO AND THE JUUKAN GORGE ROCK SHELTERS

Rio Tinto is a global mining giant with iron ore mining operations in the remote Pilbara region of Western Australia. The Pilbara region produces high-grade ore on a massive scale, which is largely exported for the produc-tion of steel. Rio Tinto's Brockman 4 mine is on the traditional lands of the Puutu Kunti Kurrama and Pinikura people (PKKP).

Since 2003 the company has engaged with the PKKP people in relation to the Juukan 1 and Juukan 2 rock shelters on the Brockman lease.[3] In the period since then a number of archaeological surveys have been conducted and understanding of the cultural significance of the shelters has grown. By 2014 it had been established that human activity on the site could be dated to 43,000 years and that Juukan 2 was one of the most archeologically sig-nificant sites in Australia. Archaeologists found, for example, a 28,000-year-old tool made from bone and remnants of a 4000-year-old plaited hair belt.[4] These finds provided new insights regarding the diversity and complexity of tools of the era and the timing of tool use.

Despite a stated commitment to the preservation of heritage in and around mining sites, Rio Tinto destroyed the rock shelters in May 2020. The blasting of the shelters was conducted to access some high-grade ore and thereby earn an extra US$135 million. For context, Rio's iron ore division had total revenue of US$24 billion in 2019.[5]

Shareholder and community anger over the incident was aggravated by the apparent hypocrisy. On the one hand Rio Tinto trades on its close and respectful relationship with traditional owners; annual reports feature pho-tographs of CEO Jean-Sebastian Jacques with indigenous people. Yet during the inquiry he claimed not to have known about the significant rock shelters on the Brockman lease.

The board review found that the destruction of the rock shelters was the result of numerous decisions and communication failures since 2014 but stopped short of pinning blame on any one individual. It was a case of everyone and no-one being responsible.[6] In the end, three senior executives were each seen as partly responsible: the CEO, the iron ore boss Chris Salis-bury and the corporate affairs executive Simone Niven. All three were given financial penalties but held onto their executive positions.[7]

> The case study highlights that group accountability is not true account-ability. When everyone is responsible, balls get dropped because no-one is paying sufficient attention. True accountability requires individual own-ership of an issue. The fact that no senior executive at Rio Tinto had clear ownership of heritage is the clearest possible statement that it was not a genuine priority.

This section will explore the current state of knowledge about accountability and how it affects behaviour. Research into accountability exploded in the 1980s and 1990s, and a significant review paper was published in 1999 by Lerner and Tetlock.[8] This literature identified that under certain conditions, accountability is associated with better outcomes. Interestingly, accountability can reduce a number of the biases that are particularly problematic in risk management such as overconfidence and groupthink. Research suggests that accountability works because individuals are concerned about their image and status and seek approval in the eyes of others. As accountability entails the expectation of a future evaluation, individuals position themselves to defend their decisions and behaviour. When people expect to justify their actions, they want to avoid appearing foolish. They prepare for evaluation by search-ing for reasons to justify their actions, so they analyse a wider range of relevant information, pay more attention to this information, anticipate counterargu-ments and are more self-reflective. In a management setting, we might expect that accountable persons would show more care and diligence: they might delegate responsibility in a more rigorous fashion, and follow up to check that tasks have been carried out well; they might be more diligent in responding to red flags that indicates all is not well in their area of accountability. Account-ability seems to invoke more 'system 2' or analytical thinking, as opposed to the automatic style of thinking that is associated with many of the behavioural biases.

Notice that monetary rewards and sanctions are not essential for accountabil-ity to be effective. Evaluation, even with no financial consequences, can make a difference to people's behaviour, making them more productive or improving their judgements. It's also important to note that accountability is a state of mind. Different people in the same situation might perceive or experience account-ability quite differently.

Research into individual accountability has continued at pace so far in the twenty-first century, and a further review paper by Hall, Frank and Buckley was published in 2015.[9] This discusses a number of advantages and disadvantages that have been identified by researchers in relation to accountability. For example, accountability has been found to increase workplace stress, but this is not necessar-ily a problem. Moderate amounts of stress can increase work engagement but there is potential for stress to become a problem at high levels. High levels of stress can be experienced if, for example, executives have accountability for the actions of others over whom they do not have direct authority. This is potentially a concern for executives in risk/compliance/assurance roles, but political skill might help accountable executives handle this problem.

When executives are accountable, there is an obligation to demonstrate that they have taken sufficient care in discharging their duties. As a consequence, executives may feel the need to allocate energy and resources to documenting evidence of activity or justifying decisions, resources that could be more productively used elsewhere. The academic literature has identified that resource waste is one of the potential downsides of accountability and, even worse, gaming or manipulating performance measures in order to appear effective.

BOX 4.2 REGULATING FOR EXECUTIVE ACCOUNTABILITY

To address public concerns about lack of executive accountability, the UK introduced a new regime designed to regulate accountability: the Senior Managers' and Certification Regime (SMCR).[10] This novel approach has been endorsed by the Financial Stability Board.[11] Australia[12] and Hong Kong[13] have already introduced similar regulations while others are seriously considering the same path.

The SMCR was initially introduced for banks in 2016 and has since been rolled out more broadly in the UK financial services industry. Senior managers must be assessed as fit and proper under the regime and their responsibilities clearly defined. Such clarity, along with obligations to take reasonable steps to fulfil these responsibilities, is intended to focus the minds of executives. In the event that problems emerge in their portfolio the accountable managers can easily be identified and sanctioned.

Sanctions can be imposed, for example, through the remuneration system as discussed in Section 4.2.4. Under the SMCR there is the possibility of regulatory fines imposed on individual executives and also jail sentences. But these sanctions are only part of the story. Accountability works to a large extent because people, being social creatures, are concerned about their reputation and status. Having clear individual accountability when things go awry means that the mechanisms of shame and humiliation are invoked. Fearing potential future shame, executives respond by discharging their managerial duties with greater care and diligence.

These novel regulatory moves have, perhaps unsurprisingly, created controversy. Concerns were raised, for example, about the willingness of executives to accept roles with this heightened level of scrutiny and a loss of collegiality in senior executive teams as each manager focused on their own area of accountability. But our evaluation of the Australian regime suggest that the drawbacks of individual accountability have been outweighed by the benefits.[14]

In 2019 UK Finance, an industry body, produced a report[15] evaluating the industry's experience of the SMCR to date.

> *'Overwhelmingly there is a perception within firms that there has been meaningful change. There was also evidence of real change taking place, with particular emphasis on a change in culture and behaviours. In addition, respondents reported that the implementation of the SMCR had brought the added benefit of requiring firms to definitively clarify the roles and responsibilities of senior managers. However, there was some input that suggested that the SMCR had led to too much complexity and a focus on recording evidence of decisions and actions. The report also concludes that the industry has become more risk averse, although there is a debate whether this amounts to a real change in risk appetite or alternatively more consideration of risk in decision making'.*
>
> UK Finance (2019) SMCR: Evolution and Reform
> (used with permission)

While accountability in general has many benefits, as well as some negative consequences, it's an open question as to whether accountability can be regulated. As accountability is a state of mind rather than a state of affairs, we need to know whether new accountability regulations can induce greater felt accountability. This is likely to be a function of the exact regulatory design and the effectiveness of the regulators in enforcing the regulations, but early evaluations suggest that this is a promising way forward for risk governance.

4.2 Remuneration and performance measurement

Accountability is often implemented through remuneration and performance measurement, making these some of the most important elements of the governance system. Arguably the choices that are made in this regard will have far-reaching consequences for the behaviour of employees and managers. Performance targets can be powerful drivers of behaviour if they are the basis for remuneration, sanctions, promotion and status within the firm. For this reason, it is imperative that performance evaluation systems are designed to provide the appropriate incentive(s) to add value from the perspective of shareholders and other legitimate stakeholders.

Performance-based pay is designed to align the incentives of external stakeholders and employees. By linking pay to outcomes that are in the interests of the company (such as higher revenues or profits), executives are given incentives to work hard for the benefit of its stakeholders. Performance pay is therefore a mechanism designed to alleviate agency risk. It is particularly relevant in cases where there are significant information asymmetries i.e. where it may be difficult for external stakeholders to monitor the actions of executives directly.

4.2.1 Components of executive compensation

The field of executive compensation is vast and Murphy (2012) provides a great overview of the field.[16] Table 4.1 presents the major forms of executive compensation, although even this list is incomplete because it excludes retirement benefits and perquisites such as health benefits.

From the perspective of executives, base salary in the form of cash is the most attractive form of remuneration as it is riskless. In contrast, variable remuneration either in the form of cash bonuses or the award of shares/options, is paid only when certain criteria are achieved. For example, payment might depend on achieving certain profit or sales targets, which are only partially controlled by the executive. In an economic downturn, for example, profit targets may be unattainable despite the best efforts of the executive. In this way the executive is forced to bear some risk, and this will affect the value that the executive places on the variable remuneration.

From the perspective of the company, it is this variation that is part of the attraction. Variable remuneration provides operational flexibility since it is usually paid only when the company can afford to pay executives well. Not only does variable remuneration protect against insolvency, but it provides explicit incentives for executives to behave in a specified manner. The choice of performance criteria is therefore crucial to ensure that the incentives are operating as intended. The performance criteria send a strong, salient signal to executives as to what the organisation most values and how they should direct their effort. A final benefit of variable remuneration is the ability to attract and retain the best people. Just as a tennis tournament can attract the best players by offering them higher rewards, organisations that pay for performance tend to attract the best executives or at least those who are confident in their abilities.[17]

Deferred compensation and shares/options are important for creating long-term incentives. The benefits 'vest' to the executive on a future date, often years in the future, at which point cash is paid, shares may be sold and options may be exercised. If the executive resigns prior to the vesting date these benefits may be forfeited, so they create incentives for loyalty. Deferrals also make it easier to impose sanctions if the performance is later found to have been overstated. Restricted shares vest once the vesting period has elapsed. Performance shares have an additional performance hurdle that must be met before vesting can occur.

From the perspective of the executive, shares are riskier than cash because their value depends on the share price. But shareholders often prefer to offer share-based incentives, which have the potential to better align the interests of executives with their own. Options are so named because they provide the executive with the 'option' or right to purchase[18] shares at a pre-determined

TABLE 4.1 Forms of Executive Remuneration

Form	Issues to Consider
Base Salary	• Payable in cash, no risk to the executive • No explicit incentive to perform • No operational flexibility for company
Cash Bonus	• A vehicle for short-term incentives • Useful for attracting high-performing executives • Risk to the executive (achieving targets may not be possible for reasons outside the control of the executive) • Provide operational flexibility for company • Choice of performance criteria crucial, often linked to accounting profits • Clawback of bonuses after payment can be difficult, even if misconduct is discovered.
Deferred Compensation (sometimes called restricted debt)	• Similar to cash bonus but deferral means that the compensation can be withdrawn, via malus provisions, if misconduct is discovered • Company has the use of funds until vesting date • Encourages loyalty until vesting date • Delay is unattractive to executives and also riskier (cash may be lost or reduced in the event of company insolvency) so deferral premium may be needed
Shares and Options	• Only granted/awarded when trading conditions allow, giving operational flexibility • Vesting date usually years into the future so creates longer-term incentives • Riskier for the executive than cash, since value can fall significantly, for reasons outside their control, so executives apply significant valuation discount • Potentially better alignment of interests between executives and external shareholders, since outcome depends on share price • Can have performance hurdles built in i.e. shares/options only vest if certain criteria achieved e.g. share price has to outperform the market index or peer firms. • Possibility of malus provisions, which apply prior to vesting • Applicable mainly for listed firms • Challenge of valuing restricted options at the time of grant • Possible tax benefits (relative to cash) depending on jurisdiction • Encourage loyalty until vesting date • Administrative complexity • Options encourage executive risk-taking

price, known as the exercise price. In the most common case of 'at-the-money' options, the exercise price is set equal to the share price at the time that the option is granted. For example, an option might be granted with a term of 5 years, vesting after 3 years, with an exercise price of $10. After 3 years and any time before expiry, the executive can exercise the right to buy shares at $10. If the market price is above $10 then this can be an attractive opportunity, because (s)he can immediately sell at the market price, making a profit. If, however, the share price is never above $10 during the vesting period from year 3 until expiry, the option is worthless. For this reason options are the riskiest of all from the perspective of the executive. The higher the risk and the more risk averse the executive is, the greater the discount rate that executives apply when valuing the incentives from a personal perspective.

The use of options in executive remuneration is interesting because of the link with riskier investment and financial policies.[19] Unlike shares, the value of options rises with share return volatility, providing incentive for executives to take more risk. Taking higher risk is not necessarily a bad thing and is a good thing in the right circumstances. Leading up to the GFC, however, financial institutions with more options in CEO compensation contracts took greater risks. This resulted in potential solvency problems that left these firms with no other option but to use the emergency financial assistance provided by the Federal Reserve. The lesson here is that options should be used carefully and with careful risk governance to ensure that risk-taking is appropriate given the appetite of the organisation.

The concepts of 'clawback' and 'malus' are important for understanding incentives. Clawback refers to the recovery of benefits, such as cash bonuses, after they have been paid. Clawback would be considered appropriate in cases where evidence of misconduct emerges, such as fraud. For example, executives might misrepresent the financial situation of the company in order to qualify for a bonus. If this is later discovered and the financial results have to be downgraded, then that might be grounds for recovery of the previously paid bonus.

Unfortunately, there have often been legal difficulties in recovering benefits after payment, and this has encouraged the growing popularity of deferrals and malus provisions. Malus provisions apply to benefits that have been awarded but not yet paid. If misconduct emerges during the deferral period, the benefit can be reduced or withdrawn entirely.

4.2.2 Time trends in executive compensation

Figure 4.1 shows the composition of total compensation for CEOs of S&P500 companies over time.[20] The most notable rise in CEO compensation occurred during the 1990s, fuelled by an explosion in the popularity of option grants. This was driven in part by increasing demands from shareholders for pay/performance sensitivity.[21] It should be noted, however, that options are risky from the executive

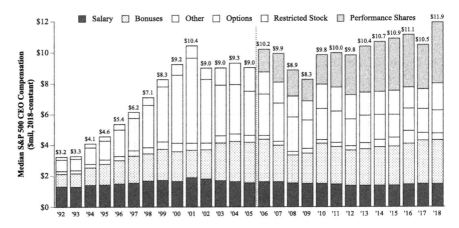

FIGURE 4.1 The Composition of CEO Pay Over Time

Source: Professor Kevin Murphy, used with permission.

perspective so the rise in compensation is not as marked if the analysis is performed on a risk-adjusted basis. In financial year 2018 total CEO compensation reached a new high, this time driven by granting of shares.

This century there has been a trend away from options and towards shares, especially performance shares. This switch is most likely a result of changes to the accounting treatment of options.[22] As of 2018, CEO compensation in large US firms is comprised approximately 50% of share awards and 14% of option grants.[23]

In the US the stock market climbed in spectacular fashion from 2009 to early 2020, so CEOs whose shares and options vested during this period pocketed large sums of money. Since a rising tide lifts all boats, even those with mediocre captains, this benefit appears out of step with the pay-for-performance principle. A solution is to ensure that vesting occurs only if other hurdles are met as in the case of performance shares e.g. share price performance exceeds the market or a group of peers. This approach has become popular but is not universally applied.

International comparisons superficially show that CEO remuneration is higher in the US than other countries. According to analysis conducted in around 2012, this gap was decreasing and could be explained largely by differences in firm size, industry, firm and board characteristics. Larger firms understandably pay CEOs more, and there are many large US firms. US firms tend to have higher institutional ownership and more independent boards than their non-US counterparts, and both these factors are associated with greater use of share-based compensation. Certainly, US firms make greater use of share-based compensation for their executives, but once adjusted for risk, the gap in favour of US CEOs disappears.[24] It would be interesting to revisit that comparison using up-to-date data.

4.2.3 Controversies in executive compensation

Are senior executives paid too much? Is there too little pay-performance sensitivity? These are some of the most contested questions in the executive compensation literature. Those in the 'efficient contracting' camp argue that the observed level and composition of compensation reflects the state of the market for managerial talent and that the incentives reflect attempts by directors to optimise firm value. The rapid rise in CEO salaries is, they maintain, no different from the rapid rise in salaries for other highly talented individuals, similar to certain entertainment and sport stars. Rockstar CEOs, like their counterparts in entertainment and sport, have the capacity to dramatically improve the performance of the firms they manage, benefitting all stakeholders. The massive disparity between executive pay and that of lower-level employees is seen as an important incentive encouraging employees to aspire to higher levels. Such disparities are called 'tournament' incentives,[25] just as in tennis or golf tournaments there is a vast disparity between the earnings of the top players and those that get knocked out in the early rounds.

On the other hand, the 'managerial power' camp argues that executive compensation is excessive and serves managerial interests. They argue that rent-seeking[26] managers take advantage of the fact that directors too readily agree to excessive compensation contracts. This happens because directors are paying executives not with their own money but with shareholder funds. In other words, directors are failing in their duties and not adequately protecting the interests of shareholders. Rent extraction is most easily accomplished through forms of compensation that are difficult for small shareholders to observe or understand. Examples include deferred pay, perquisites, loans, excessive severance payments and options that are not indexed for the market or industry.

This managerial rent extraction seems particularly relevant when hiring CEOs externally. Externally hired CEOs are uniquely positioned to maximise their compensation because of the way that recruitment and negotiation processes work, as explained by Murphy (2012). The executive search process typically leads to only a small number of potential candidates, leaving the company in a weak negotiating position. In addition, it is common for prospective CEOs to hire professionals to negotiate remuneration on their behalf. Arguably, one of the best protections against excessive compensation is to develop executive talent internally, avoiding the need for external recruitment.

4.2.4 Pay/performance sensitivity

Logically it's easier to justify high CEO pay when it is associated with excellent relative performance. But the case for 'managerial power' is strengthened by evidence of downward rigidity in CEO compensation. Downward rigidity, or pay without performance, is the degree to which executive pay is less sensitive to a decrease in firm performance than it is to an increase. Research has not only documented this phenomenon but also finds that better governance, through long-term institutional investors, helps to reduce it.[27]

Pay-performance sensitivity can come through share-based remuneration, but another mechanism is variation in cash bonuses. An Australian report on CEO remuneration in 2019[28] highlighted that bonuses were consistently paid out near the top end of their maximum value. Despite a number of cases where firms had reported disappointing and even scandalous results, CEO cash bonuses were still paid. The purportedly 'at-risk' portion of remuneration was in fact being treated more as an entitlement. The lesson here is that some directors need to work harder at imposing negative consequences on executives when performance is poor.

This asymmetry in executive remuneration – the 'heads I win, tails you lose' phenomenon – is particularly problematic for risk management. Asymmetry creates incentives for executives to take unnecessary risks at the expense of shareholders.

In addition to the asymmetry problem is the fact that the negative consequences of risk are often not seen in the short-term but become apparent over time. So, a rent-seeking executive could manipulate this situation to her advantage. By taking large risks in a benign economic environment, executives can generate short-term returns for the firm – and rewards for themselves – at the expense of disastrous longer-term outcomes once the business environment deteriorates. The self-interested executive can avoid these longer-term negative consequences by receiving her cash bonuses, selling her shares and exercising her options before the disastrous outcomes for the firm become apparent. This dynamic, illustrated in Figure 4.2, is considered to be one of the underlying causes of the global financial crisis of the mid-2000s.[29] Derivatives aficionados

FIGURE 4.2 Short-term Profits, Long-term Disaster

will recognise this profile as a short, out-of-the-money option. Most years the option grantor receives a premium but occasionally (s)he incurs significant losses when the option is exercised.

A variation on this theme occurs when short-term profits are generated through misconduct or fraud. In numerous cases, including Commonwealth Bank of Australia, executives generated short-term profits for some years by selling inappropriate products to vulnerable customers (see Chapter 12). Eventually the exploitation of customers came to light, resulting in fines, expensive remediation programs and reputational damage. Not surprisingly, these unethical business strategies were initially hidden. By the time that problems became apparent, the executives in charge had pocketed their bonuses and sold their shares at a profit.

In the Royal Commission into financial services misconduct in Australia, Commissioner Hayne, a former chief justice of the High Court of Australia concluded as follows: 'One simple, but telling, observation informs those inquiries. All the conduct identified and criticised in this report was conduct that provided a financial benefit to the individuals and entities concerned. If there are exceptions, they are immaterial'.

A couple of alternative solutions have been proposed to this problem by the financial services industry. The Financial Stability Forum produced guidance on the design of incentives after the global financial crisis, and additional guidance was provided in response to the misconduct scandals that emerged later.[30]

If our measures of risk were perfect then this problem could be easily addressed; rewards could be linked to risk-adjusted profits. Unfortunately, some risks are difficult to measure accurately, so risk-adjusted performance measures do not completely solve the problem. Where rewards are based on risk-adjusted performance, executives will have an incentive to hide or minimise risk making the measurement problem even worse. As will be discussed later, conduct and compliance risks are particularly prone to this problem.

The second proposal in Table 4.2 relates to pay/performance sensitivity. As previously explained, downward rigidity is often observed in relation to variable remuneration. In other words, too often executives receive their so-called variable remuneration regardless of performance. Responsibility rests with directors to ensure that this does not happen and to impose meaningful consequences when appropriate.

4.2.5 The balanced scorecard and gateways

The 'balanced scorecard' has been a controversial solution for addressing risk. According to the Financial Stability Board (2018):[31]

> The processes for managing misconduct risk through compensation systems should include, at a minimum, ex ante processes that embed non-financial assessment criteria such as the quality of risk management, degree

TABLE 4.2 Aligning Variable Remuneration with Risk

Proposal	Issues
Base variable remuneration on risk-adjusted profits	• Some risks are difficult to measure • Executives then have incentive to hide/minimise risk
Variable remuneration should be cut following unsatisfactory outcomes	• Requires effective governance to offset managerial power • Evidence of 'downward rigidity'
Base variable remuneration on 'balanced scorecard' with both financial and non-financial performance criteria	• Signalling benefit that non-financial criteria matter to the organisation • Non-financial performance criteria difficult to measure • Gaming/faking of non-financial criteria compromised managerial information, leads to inappropriate rewards and adversely impacts on firm culture
Gateway conditions i.e. eligibility for variable remuneration depends on meeting risk/compliance requirements	• Similar to balanced scorecard mentioned previously. Short-term risk and compliance measures are systematically biased due to monitoring difficulties.
Longer deferrals with malus provisions to cover misconduct and unexpected risk outcomes	• Higher deferral premium may be needed to compensate executives • May effect ability to attract/retain high-performing executives
Greater use of share-based remuneration (shares and options) with longer vesting periods	• Value of shares/options will suffer if risk managed poorly, so accountability is built in • More risk to executive so heavily discounted • Extend vesting period beyond term of office

of compliance with laws and regulations and the broader conduct objectives of the firm including fair treatment of customers, into individual performance management and compensation plans at all levels of the organisation and as part of the broader governance and risk management framework.

The Balanced Scorecard is a system of performance measurement used when executives have multiple, potentially competing objectives. The concept of the Balanced Scorecard was introduced by Kaplan and Norton (1992).[32] A benefit of this approach is the ability to capture a range of performance criteria that might reflect the interests of multiple stakeholders, rather than focusing solely on financial criteria. Customer outcomes, for example, are important for most organisations and including this criterion can potentially help to address conduct risk. It signals to executives that business practices that boost profits at the expense of the customer are not valued by the organisation.

In practice implementation problems have been significant due to the problems in measuring non-financial criteria in the short term. Commonly used measures of customer satisfaction, such as the Net Promoter Score (NPS),[33] are ineffective in some contexts. It is a useful measure in businesses where the customer is in a good position to assess the quality of a product or service, such as a restaurant or a hair salon. But in industries where products are complex and opaque and customers lack sophistication, the NPS is a very poor measure. A customer might be served by a crook who exploits them for personal gain, but if the exploitation is conducted with charm then the NPS is likely to be high. The misconduct towards customers may not be detected for months, years or ever. Putting it bluntly, many customers don't realise they're being screwed.

A study conducted by the Australian Securities and Investment Commission (ASIC) perfectly illustrates the problem in the context of financial advice.[34] ASIC identified problems in the ability of customers to assess the quality of financial advice. While 86% of consumers considered the advice they received to be good, ASIC assessors rated only 3% of the advice reviewed as good, with the remainder rated as only adequate or poor.

Customer turnover data and complaints data suffer from a similar problem if customers have difficulty evaluating the quality of the product or service received. Complaints data can also be exposed to the risk of manipulation by executives, especially if the data are used for determining their rewards. For example, an executive might find ways of placating an unhappy customer, to prevent them making a formal complaint. While the individual customer walks away satisfied, the underlying business practice that led to the dissatisfaction continues. Other customers who lack the motivation to express their dissatisfaction remain dissatisfied, and the complaints data shows nothing.

Goodhart's Law: when a measure becomes a target, it ceases to be a good measure.

These examples highlights a much broader problem with performance measurement: linking measures to reward tends to reduce their usefulness. This was the insight of Goodhart, a British economist, and the harder something is to measure, the more that Goodhart's Law applies. When measures are linked to reward, people often find ways to manipulate or game the measure, destroying using management information. Even worse, if it becomes common knowledge that the risk/compliance measures tend to be gamed, then this could have an adverse impact on risk culture. If performance measures can be gamed, then it's a short step to gaming other policies; the espoused risk policies are increasingly seen as a joke.

Staff engagement and culture surveys can also lose their value once the scores are used for decisions about reward or promotion, as explained in Chapter 3. By linking staff surveys to remuneration outcomes, the risk is that a) remuneration outcomes will be determined incorrectly such that poor conduct and gaming behaviour will be rewarded and b) the surveys lose their value as a management tool. The usefulness of management information will be destroyed, for no clear benefit.

In one organisation there had been a series of severe technology outages, known as Sev-1 outages. It was decided to set a key performance target for Sev-1 outages near zero. Staff in the technology area were informed that no bonuses would be paid unless the target was reached. The target was achieved, but this was done by refusing to classify any outage as Sev-1, even when there had been no connectivity for an hour. This is yet another illustration of the power of Goodhart's Law.

Increasingly we see that balanced scorecards are used not just for senior executives but for employees throughout the organisation. Due to the difficulty of measuring the non-financial criteria, manager ratings from the annual performance review are often fed into the scorecard. An example of such a criterion would be 'Behaviour is consistent with organisational values' where the manager applies a subjective rating. There is often doubt as to whether these ratings are credible and academic researchers have documented a range of problems with subjective management ratings due to various biases. Centrality bias is the tendency to give all employees a similar rating, despite variation in actual performance, while leniency bias is the tendency to give higher performance ratings than is warranted. In both cases the managers might be inclined to give most employees the same high rating, thus avoiding the need to justify low ratings to disgruntled employees. As an educator who often has to justify low grades to students, this author has a great deal of sympathy for the problem, but without a healthy variation in ratings, the whole system becomes pointless and potentially counter-productive.

Particularly worrying is the case where managers' own incentives and preferences can influence their ratings. Due to the large amount of managerial discretion in the ratings and the desire to retain top performers in sales/profits, managers may give a high rating despite poor behaviour in the risk/compliance domain.[35] Even more worrying, subjective performance ratings can be prone to favouritism, collusion and extortion.

The classic work on incentivising in multi-task contexts, where executives have more than one performance criteria, is Holmstrom and Milgrom (1991).[36] While this paper predates the term 'balanced scorecard', it addresses the fact that executives and employees are often evaluated on multiple dimensions. Even in a simple manufacturing workplace, the number of widgets produced is not the only thing that matters; quality, however defined, also matters. But crucially, quality is usually more difficult to measure than quantity. Holmstrom and Milgrom predicted that since some performance criteria are more objectively assessed than others, agents will direct more attention to those criteria and less attention to criteria that are imperfectly or subjectively measured. So even if quality and quantity have equal weighting, workers will inevitably focus on the more easily measured criteria: quantity. Since quality suffers when workers rush to achieve high quantity, quality will inevitably suffer.

This ground-breaking theoretical work predicted that:

> More generally, the desirability of providing incentives for any one activity decreases with the difficulty of measuring performance in any other activities that make competing demands on the agent's time and attention.
> *(Holmstrom and Milgrom, 1991, p. 26)*

We attempted to test this theory in an experimental study with finance professionals at Macquarie Business School.[37] In this study we investigated a simplified balanced scorecard with just two performance criteria. The first, transaction volumes, is easily measured while the second, compliance with policy, is much more challenging. Compliance risk is a significant issue in financial institutions because they are so heavily regulated; internal policies proliferate to ensure that the institution as a whole meets its legal obligations and also to ensure that its own objectives are achieved. An employee might be expected to comply with policies relating, for example, to anti-money laundering, responsible lending, credit limits, customer/product suitability, cyber-safety etc. Compliance is systematically overstated since staff will take steps to conceal policy violations while controls and monitoring activities are imperfect.

It is important to recognise that employees must weigh up the competing demands of compliance and sales. Compliance with policy will require that the employee reject some profitable opportunities, reducing sales and creating a fundamental tension between the two activities. Applying the theories of Holmstom and Milgrom (1991) to this setting, we predicted that an employee working under a balanced scorecard would focus more attention on sales volumes and less attention on compliance. A balanced scorecard arrangement that rewards both sales and compliance will therefore have worse compliance outcomes than the fixed remuneration alternative. This deterioration of compliance outcomes should, however, be offset to some extent by an improvement in sales activity due to the effort-inducing nature of the incentives. We also considered a gateway arrangement where participants would not receive any variable reward if they violated the compliance target.

The study concluded that the highest rates of compliance are achieved under fixed remuneration. Interestingly, most but not all (87.5%) participants complied when there was no variable remuneration and hence no monetary reward for violating the policy. The fact that some would breach policy even in this scenario can perhaps be explained by the fact that they are motivated to achieve high sales simply for the buzz of high performance, even with no financial reward. Once variable remuneration was introduced in the lab with the balanced scorecard, the proportion of people choosing consistently to comply dropped by 16.3%. In other words, the pressure for them to achieve high volumes produced more policy violations, even though compliance was specifically rewarded in the balanced scorecard. The proportion of people complying fell even further, by 29.2%, under the gateway condition.

We found only partial support for the hypothesis that the multi-task performance pay structures promote productivity. Both the balanced scorecard and the gateway treatments produced a significant increase in the number of transactions, but many of these transactions were inconsistent with the stated policies of the hypothetical workplace. Only the gateway treatment produced a significant increase in the number of 'good' transactions.

Multi-dimensional reward systems rely on measuring and comparing performance on multiple criteria. This raises an important question: is the poor behaviour we observed a consequence of the monetary reward or the underlying performance measurement and ranking? Some may argue that even without monetary incentives linked to sales, violations of policy would still occur since employees are motivated by the desire for non-monetary rewards such as rankings.

Again we tested this in our experimental study. We gave participants feedback on their performance, relative to peers, for both sales and compliance. We found that individuals anticipating ranking feedback were more productive, even when the ranking had no monetary consequences. In this situation the number of participants choosing to consistently comply remained unchanged but those who sometimes violated policy were less compliant.

4.2.6 Deferrals and share-based remuneration

Given the extraordinary difficulty of measuring risk/compliance outcomes in the short-term, it seems that both the balanced scorecard and the gateway are doomed to fail. Arguably if risk is going to be incorporated effectively into remuneration systems, it has to be done when the relevant information is available, that is, in the longer term. When negative information eventually comes to light, that is the best time to make the appropriate adjustments. Practically speaking, this can most easily be achieved through long-term incentives. Specifically, for risk governance, organisations wanting to offer incentives should focus on deferrals with malus clauses and restricted shares/options.

Already some research has been published that supports the use of deferrals. The accounting literature has investigated the role of provisions that allow companies to recoup incentive payments following an accounting restatement. Restatement of financial reports can indicate that executives have gamed the system by initially overstating profits to earn a bonus. US studies[38] have examined firms that introduced these provisions and find that the incidence of accounting restatements falls. In other words the executives, fearing the future loss of rewards, are less likely to engage in reporting misconduct and the quality of earnings improves.

Of course, executives don't find long-term incentives as attractive as their short-term cousins. A dollar now is always preferable to a dollar in the future, especially if it can be withdrawn for bad behaviour. This naturally raises questions about the need to offer deferral premiums, that is, higher overall pay to compensate. It also raises questions about the ability to retain/attract the best. Again we turned to our experimental laboratory at Macquarie Business School to answer these questions.[39] Our initial focus was on students, since many organisations recruit university graduates and the ability to attract good graduates is an important consideration.

Similar to the experiment described previously, we used an experimental design where participants were judged for both their productivity and their compliance with policies in a hypothetical workplace. Whereas productivity was measured perfectly, compliance was imperfectly measured; not all transactions were checked or audited for compliance with policy prior to payment. We allowed participants to choose between three different remuneration schemes, reflecting the reality that in the real world, people gravitate over time to organisations that offer them desirable remuneration.

Table 4.3 summarises the three remuneration schemes in the experiment. In schemes 1 and 3, participants received their payment immediately whereas in scheme 2, the payment was deferred by a week. In scheme 2 we offered higher payment to compensate for the delay. In the schemes with immediate payment

TABLE 4.3 Experimenting with Deferrals

Remuneration Scheme	Participants who chose the scheme...
1. Variable with Immediate Payment; Audit rate 20%	• Displayed the lowest rates of compliance • Were less likely to be compliant • Were more likely to be male
2. Variable with Deferred Payment; Audit rate 90%; Deferral Premium	• Displayed the highest rates of compliance • Displayed the highest productivity • Were more likely to be productive
3. Fixed Payment; Audit rate 20%	• Displayed the lowest productivity • Were more likely to be unproductive • Were more likely to be female

the audit rate was 20%, but this increased to 90% in scheme 2, reflecting the fact that monitoring tends to improve when more time is available.

We observed the highest productivity and the highest rates of compliance in scheme 2 with deferrals. The selection effects proved to be important because people selected into the various remuneration schemes according to ability and propensity to violate the policies. We were able to judge the abilities/propensities of participants because of their performance in early rounds, prior to the selection stage. Scheme 2, with deferred payment but better monitoring of behaviour was disproportionately selected by productive people and, not surprisingly, produced the best outcomes. While some individuals prefer immediate payment of bonuses, these individuals are not significantly more likely to be productive. The finding is consistent with extant behavioural studies that have linked cognitive ability to greater patience and lower discounting of future payments.[40] This means that deferrals may therefore be helpful for selecting those with cognitive ability

While more research on deferrals is needed, the evidence we have so far appears promising. While remuneration costs are likely to be higher in total under deferrals, organisations may be willing to pay more to achieve productivity with compliance.

Greater use of share-based remuneration confers similar advantages to deferred cash. This is because the shares cannot be sold, or options exercised, until after the vesting period is completed. Malus clauses can be built in that allow the benefits to be withdrawn following unacceptable risk outcomes or evidence of misconduct.

Unfortunately, many of the share-based remuneration schemes vest after only 3–4 years, and this is arguably not long enough to address long-term threats. Adapting to climate change involves significant expenditure in the short-term but the benefits will be seen over the coming decades. Why would executives with a three-year vesting horizon bother to make these significant investments for the future, investments that will harm short-term profits and rewards?

Another problem with these plans is the potential for executives to build up significant wealth over time, creating a sense of overconfidence and immunity to risk. After a number of years in the job, several tranches of shares may already have vested and been converted to cash. With so much cash in the bank, the executive arguably becomes increasingly risk tolerant and unconcerned about future losses. Consider the cases of Lehman and Bear Stearns.[41] From 2000–08, senior executives cashed out $1.4 billion and $1 billion, respectively, from cash bonuses and equity sales. It's unlikely that their incentives were truly aligned with current shareholders in 2007, who would have benefited from a more conservative approach.

Yet another problem with many share schemes is the possibility of share price manipulation around the vesting date. A study by Edmans, Fang and Huang[42] found that vesting equity is positively associated with the probability of a firm repurchasing shares. CEOs orchestrate these buybacks not because the shares are undervalued but to boost up the share price just prior to the vesting date and therefore to maximise the value of their share proceeds. In the 2–3 years afterward, such firms typically experience more negative returns.

In order to avoid such manipulations and create a truly long-term focus for addressing long-term threats, we need radical solutions. Some have recommended very long vesting periods ending 2–4 years after the executive's last day in office.[43] The extension beyond the term of office creates incentives for the executive to continue a long-term focus till the very end of her term and maintain a sharp focus on risk.

Share-based remuneration is arguably less useful for incentivising employees at lower levels. Unlike senior executives, low level employees have little ability to influence the share price. Forcing them to take a risk, over which they have little control, may be counter-productive in the sense that employees will apply a very large discount rate. This means that employees, who see little value in the shares, are not motivated by them to any significant extent.

In fact, for lower-ranking employees there is less need to offer incentive pay at all. The possibility of promotion, not available to senior executives, should provide adequate incentive for good long-term performance. Careful consideration must be given to promotion criteria to ensure that risk and compliance outcomes play an appropriate role. Advancement is not usually something that happens annually, so it provides an opportunity for evaluation of employees over an extended period of time. Professional services firms have demonstrated the effectiveness of this method, leveraging the steep differential between salaries at high and low levels. Their junior employees work long hours, despite the lack of any explicit incentive payment, for the opportunity to rise through the ranks and perhaps to be offered partnership.

Notes

1 Lane, M. (2020). The idea of accountable office in Ancient Greece and beyond. *Philosophy, 95*(1), 19–40.
2 Hall, A. T., & Ferris, G. R. (2011). Accountability and extra-role behavior. *Employee Responsibilities and Rights Journal, 23*(2), 131–144.
3 Rio Tinto. (2020). *Board review of cultural heritage management.* Available at www.riotinto. com/en/news/releases/2020/Rio-Tinto-publishes-board-review-of-cultural-heritage-management#:~:text=The%20board%20review%20concluded%20that,and%20above%20its%20legal%20obligations
4 Sydney Morning Herald. (2020, May 26). *Blast destroys one of country's oldest know Aboriginal heritage sites.* Available at www.smh.com.au/national/blast-destroys-one-of-country-s-oldest-known-aboriginal-heritage-sites-20200526-p54wmt.html
5 Australian Financial Review. (2020, August 8). Rio Tinto's cultural indifference. Available at www.afr.com/chanticleer/rio-tinto-s-cultural-indifference-20200807-p55jmq
6 Australian Financial Review. (2020, August 24). *Everyone and no-one to blame for Rio gorge tragedy.* Available at www.afr.com/chanticleer/everyone-and-no-one-to-blame-for-rio-gorge-tragedy-20200824-p55oo9
7 Australian Financial Review. (2020, August 24). *Rio Tinto chairman backs Jacques over Juukan.* Available at www.afr.com/companies/mining/rio-tinto-chairman-backs-jacques-over-juukan-20200824-p55oll
8 Lerner, J. S., & Tetlock, P. E. (1999). Accounting for the effects of accountability. *Psychological Bulletin, 125*(2), 255.
9 Hall, A. T., Frink, D. D., & Buckley, M. R. (2017). An accountability account: A review and synthesis of the theoretical and empirical research on felt accountability. *Journal of Organizational Behavior, 38*(2), 204–224.

10 Allen, T. (2018). Strengthening the link between seniority and accountability: The senior managers and certification regime. *Bank of England Quarterly Bulletin, 58*(3), 1–10.

11 Financial Stability Board. (2018). *Strengthening governance frameworks to mitigate misconduct risk: A toolkit for firms and supervisors.* Available at www.fsb.org/2018/04/strengthening-governance-frameworks-to-mitigate-misconduct-risk-a-toolkit-for-firms-and-supervisors/

12 Australian Prudential Regulation Authority. (2018). *Information paper: Implementing the banking executive accountability regime.* Available at www.apra.gov.au/sites/default/files/information_paper_implementing_the_bear.pdf

13 Hong Kong Securities and Futures Commission. (2017) *SFC fully implements manager-in-charge regime.* Available at www.sfc.hk/edistributionWeb/gateway/EN/news-and-announcements/news/doc?refNo=17PR131

14 Sheedy, & Canestrari-Soh (2021) 'Regulating Accountability: An early look at the Banking Executive Accountability Regime (BEAR)'. Available at https://papers.ssrn.com/sol3/papers.cfm?abstract_id=3775275

15 UK Finance. (2019). *SMCR: Evolution and reform.* Available at www.ukfinance.org.uk/policy-and-guidance/reports-publications/smcr-evolution-and-reform

16 Murphy, Kevin J. (2012, August 12). Executive compensation: Where we are, and how we got there. In George Constantinides, Milton Harris, & René Stulz (Eds.), *Handbook of the economics of finance.* Elsevier Science, North Holland (Forthcoming), Marshall School of Business Working Paper No. FBE 07.12. Available at SSRN: https://ssrn.com/abstract=2041679 or http://dx.doi.org/10.2139/ssrn.2041679

17 Dohmen, T., & Falk, A. (2011). Performance pay and multidimensional sorting: Productivity, preferences, and gender. *American Economic Review, 101*(2), 556–590.

18 Call options give the right to purchase which put options give the right to sell shares. In the context of executive remuneration, call options are always used.

19 Coles, J., Daniel, N., & Naveen, L. (2006). Managerial incentives and risk-taking. *Journal of Financial Economics, 79,* 431–468; Chen, C. R., Steiner, T. L., & Whyte, A. M. (2006). Does stock option-based executive compensation induce risk-taking? An analysis of the banking industry. *Journal of Banking & Finance, 30*(3), 915–945; Gande, A., & Kalpathy, S. (2017). CEO compensation and risk-taking at financial firms: Evidence from US federal loan assistance. *Journal of Corporate Finance, 47,* 131–150.

20 Figure 4.1 was sourced directly from Professor Kevin Murphy and is used with his permission. Compensation data are based on all CEOs included in the S&P 500 using data from ExecuComp. CEO grant-date pay includes cash pay, payouts from long-term pay programs, and the grant-date value of stock and option awards (using company fair market valuations when available and otherwise using ExecuComp's modified Black Scholes approach). Monetary amounts are converted to 2018 constant US dollars using the consumer price index.

21 Murphy (2012) argues in 5.2.3 that the dramatic increase in option grants during the 1990s resulted from low 'perceived cost' from the perspective of the companies granting them. For the company there is no cash outlay, and (prior to the 2006 changes in accounting rules) no accounting charge.

22 See Murphy (2012) Section 3.8.4

23 Economic Policy Institute. (2019). *CEO compensation has grown 940% since 1978.* Available at https://files.epi.org/pdf/171191.pdf

24 See Murphy (2012) Section 4.

25 Kini, O., & Williams, R. (2012). Tournament incentives, firm risk, and corporate policies. *Journal of Financial Economics, 103*(2), 350–376.

26 Rent seeking is the practice of unfairly manipulating policy or economic conditions for personal benefit at the expense of others.

27 Choi, P. M. S., Chung, C. Y., Hwang, J. H., & Liu, C. (2019). Heads I win, tails you lose: Institutional monitoring of executive pay rigidity. *Journal of Financial Research, 42*(4), 789–816.

28 Australian Council of Superannuation Investors. (2019). *CEO pay in ASX200 companies*. Available at https://acsi.org.au/wp-content/uploads/2020/02/CEO-Pay-in-ASX200-Companies-September-2019.pdf

29 Bhagat, S., & Bolton, B. (2014). Financial crisis and bank executive incentive compensation. *Journal of Corporate Finance, 25*, 313–341.

30 Initial post-crisis principles are in Financial Stability Forum. (2009). *FSF principles for sound compensation practices*. Available at www.fsb.org/wp-content/uploads/r_0904b.pdf The Financial Stability Board replaced the Financial Stability Forum. Further guidance on compensation was provided in Financial Stability Board (2018). *Supplementary guidance to the FSB principles and standards on sound compensation practices*. Available at www.fsb.org/2018/03/supplementary-guidance-to-the-fsb-principles-and-standards-on-sound-compensation-practices-2/

31 Financial Stability Board. (2018). *Supplementary guidance to the FSB principles and standards on sound compensation practices*. Available at www.fsb.org/2018/03/supplementary-guidance-to-the-fsb-principles-and-standards-on-sound-compensation-practices-2/

32 Kaplan, R., & Norton, P. D. (1992). The balanced scorecard: Measures that drive performance. *Harvard Business Review, 83*(7/8), 172–180. Available at http://simsrad.net.ocs.mq.edu.au/login?url=https://search.ebscohost.com/login.aspx?direct=true&db=heh&AN=17602418&site=ehost-live

33 The NPS is calculated based on responses to a single question: *How likely is it that you would recommend our company/product/service to a friend or colleague?* The scoring for this answer is most often based on a 0 to 10 scale. Those who respond with a score of 9 to 10 are called promoters; those who respond with a score of 0 to 6 are labelled detractors. The Net Promoter Score is calculated by subtracting the percentage of customers who are detractors from the percentage of customers who are promoters.

34 Australian Securities and Investments Commission. (2019). *Disclosure: Why it shouldn't be the default*. Report 632. Available at https://asic.gov.au/regulatory-resources/find-a-document/reports/rep-632-disclosure-why-it-shouldn-t-be-the-default/

35 Bol, J. C. (2011). The determinants and performance effects of managers' performance evaluation biases. *The Accounting Review, 86*(5), 1549–1575; also Delfgaauw, J., & Souverijn, M. (2016). Biased supervision. *Journal of Economic Behavior & Organization, 130*, 107–125.

36 Holmstrom, B., & Milgrom, P. (1991). Multitask principal-agent analyses: Incentive contracts, asset ownership, and job design. *Journal of Law, Economics and Organization, 7*, 24.

37 Sheedy, Elizabeth A., Zhang, Le, & Steffan, Dominik. (2019, May 15). *Scorecards, rankings and gateways: Remuneration and conduct in financial services*. 2019 Financial Markets & Corporate Governance Conference. Available at SSRN: https://ssrn.com/abstract=3317344

38 Chan, L. H., Chen, K. C., & Chen, T. Y. (2013). The effects of firm-initiated clawback provisions on bank loan contracting. *Journal of Financial Economics, 110*(3), 659–679; also Dehaan, E., Hodge, F., & Shevlin, T. (2013). Does voluntary adoption of a clawback provision improve financial reporting quality? *Contemporary Accounting Research, 30*(3), 1027–1062.

39 Sheedy, Elizabeth A., Zhang, Le, & Liao, Yin. (2020, February 5). *Deferred pay in financial services: Compliance, productivity and attracting talent*. Macquarie Business School Research Paper No. February 2020. Available at SSRN: https://ssrn.com/abstract=3535347 or http://dx.doi.org/10.2139/ssrn.3535347

40 Frederick, S. (2005). Cognitive reflection and decision making. *Journal of Economic perspectives, 19*(4), 25–42; Dohmen, Thomas, et al. "Are risk aversion and impatience related to cognitive ability?" *American Economic Review* 100.3 (2010): 1238–60; Ackert, L. F., Deaves, R., Miele, J., & Nguyen, Q. (2020). Are time preference and risk preference associated with cognitive intelligence and emotional intelligence?. *Journal of Behavioral Finance, 21*(2), 136–156; Bayer, Y. A. M., & Osher, Y. (2018). Time preference, executive functions, and ego-depletion: An exploratory study. *Journal of Neuroscience, Psychology, and Economics, 11*(3), 127.

41 Bebchuk, L. A., Cohen, A., & Spamann, H. (2010). The wages of failure: Executive compensation at Bear Stearns and Lehman 2000–2008. *Yale Journal on Regulation, 27*, 257.
42 Edmans, A., Fang, V. W., & Huang, A. (2017). The long-term consequences of short-term incentives. *European Corporate Governance Institute (ECGI)-Finance Working Paper*, (527).
43 Bhagat, S., & Bolton, B. (2014). Financial crisis and bank executive incentive compensation. *Journal of Corporate Finance, 25*, 313–341; Bhagat, S., Bolton, B., & Romano, R. (2014). Getting incentives right: Is deferred bank executive compensation sufficient. *Yale Journal on Regulation, 31*, 523.

PART B

The risk management process

.

5

RISK MANAGEMENT PROCESS OVERVIEW

Understanding the risk management process is essential for all risk/compliance/ assurance professionals, as well as for those overseeing the process in senior leadership roles. The process, as embedded in international risk management standards ISO31000, is illustrated in Figure 5.1. This chapter briefly explains the process, based on the standards. The chapters that follow explore specific aspects of the process in more detail, with examples drawn from a range of industries.

5.1 Communication and consultation

Effective risk management relies on gathering relevant information and feedback, hence the need for consultation with both internal and external stakeholders and relevant experts. Consultation is particularly important when defining risk criteria and evaluating risks.

Communication is needed to promote awareness and understanding of risk. It helps ensure that members of the organisation are clear about their role in risk management. Frequent communication with internal and external stakeholders is particularly important in dynamic risk environments.

5.2 Scope, context and criteria

This step is to clarify certain features of the risk environment before proceeding to analysis.

> Scope: does the risk management apply to a program, project, or organisation? Is the focus strategic or operational?
>
> Context: what are the important contextual factors, both internal and external? External context might include regulatory, competitive, technological, economic, legal and societal factors. Internal context could take

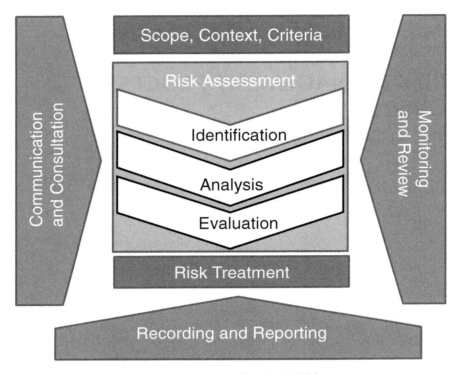

FIGURE 5.1 Risk Management Process Based on ISO31000

account of resources, strategic objectives, organisational history and culture etc.

Criteria: here we define the risk criteria that will be monitored to evaluate the significance of risk and guide decisions. The criteria must reflect the organisation's objectives and resources, as well as obligations to stakeholders. In organisations where the safety of employees and customers is a concern, criteria could include the rate of fatal and serious accidents. For a company with debt covenants based on the level of earnings, earnings per quarter would be a sensible risk criterion since a breach could lead to foreclosure.

ISO31000 does not specifically mention the term 'risk appetite', but its importance is implied. An understanding of organisational context provides an understanding of how much risk the organisation is willing to take, on key risk criteria, in order to achieve its objectives.

5.3 Risk assessment

Risk assessment includes three sub-processes: identification, analysis and evaluation. The first step, identification, is the simplest; the focus here is simply on recognising and describing risks to create a risk register. A potential challenge here is to identify emerging risks before they become serious.

Risk analysis involves detailed, often quantitative consideration of possible outcomes, including likelihood and impact. This is arguably the most difficult step in the entire risk management process, with flawed analysis leading to disastrous decisions in subsequent stages. Good risk analysis is a potential defence against biases such as overconfidence and the availability bias but is itself exposed to biases and blind spots.

Risk evaluation is the final step of the assessment process leading up to the treatment decision. We review the results of the analysis and consider the likely impact of risk on the risk criteria. This evaluation might prompt additional analysis or consideration of possible treatments and their effectiveness, having regard for cost. It might also prompt further discussion of objectives.

5.4 Risk treatment

The risk treatment stage includes selecting, planning and implementing treatments. In general there are six broad options as follows:

- Retain. No action is needed as the risk is acceptable;
- Avoid. Discontinue an activity that creates unacceptable risk;
- Increase. Take additional risk in order to pursue an attractive opportunity;
- Reduce the likelihood of an adverse event. This involves preventative controls;
- Mitigate. Impact controls reduce the consequences flowing from an adverse event;
- Transfer. Share the risk with other parties e.g. insurance.

The risk treatment stage is more complex than it first appears because treatments can introduce new risks and adverse consequences to be managed. There are usually multiple potential treatments that may be considered, all varying in their effectiveness and cost.

5.5 Recording and reporting

Effective reports aid understanding, encompass all the crucial issues as briefly as possible and support good decisions. Reports are needed to help managers keep track of the extent of risk – ensuring that it is within appetite – and to monitor risk trends. Reporting to the board is a particularly fraught issue, with the challenge being to provide relevant, insightful information without overwhelming and unnecessary detail. A fundamental principle of reporting risk is that reports should focus on the organisation's chosen risk criteria (see Section 5.2).

5.6 Monitoring and review

Successful risk management requires ongoing monitoring and review. It's an iterative process requiring constant adjustment, since risks are evolving, analysis is imperfect and treatments often have unforeseen outcomes. In this stage the organisation could consider some or all of the following:

- Were the actual outcomes for risk criteria in line with expectations, and if not, why? To what extent was the outcome due to good luck or good management? Sometimes large samples covering long periods of time are needed in order to tell the difference;
- How effective was the risk analysis for predicting possible outcomes? If not why? Did we fail to consider certain risks? How can risk analysis be refined to be more useful in future?
- Did the treatments operate in the manner expected, and if not, why? Can the treatments be refined for the future? What new treatments might we consider?
- Do we need to review the risk criteria to better address the needs of stakeholders?
- Are risk reports providing useful information to the key stakeholders?

6

COMMUNICATING AND INFLUENCING FOR RISK GOVERNANCE

Communication and consultation play an important role in the risk management process. The communication goal might be to help relevant stakeholders understand risk or to persuade them to introduce/upgrade the risk management framework. A consultation process aims to consider a range of perspectives or gather relevant information. In the context of risk governance these goals are particularly challenging because of the biases, blind spots and bonuses that impede our ability to think about and respond to risk. Efforts to communicate, consult and influence occur in an environment where the audience is sometimes hostile and often apathetic. Very few will be naturally engaged in the topic, unless in the midst of a major scandal or disaster. In this chapter we explore some possible solutions to these problems.

6.1 Dealing with hostility and suspicion

Risk governance typically benefits external stakeholders (debt providers, customers, suppliers, regulators, broader community and shareholders with a long-term view), so the hostile response is normally from within. Very few people like change, so attempts by organisations to adopt risk governance, requiring people to comply with new policies, can sometimes be met with hostility and/or suspicion. One of the advantages of a hostile audience is that they are at least engaged in the topic; in some respects this is easier to deal with than the case of apathy. Audiences who are interested and engaged are much more likely to respond to well-reasoned arguments and analysis of facts. But first you must listen.

One of the most important principles in all communication is to understand the attitudes and concerns of the audience. To maximise success, take time to understand the underlying issues, values and attitudes that might be creating hostility and suspicion. Once understanding has been gained, show that you have listened and heard by acknowledging the concerns of the audience. Then you are in a much stronger position to address those concerns and misconceptions. You may be able to provide information that corrects false impressions.

A further benefit of understanding the audience is the ability to better craft your message. You will need to frame your case/arguments in terms that are consistent with the audience's own perspectives and needs. A recent study[1] found that environmental messages need to be framed differently depending on whether the audience has more liberal political views or more conservative views. For the more liberal audience, the message described the harm and destruction humans are causing to the environment and emphasized how important it is for people to care about and protect the environment. The harm/care pictures showed a destroyed forest of tree stumps, a barren coral reef and cracked land suffering from drought. For the more conservative audience, the message appealed to notions of purity/sanctity, focusing on how polluted and contaminated the environment has become and how important it is for people to clean and purify the environment. The purity/sanctity pictures showed a cloud of pollution looming over a city, a person drinking contaminated water and a forest covered in garbage.

Dr Robert Cialdini studied the science of influencing for many years and identified six principles for influencing others.[2] One of these is the principle of **consensus and social proof**: the idea that people tend to follow the lead of others who are similar to themselves. If you can convince some people in the organisation of the benefits of risk governance, those with hostile or cynical attitudes are more likely to follow suit. Over time people will tend to either fall into line or depart.

Another Cialdini principle is **authority**, based on the idea that people are uncertain how to behave and thus look to experts for guidance. Humans have a strong tendency to agree with others they admire, so find an authoritative, credible and admired spokesperson who can present the case for risk governance persuasively.

Yet another Cialdini principle is **liking**. You are much more likely to influence/persuade if you are liked by the audience. Liking often develops from finding common ground such as shared interests. It can also grow in the presence of genuine praise. Simple things like smiling and friendliness can go a long way. Never use offensive language.

The principle of liking relates to yet another principle – **reciprocity**. If an individual gives us something, not only are we more inclined to like them; we feel obligated to reciprocate. You can use this principle to your advantage, whether or not your audience is hostile. By doing something for them, helping them achieve their goals, they are much more likely to reciprocate by helping you with your risk governance goals.

Following a gracious act on your part, you are in a strong position to ask your audience to take a small step in assisting you. While they may not be on board with every aspect of risk governance, they may be willing to put a toe in the water. Asking for a minor contribution, such as a small information request or feedback on a short report, would rarely be rejected, especially as these requests demonstrate respect for their expertise or perspective. Having agreed to a small request, people are then more likely to respond favourably to much more significant requests. This is due to the principle of **commitment and consistency**; it turns out that people like to be self-consistent.

6.2 Dealing with apathy and overconfidence

Apathy and overconfidence are some of the most pervasive challenges for risk governance communication. Very few people have a natural interest in risk governance and therefore the goal is to engage the audience.

Here too, understanding your audience is key. The more you can understand what issues concern them, the more you can engage them by linking your communication to those issues. But your message will almost certainly need strong emotional hooks to get attention. Use emotionally involving scenes, vivid visuals and lively/rich language including metaphor. Dramatized case examples and testimonials may cut through; consider using video rather than just written communication. Many businesspeople find this communication style uncomfortable, being more familiar with written communication that is in a constrained and guarded style. The influencing techniques of Cialdini, mentioned earlier, can also be used effectively for apathetic and overconfident audiences.

6.3 Use of storytelling

One of the most noticeable trends in communication recently has been the use of narrative or storytelling. Indeed, a number of case studies are used in this book. Organisations increasingly use storytelling methods because they are so compelling, engaging and disseminate well. For example, messages told in story format get shared more on social media. Stories can help the audience to understand the risk through simplification and highlighting cause and effect. Risk management stories are particularly helpful because they make complex and abstract concepts much more relatable and concrete.

Storytelling works well both for breaking down hostility and engaging those who are apathetic. A well-told story transports us to another world and involves us. Stories inhibit the normal process of counterargument invoked by a traditional persuasive message. They make people more open to alternative points of view and more likely to revise their preconceived ideas. This is one of the reasons why novels and cinema have often been powerful agents of change in society.

While narrative has enormous power, it is not a panacea and doesn't apply to every situation. Non-narrative forms of communication (didactic, expository) can be seen as more objective and credible. There is a danger that narrative can over-simplify and distract from the intended message. They can also be seen as manipulative or as propaganda. Both approaches can be valid depending on the situation.

6.4 Appealing to fear

A fear appeal is a communication that attempts to persuade people to change their behaviour by highlighting the negative consequences of the behaviour and invoking a fear reaction. A television commercial showing a horrific car crash is a fear-based message designed to encourage drivers to slow down or avoid drunk driving. Cigarette packaging showing an image of a diseased lung is designed to discourage smoking. Similarly, a staff video that makes salient the potential for customer harm and reputational damage could be used to promote staff compliance with policies designed to protect customers.

Fear appeals are controversial and have been much studied in the academic literature. Some claim that fear-based messaging can backfire, because instead of invoking fear they invoke denial. One of the barriers to the success of fear appeals is that behavioural biases can make them less effective. A young smoker may have a sense of invulnerability or over-optimism that (s)he will not personally be affected by smoking-related disease. If the consequences of the behaviour occur in the long-term, then short-termism may cause the person to focus more on the pleasure of the moment than bad outcomes that are decades in the future.

A major meta-analysis of the effectiveness of fear appeals was published in 2015[3] and provides strong evidence to support this approach. The meta-analysis assessed 127 studies collected from diverse populations. Fear appeals are generally effective for changing attitudes, intentions and behaviours and there was no evidence that they produce negative outcomes. Fear appeals are most effective when they are accompanied by efficacy statements, that is, assurances that action can be taken to address the risk and the recipients are capable of performing the recommended actions. The effect of fear appeals is greatest for cases of high severity and high susceptibility, that is, where the message emphasises the recipient's personal risk for negative consequences and those consequences are severe. Their effect is greater for one-time behaviours (e.g. getting vaccinated) than for repeated behaviours (e.g. regular exercise).

6.5 General principles

- Start with understanding your audience and their concerns. Tailor the message accordingly;
- People who are interested respond to rational appeals (expert quotes, documentation and statistics);
- People who are not involved or apathetic need emotional appeals e.g. dramatized case examples and testimonials;

- Fear-based messages are good for getting attention. To maximise their effect, also offer concrete and achievable strategies to address the risk and assurances that the audience is capable of implementing the strategies;
- Use stories to engage the audience, make abstract risk concepts relatable and break down hostility/suspicion;
- Give careful consideration to the tone of your message. Serious is the safest but do not preach or dictate. Sometimes a light, humorous, ironic or dramatic tone can work;
- When arguing a case, start with strongest points first;
- Ensure that your message is clear to the target audience. Ideally you should test your communication first on a small representative sample or get another opinion;
- Think about how you will first capture, and then maintain attention throughout. Apart from fear, other useful tools are change, novelty and mystery;
- Think carefully about your call to action. Make it very clear, concrete and achievable. For example, rather than ask people to stop smoking, ask them to commit to a smoke-free week;
- Use role models and credible authorities where relevant;
- Make every possible effort to meet your audience more than halfway e.g. use the communication medium or meeting location that they are most comfortable with;
- Provide good evidence for threats and benefits.

BOX 6.1 COMMUNICATING LOW PROBABILITY EVENTS

Effective communication is one of the ways we can best influence people to make good risk choices. It turns out that small changes in the way we communicate can make a big difference in the way people respond. Consider these two statements about the risks associated with using a vaccine that protects children from a fatal disease.

> Statement 1: the vaccine carries a 0.001% risk of permanent disability.
> Statement 2: one of 100,000 vaccinated children will be permanently disabled.

Which statement has greater impact on you? If you're like most people, the second statement is much more impactful, even though the two statements are mathematically equivalent. It conjures up an image of the one child who is permanently disabled while the 99,999 safely vaccinated children are downplayed. This is an example of what psychologists call 'denominator neglect'.[4] Low probability events are taken more seriously when they're expressed in terms of frequency or numbers, like in Statement 2. When we express risk in terms of percentages or probabilities, the impact is reduced. Probabilities are abstract for most people but numbers are more vivid.

Here's another example. In a research study, people were asked to judge which of two situations was more risky:

> Case 1: a disease that kills 1,286 people out of every 10,000 (Notice that here the risk is expressed as a frequency.)
>
> Case 2: a disease that kills 24.14% of the population (Here the risk is expressed as a probability.)

People tended to judge the first case as being more risky, although here the disease kills fewer than 13% of the population and is mathematically much less risky. This is yet another example of how people struggle to make accurate judgements about risk.

What does this mean for communication habits? We need to get into the habit of communicating risk information appropriately, depending on the situation. If there's a danger that people are neglecting a risk, we need to think of ways to make the bad outcome more vivid. Using frequencies rather than probability is one way to do that. Using rich and vivid descriptions of the bad outcome is another way to focus attention where it's needed. Terrorists are masters at this because they work to construct bad outcomes and media images that are extremely vivid and distressing, even though the probability is vanishingly low.

In other cases the danger is the opposite. People can be unduly concerned about bad outcomes – like shark or terrorist attacks. In that case it's helpful to put the dreaded outcome into context and make the good outcomes more salient. For example if someone is terrified of swimming at the beach because of sharks you could say: out of ten million people swimming at the beach, one person will be attacked by a shark, a few people will drown, some thousands will have a minor mishap like sunburn, but more than 9,990,000 will have a fun time and be healthier for getting some exercise and Vitamin D. Why would you want to miss out on that?

So next time you need to communicate about risk, think about your goal and the context. And adapt your message appropriately.

6.6 Quantitative information

Presenting numerical information can be challenging, especially for non-technical audiences with poor numeracy. It's important to:

- Highlight the most important information;
- Pre-test symbols and graphics;

- Use risk visualization wherever possible;
- If you state probabilities as 1 chance in X, keep X consistent. For example, there is one chance in 10 of insolvency this year, 3 chances in 10 of achieving our target profit;
- Express as absolute risks (1 in 10) as opposed to relative risk (10%) and do not use decimals;
- Use analogies i.e. 1 in 1,000,000 is difficult to conceptualise. An analogy would be that this is equivalent to 30 seconds in a year;
- Presenting uncertainty about risk estimates is challenging. It increases the perceived trustworthiness but reduces the perceived competence of the source. Best to address uncertainty head-on. Acknowledge it, explain why it exists, describe what, if anything can be done to get a better handle on it and explain how the risk can be reduced in the meantime;
- Avoid cumulative distribution functions as very few people understand them;
- Provide simple interpretive text to complement figures and charts.

Notes

1 Feinberg, M., & Willer, R. (2013). The moral roots of environmental attitudes. *Psychological Science*, *24*(1), 56–62.
2 Cialdini, R. (2014). *Influence: The psychology of persuasion* (Revised ed.). Harper Collins.
3 Tannenbaum, M. B., Hepler, J., Zimmerman, R. S., Saul, L., Jacobs, S., Wilson, K., & Albarracín, D. (2015). Appealing to fear: A meta-analysis of fear appeal effectiveness and theories. *Psychological Bulletin*, *141*(6), 1178.
4 See discussion of this in chapter 30 of Kahneman, Daniel. (2011). *Thinking, Fast and Slow*. Allen Lane.

Further reading and resources

Cialdini, R. (2014). *Influence: The psychology of persuasion* (Revised ed.). Harper Collins.
Cialdini, R. (2016). *Presuasion: A revolutionary way to influence and persuade*. Random House Books.
Lundgren, R. E., & McMakin, A. H. (2018). *Risk communication: A handbook for communicating environmental, safety, and health risks*. John Wiley & Sons. See Chapter 22 for information about communicating in a crisis.
Perloff, R. (2016). *The dynamics of persuasion: Communication and attitudes in the 21st century* (6th ed.). Routledge.

7
CONTEXT, CRITERIA AND RISK APPETITE

This phase of the risk management process clarifies certain features of the risk environment; it's a critical step before proceeding to analysis. We consider the following:

> Context: what are the important contextual factors, both internal and external?
> Criteria: what are the risk criteria that are of concern?
> Risk Appetite: what is our appetite for risk on the chosen criteria given our context?

7.1 Context

External context might include regulatory, competitive, technological, economic, legal and societal factors. Internal context could take account of resources, strategic objectives, organisational history and culture etc.

One of the most common questions about risk governance is whether it can be applied to smaller or unlisted organisations. Much of what is written about risk governance seems to fit primarily in the context of large, listed firms. This section gives explicit consideration to some other organisations, exploring their internal contexts.

7.1.1 SMEs

Small and medium-sized enterprises (SMEs) have advantages and disadvantages when it comes to risk governance. On the one hand, incentive conflicts are usually minimal because the manager and the owner are one and the same. The owner/manager plays an active role in decision making and is well-informed of all the risks facing the business. The owner/manager is the primary stakeholder and (s)he intuitively grasps the importance of risk management for achieving success. Moschella, Boulianne and Mignan (2020)[1] find that entrepreneurs view risk management 'as a mindset that emphasizes: 1) the preservation of key assets, 2) the creation of competitive advantages, and 3) the development of business opportunities'. SMEs also tend to regard their own reputations and their employees as some of their most important resources. Both managers and employees tend to be highly committed to the success of the organisation. Personal relationships and small size tend to increase the level of accountability and motivation.

Against these strengths one must also consider the fact that small size can be a disadvantage. SMEs are unlikely to be able to employ risk specialists. Lack of resource and expertise often means that risk management is intuitive and informal. Does this matter?

To some extent the lack of formal risk policies and procedures is offset by the fact that owner/managers have a very firm grip on the culture and values of the SME organisation. A strongly conveyed culture helps employees understand what they ought to do without the need for extensive documentation. SMEs tend to make use of 'interactive controls' whereby the owner/manager reduces risk by working on the front lines alongside employees.

Another way that SMEs address their lack of formal risk management resource is to rely on accountants, whether on staff or external. Financial risk is usually a primary concern due to capital constraints and shoestring budgets. Owner/managers view accountants as helpful for identifying business problems, for challenging assumptions and bouncing ideas off. External providers of capital, such as banks, can often play an advisory role.

It's worth noting that many owner/managers are quite risk tolerant, indeed this characteristic could be considered a prerequisite for entrepreneurship. Optimists are much more likely to be entrepreneurs and this gives them a resilience to cope with adversity and the ability to enthuse/motivate those around them. But this strength can become a liability due to the optimism bias, which is associated with misguided overconfidence and disaster.

Kahneman[2] describes a Canadian investor's assistance program that was designed to help inventors avoid being caught by the optimism bias. The program provided each inventor with an objective assessment of the commercial prospects of their idea, based on 37 criteria. Each one was given a letter grade from A to E with E being the least likely to succeed commercially. Over 70% of the inventions received a grade of D or E i.e. forecast of failure. The assessments proved to be rather accurate: only 5 of 411 projects that were given a grade of E reached commercialisation and none were successful. Despite this, 47% continued development efforts even after being told that their project was hopeless and on average these persistent individuals doubled their initial losses before giving up.

While entrepreneurs typically lack an expert board of independent directors, it remains essential to obtain challenge in some form. Owner/managers need critical friends who can help them avoid entrepreneurial wishful thinking.

7.1.2 Start-ups

Many of the risk governance issues for SMEs apply equally to start-ups, especially the possibility of optimism bias.

For start-up ventures, an upfront risk assessment can be useful to help design the business and financing model. Businesses at an early stage of development are usually considered highly risky, making it difficult to access debt capital. The upfront risk assessment can also be useful when pitching to potential investors, whether debt or equity.

The 52 Risks® framework[3] is a free tool that can be used by businesses at every stage to systematically consider the broad universe of risks. Users can discuss each risk category, identifying the relevant risks in each, rate each risk and agree on action to be taken. This can be the basis of a simple action plan or risk management strategy for the venture.

Each identified risk should be allocated to a specific individual to provide accountability. Strategic and operational risks might be allocated to the CEO or key executives. Financial risks are usually allocated to the CFO, finance director or finance manager.

BOX 7.1 PROJECT RISK AND THE PLANNING FALLACY

Nobel prize winner, Dan Kahneman,[4] tells an incredible story about a project he was once involved in. A team was assembled to design the curriculum and write a textbook to teach judgement and decision making in Israeli high schools. The team had met every Friday afternoon for about a year at this point. By now they had a detailed outline of the syllabus, had written a couple of chapters and had run a few sample lessons in the classroom. Dan decided to use a simplified Delphi process. He asked everyone on the team to write down, on a piece of paper, an estimate of how long it would take to complete the textbook. The estimates ranged between 1.5 and 2.5 years, averaging about 2 years.

Then Dan decided to try a different approach. He asked Seymour, an expert on curriculum development who was a member of the team, to reflect on other similar projects; projects that had developed a curriculum from a clean sheet of paper. He asked Seymour how long it took those other teams to complete the task. Seymour fell silent for a while, but when he finally spoke he admitted, with some embarrassment given his previous answer in the Delphi process, that about 40% of similar teams never completed their projects. Of the ones that did, it took them between 7–10 years. Dan asked another smart question. 'When you compare our skills and resources to those of the other groups, how good are we? How would you rank us in comparison with those teams?' Seymour's assessment was that the project team was below average but not by much.

What's amazing about this story is that the team continued to persevere, despite this very discouraging information. In fact they carried on as if nothing had happened. The book took 8 years to complete from that point and the Ministry of Education that had originally commissioned the curriculum never used it! It's a stunning example of the planning fallacy, where people systematically underestimate the cost and time to complete large projects. You've probably experienced it yourself, and the author experienced it right while writing this book! It's a rare project that comes in on time and within budget and to specification.

In Dan Kahneman's telling of the story, he admits that the biggest problem was the failure of the team to allow for unknown unknowns. They could not foresee all of the events that caused the project to drag out for so long including divorces, illnesses and bureaucratic crises. So what is the solution to the planning fallacy? It's called reference class forecasting and consists of 3 steps.

> Step 1 is to identify an **appropriate reference class**, be it kitchen renovations, large railway projects or curriculum development projects.
> Step 2 is to **find out the typical outcomes** for that reference class and use this to generate a baseline prediction.
> Step 3 is to then **make an appropriate adjustment** to that baseline prediction depending on the specific circumstances of the project.

7.2 Criteria

The goal of risk management is to ensure that an organisation achieves its objectives, but what are the criteria for success? On what basis can the organisation say that success is achieved or not? It's important to be clear about this. Any organisation must determine, in consultation with stakeholders, which objectives it is committed to reaching. This will in turn determine the criteria for risk management.

Risk criteria are the significant factors that determine success or failure in the organisation. They will be the focus of risk management attention, monitored to evaluate the significance of risk and guide decisions. Risk criteria should reflect the organisation's values, policies, and objectives, should be based on external and internal context, should consider the views of stakeholders and should be derived from standards, laws, policies and other requirements.

For a company with debt covenants based on the level of earnings, maintaining earnings per quarter would be a sensible business objective since a breach could lead to foreclosure or renegotiation of the credit facility. The risk criteria would be anything that causes earnings to fall including either a drop in sales or increase in costs.

For SMEs, survival is driven to a large extent by liquidity – having sufficient cash or liquid assets to continue operations. In this case a key business objective is to maintain an amount of cash in the bank or utilisation of the overdraft facility below a certain level. The cash balance could be driven by several different risk types, from strategic to operational. Here the important thing is not so much the source of risk but the likelihood of achieving objectives according to the various criteria selected.

In most jurisdictions, there are occupational health and safety laws affecting organisations. This means that the safety of employees and customers is a concern by virtue of legal requirements, if not a natural concern for wellbeing. There-fore, risk criteria are the things that tend to increase the rate of fatal and serious accidents e.g. staff shortages in the context of a hospital leading to staff working excessive hours.

Increasingly even listed companies are committed to achieving environ-mental, social and governance (ESG) criteria. These criteria go beyond short-term shareholder benefit, although many shareholders, especially those with a longer-term perspective, also support these objectives. A growing number of investors are now signatories to the Principles for Responsible Investment, sup-ported by the United Nations,[5] and a growing academic literature is exploring the phenomenon of ESG investing.[6] For example, under the broad category of the environment, issues such as sustainable land/water use, production of green-house gases and biodiversity could be considerations. Depending on the business context, any one of these could become a business objective. If reduction in emissions is chosen as a business objective, then the relevant risk criteria would be issues that prevent the organisation from meeting its emissions targets e.g. a project to adopt renewable power is delayed.

7.2.1 Public sector

Public sector organisations are typically focused on a particular service mission. Health and education departments have a mission to deliver health and education services to their communities; regulatory bodies have a mission to prevent illegal practices in the sector within which they operate. In that sense the mission tends to define the primary risk criteria (see Section 7.2). In education for example, the primary risk criteria would be issues preventing children from completing their education and achieving specified outcomes e.g. poor teacher quality, over-crowded classrooms, lack of support for children with additional learning needs.

Other risk criteria would relate to meeting legal and policy obligations. For example, in the education context, schools owe a duty of care to protect the safety of pupils and must take reasonable care to ensure that it employs compe-tent employees and provides safe premises. Failure to do this can result in litiga-tion. Public sector agencies are particularly open to legal consequences because aggrieved 'clients' correctly understand that any penalties will be paid out of government funds. A goal for the organisation would be to reduce the number of legal claims and the risk criteria are the factors that might instead produce further claims e.g. lack of training for staff in health and safety issues, lack of resources for enhancing the safety of playgrounds.

The final set of risk criteria would typically relate to efficiency and use of resources, since almost all government agencies have funding constraints these days. Over time the public sector is expected to achieve more with fewer resources so the targets would be efficiency related. Risk criteria would be factors that cause project delays and cost over-runs.

To summarise, the focus on objectives and risk criteria is arguably the most effective way of attacking risk appetite. Leaders should start by articulating the organisation's objectives and the associated risk criteria. Ranking the objectives and identifying which ones take priority can also be a useful exercise, as can be assigning probabilities. For example, a firm might say that a core objective is to ensure that EBIT does not fall below $x in order to fund business growth, with 80% confidence. In other words, the firm is willing to tolerate only 20% chance of failing to meet this particular criterion that relates to the objective of business growth. In addition, the firm may have an objective relating to solvency that takes priority over business growth. Here the objective is to ensure that EBIT does not fall below $y in order to meet debt servicing requirements, with 95% confidence i.e. only 5% chance of failure can be tolerated.

A clear understanding of objectives, risk criteria and their relative priorities is very useful for leaders and should be the starting point for any discussion about risk appetite. From here the next step is to build an understanding of the factors that might prevent achievement of the objectives (see Chapter 8 on risk assessment) and this understanding informs the choice of appropriate limits on business activities. These limits would be considered as 'controls' and form part of the armoury for treating risk as explained in Chapter 9.

7.3 Risk appetite

Interestingly, ISO31000 never mentions the term 'risk appetite'. It does say, however, that 'the organisation should specify the amount and type of risk that it may or may not take, relative to objectives'. This may be interpreted as a recommendation to create a risk appetite statement (RAS), since risk appetite is the amount of risk an organisation is willing to take in order to achieve its strategic objectives and implement its business plans.

An RAS is a document that should be used to communicate the organisation's risk appetite internally, providing useful operational guidance for the conduct of business and to avoid any breaches. A well-constructed RAS should help avoid situations where risks are taken inadvertently or without adequate controls. When breaches of appetite occur, this should trigger contingency plans and mobilise additional resources or managerial interventions to ensure that risk is reduced to acceptable levels. Ideally the RAS cascades throughout the organisation, translating into specific targets and limits at the business unit level.

The RAS can also be used for accountability, with individuals and/or businesses being penalised for breaches as appropriate.

A typical approach is to identify all the material risk criteria (see Section 7.2) that are relevant to the organisation and to specify a risk appetite for each one. For example, a bank might have a separate risk appetite for liquidity, market, credit and operational risks because of their relevance to the objective of maintaining solvency. Risk appetite may also be specified for sub-categories, for example, within operational risk the appetite may be stated separately for internal fraud, cyber risk and so on. A resources firm might make statements of risk appetite for each of: commodity price risk, currency risk, health and safety, climate risk etc.

Like many risk governance structures, the RAS is attractive in theory but implementation can be problematic. It's important to note that due to commercial concerns, many organisations do not make their RAS publicly available, making scrutiny difficult. One of the biggest challenges lies in the fact that too often, the RAS is much too vague. With no clear or measurable targets, it is very difficult to determine whether a breach has occurred. If an organisation has 'medium-low' appetite for cyber risk, what does that mean in practice?

An RAS should be concrete enough to guide actions across the organisation. It will speak to both the likelihood and the impact of risk, in a manner that can be objectively assessed. Having said this, it can be useful in an RAS to have an overarching attitude statement for each material risk, but this should be combined with objective measures.

According to its 2019 annual report, Network Rail, the owner/operator of British railway infrastructure, provided the following attitude statement:

> Network Rail has no appetite for safety, health or environmental risk exposure that could result in serious injury or loss of life to public, passengers and workforce or irreversible environmental damage. Safety drives all major decisions in the organisation. Network Rail will consider options to reduce safety risk where the business case goes considerably beyond our legal obligation to reduce risk so far as is reasonably practicable.

This statement of intent is then complemented with several measures based on the frequency of: train accidents, fatalities to employees and contractors, fatalities and serious injuries to passengers.

In the case of cyber risk, appetite could be set in terms of the frequency of service disruption events due to distributed denial of service attacks. In addition, appetite should be expressed in terms of impact(s), preferably in common units such as dollars. Risk events can often have multiple impacts, with some of those impacts felt immediately and others experienced longer term, so the total impact expressed in dollars can take some time to evaluate.

For a bank, a core objective is likely to be maintenance of capital adequacy in order to protect depositors and other stakeholders against possible insolvency. A bank might say, with regard to the objective of capital adequacy, that its risk criteria are to maintain both quantity and quality of capital substantially over regulatory minimums to ensure that the institution can withstand extreme but plausible scenarios to 99.95% confidence in any given year. On the basis of these risk criteria the bank can then determine a specific limit relating to the ratio of tier 1 capital to risk-weighted assets, say, no less than 10%.

The bank would then proceed to investigate the risks that might prevent this objective from being achieved and to understand how these risks might interact with one another. This task of risk assessment is the topic of Chapter 8. Finally, risk limits related to specific criteria would be chosen to help ensure that the bank can protect against possible insolvency. These might include limits on the extent to which loans can be made to specific industries or to customers in certain geographical locations. They might also include limits on the extent to which the bank can take speculative bets on currency movements. Its appetite for, say, credit risk can be expressed in terms of dollar losses in a financial year. For example, losses of $1 billion might be possible one year in 20 while losses of $0.2 billion might be possible one year in 5.

Another challenge for the RAS is dealing with changes in appetite. After the RAS is set by the board, there may well be new developments that justify a review. This could be because of unexpected changes to the business environment or because managers identify new high-risk opportunities with significant benefits. There is a danger that slavish devotion to staying within risk appetite may not be in the best interests of stakeholders. Some flexibility is required to ensure that risk appetite decisions can be reviewed where there is sound justification. This should be done prior to the breach occurring.

Notes

1 Moschella, Jason, Boulianne, Emilio, & Magnan, Michel. (2020, July 7). *Risk management in small-and medium-sized businesses.* Available at SSRN: https://ssrn.com/abstract=3379010 or http://dx.doi.org/10.2139/ssrn.3379010
2 Kahneman, D. (2011). *Thinking, fast and slow.* Macmillan, see Chapter 24.
3 This framework, developed by retired CRO Peter Deans, can be found at www.52risks.com/about-the-52-risks-framework/
4 Kahneman, D. (2011). *Thinking, fast and slow.* Macmillan, Allen Lane, Chapter 23.
5 For more detail on the Principles for Responsible Investment see: www.unpri.org/pri/about-the-pri
6 Daugaard, D. (2020). Emerging new themes in environmental, social and governance investing: a systematic literature review. *Accounting & Finance, 60*(2), 1501–1530.

Further reading and resources

COSO. (2020). *Risk appetite: Critical to success.* Available at www.coso.org/Documents/COSO-Guidance-Risk-Appetite-Critical-to-Success.pdf

8

RISK ANALYSIS

Good risk analysis can help to avoid the biases and blind spots that so often lead to poor risk management decisions. Both quantitative and subjective forms of risk analysis are explored in this chapter.

8.1 Quantitative risk analysis

Quantitative risk analysis is one of the most useful tools for avoiding the biases and blind spots of subjective methods. Good models help us to consider plausible but more extreme possibilities that may be ignored due to availability bias or over-optimism. One of the major advantages of quantitative models is that the underlying assumptions are obvious and therefore open to scrutiny. They can be used to visualise risk, helping to build risk awareness. They can help us to account for interactions between multiple risks to see the net effects, something that would be difficult to achieve with subjective approaches alone. Quantitative risk models allow us to measure the costs and benefits of risk treatments; these can help make a business case for risk treatments such as additional capital, investment in new controls or perhaps the purchase of insurance contracts. Without a solid business case, many risk management treatments will be left on the shelf.

It is true, however, that uncritical and unthinking use of quantitative models can be disastrous, just as unthinking use of satellite navigation systems has, on occasion, led to 'death by GPS'.[1] But this is not an argument for abandoning the use of quantitative models altogether, just as it would be foolish to abandon the use of GPS systems. We need models that help users engage System 2 thinking: the analytical and reflective style that helps us apply judgement to the signals from the models. We need more model users who are trained in the statistical methods that are the foundation of risk analysis.

Even senior leaders need to have a basic understanding of quantitative methods if they're being used to make important decisions. Without a basic understanding, how can a leader interpret reports? Or ask those searching questions? Or probe those assumptions? Thorough training in statistical methods is beyond the scope of a book such as this, but examples will be used to illustrate the benefits of the approach. The risks that are most amenable to quantitative analysis are those for which we have plentiful historical data available. Foreign exchange risk is a good example of this.

8.1.1 Case study: Larry's Luxury Food and Wine (with accompanying spreadsheet)

We start with an overview of scope, context and criteria. Larry's Luxury Food and Wine is a medium-sized business that imports and distributes food and wine from Europe to Australia. Larry sells his products to delicatessens, gourmet grocery stores and retailers of fresh food throughout Eastern Australia. He's very proud of the business he's spent 20 years building up from nothing. Every year Larry travels to Europe to source the best products that will appeal to the discerning Australian consumer. He builds close partnerships with suppliers and the sales team has developed links with many independent retailers.

Larry's revenues have grown solidly over the past few years. Gourmet food products were once purchased only by very affluent consumers but they're becoming more mainstream. As people travel more and watch celebrity chefs on TV, they're choosing to buy more luxury food items. Gourmet chocolate or cheese can be seen as an affordable luxury, a comfort purchase, a small indulgence.

With low barriers to entry in the industry, competition is intense. Larry is competing with other food importers and also with local producers. Australia now produces excellent cheese, wines, olive oil and even truffles! What about external stakeholders? Larry is the only shareholder in the company, which simplifies things somewhat. However he does have to consider the bank that has provided debt capital.

Coming to the internal context, Larry has a great team for managing the import and distribution part of the business. He also has a dedicated sales team led by his son Lenny. Beyond that, resources are fairly thin on the ground. Larry's strategy is to pursue growth and build up the value of the firm over time. He wants to leave the company in great shape for Lenny. As for culture, this is a family-based firm that values relationships and quality products. With European heritage, Larry and his family have a deep appreciation for European producers who are committed to the highest standards of production. They want to share their love of European food and wine with Australians.

Last year Larry oversaw a significant expansion of the business into the state of Queensland. He set up a new Brisbane sales office and warehouse. The expansion was expensive and Larry had to take on additional debt to pay for it. The expected uplift in sales has not yet been as strong as he'd hoped. Larry is now worried about a possible depreciation of the Australian dollar, which could hurt the business and make it difficult to keep his bankers onside. Has he over-reached with the expansion into Queensland?

Based on this background the business objective becomes obvious. For Larry the single most important issue right now is survival – the ability to service debt and pay his loyal staff. The criterion he will track most closely is cash holdings.

To better understand Larry's foreign exchange risk, let's start with historical data for the Australian dollar in terms of the Euro, as shown in Figure 8.1. We have monthly observations going back to 1999 when the Euro was first created. Since then the exchange rate has traded as low as 49 Euro cents back in December 2008 and as high as 86 Euro cents in July 2012.

Remember that we're defining risk as 'uncertainty relative to objectives'. It's useful to consider how variations in the exchange rate influence Larry's cash flows and the need to meet debt repayments and other commitments. Right now, as of 1 December 2020, the exchange rate is at 0.6177 Euro per Australian dollar. Larry buys 10,000 cases of food and wine from his suppliers each month. Paying 200 Euro per case, this is equivalent to 323.78 Australian dollars at the current rate (200/0.6177=323.78). He sells each case for 400 Australian dollars giving monthly revenues of 4 million Australian dollars and all his other costs are in Australian dollars. Variable costs are $28 a case. Fixed costs are $300,000 a month. With a debt of $20 million, at 6% per annum simple interest, he's paying $100,000 a month in interest. The earnings for the month come out at $82,182.

FIGURE 8.1 Australian Dollar in Terms of the Euro

Larry is extremely worried by the downward trend in the value of the Australian dollar over the last couple of years. In the last year the exchange rate briefly touched as low as 0.5605 Euro per AUD. If the exchange rate fell to 59 Euro cents, for example, Larry would be trading at a monthly loss of more than $69,000. But he currently has cash on hand of $1 million, so he's not likely to become insolvent in the next month.

What Larry really needs is an analysis over the longer term, say over the next year, to see how his cash flows might unfold. Simulations are the ideal way to conduct risk analysis because we can quickly and easily consider many possible scenarios. This is important for risk analysis because we care about plausible yet extreme cases. We also don't want to be limited only to scenarios that have occurred in the past. Monte Carlo simulation is a method for generating thousands of hypothetical scenarios that may or may not be based on history. The software to do this is cheap and simple to use; for simple models you can use an Excel spreadsheet as demonstrated in the provided example. Another important advantage of Monte Carlo, which will become obvious in Chapter 9, is the fact that one can easily adapt the analysis to investigate possible risk treatments. In many situations, real options, such as the option to reduce or expand operations, play an important part in risk management. These real options can be analysed with ease in the simulation setting.

This example simulates 1,000 possible paths for the exchange rate for the next year, at monthly intervals. Each path can be thought of as a possible scenario for the exchange rate and the implications for earnings are then easy to calculate and visualise. In this simulation we assume that the exchange rate follows a normal distribution.[2] We also have to make assumptions about the average and standard deviation of the exchange rate returns. Initially these are set to values that reflect the historical sample, so our simulation will be consistent with history but, by considering a much large range of possibilities, we get a better understanding of what can potentially happen.

The first 200 simulated paths have been graphed in Figure 8.2. Notice how every path starts at the same place, the current exchange rate, but by the time we get 12 months into the future there is quite a bit of divergence. A few paths end up above 75 Euro cents and a few below 50 Euro cents. But most paths end up somewhere in the middle. If you look in the spreadsheet you'll notice that every time you hit Enter, Excel generates a new set of currency paths so the results will be slightly different each time but the overall message should be the same.

Finally, we come to the really interesting bit from Larry's perspective: cash flows. Table 8.1 presents the distribution of possible cash outcomes in each of the 1,000 scenarios at the end of 12 months. We normally ignore the maximum and minimum values as these represent extreme cases with only 1/1000 probability, and our sample is not large enough to estimate these values reliably. The 95th percentile is a measure of a more possible but very favourable outcome and is approximately $5.5 million. That is, 95% of the scenarios are less favourable than this value and 5% of cases are more favourable. To achieve a cash position this

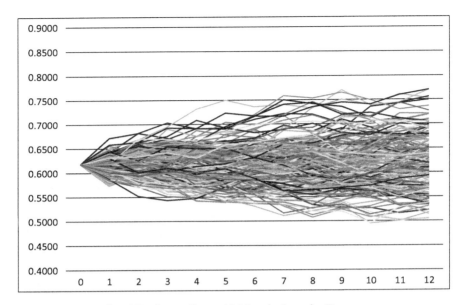

FIGURE 8.2 Simulated Exchange Rates 12 Months into the Future

TABLE 8.1 Simulated Earnings and Cash Position

	Earnings for next 12 months	*Cash after 12 months*
Maximum	$ 7,419,892.77	$ 8,419,892.77
95th Percentile	$ 4,513,287.72	$ 5,513,287.72
Median	$ 942,627.56	$ 1,942,627.56
5th Percentile	-$ 2,896,749.24	-$ 1,896,749.24
Minimum	-$ 6,112,800.82	-$ 5,112,800.82

favourable, the earnings for the year would be $4.5 million, adding considerably to his current cash holdings.

The 5th percentile, approximately -$1.9 million, is a possible but unfavourable outcome that would arise if earnings for the year were -$2.9 million. That is, 5% of the scenarios are less favourable than this value and 95% of cases are more favourable. Overall, Larry can be 90% confident that the cash outcome after 12 months will be somewhere between -$2.8 million and $4.9 million. This analysis assumes that market conditions remain at 'typical' levels in terms of the degree of turbulence.

Larry is particularly concerned about the possibility of cases where his cash position after 12 months is lower than $100,000. Anything below this threshold represents a disastrous outcome for the business, an outcome that could quickly lead to insolvency. One of the strengths of the quantitative risk analysis is that it allows him to identify the likelihood of this occurring and to visualise it as shown in Figure 8.3. Risk visualisation is a particularly powerful tool for building understanding.

This histogram highlights the range of simulated possibilities one year from now. Some of the outcomes are quite positive – if these eventuated Larry would be able to pay off quite a lot of the debt. But with around a one in five chance of a cash flow catastrophe, Larry is worried about the survival of the business. The analysis is a wake-up call for Larry to appreciate the extent of the risk he currently faces and to consider possible treatments.

Another major advantage of the simulation is that it's very easy to make changes to the assumptions underlying the analysis. In this analysis Larry assumes the standard deviation of monthly returns (a measure of market turbulence) to be 2.7% per month (equivalent to around 9% per annum). This assumption is based on the entire twenty-year historical sample, but market turbulence can be much higher at times.

This highlights the fact that Monte Carlo simulation is not limited to history; the analyst can test a range of possible future environments by adjusting the parameters. In other words, scenario analysis can be conducted within the simulation context by changing the parameters. If Larry increases standard deviation to 3.5% per month, similar to the values experienced in the 2008–09 financial crisis, then the probability of catastrophe increases to more than one in four.

8.2 Analysing risk interactions

One of the most common mistakes people make in risk analysis is to forget that they have multiple risks. What makes things even more complex is that those

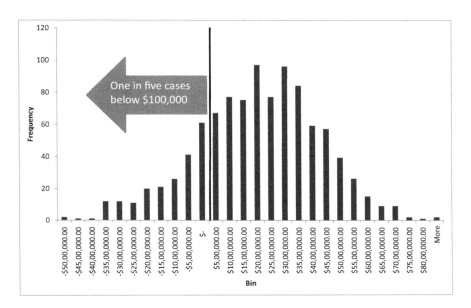

FIGURE 8.3 Histogram of Cash Position After 12 Months

risks sometimes interact with one another. In 2002, Muelbroek proposed integrated risk management as a potential alternative to the siloed approach.[3] Integration here refers to the aggregation of risks across the firm, taking account of possible dependencies. Rather than considering one risk at a time, all risks are viewed together within a strategic framework, just as asset managers consider a portfolio of investments having regard for correlations between the assets in the portfolio.

Quantitative risk models should account for interactions and the methods for achieving this are well understood. This book does not provide training in the statistical methods for doing this but highlights their importance with several examples.

8.2.1 Interactions at Singapore Airlines

Imagine an airline, like Singapore Airlines, for whom jet fuel is one of the most significant costs. This is a significant risk for an airline so, like many airlines, Singapore Airlines purchases futures as a hedge to protect against the possibility of an increase in the cost of jet fuel. Simply put, this is a contract to buy jet fuel at a fixed price for delivery in the future.

In the COVID-19 crisis of 2020, demand for flights was greatly reduced so Singapore Airlines had to cut back its scheduled services. This meant that jet fuel requirements were greatly reduced. Often during a period of economic weakness, the price of commodities, such as jet fuel, tends to fall. This is exactly what happened during the COVID-19 crisis. But Singapore Airlines had purchased jet fuel for future delivery, so the future contracts generated losses, which could not be offset against fuel purchases. Rather than reducing risk, the hedging strategy aggravated the airline's losses during the crisis. Reports indicated that Singapore Airlines would lose some 1.26 billion Singapore dollars when the financial year ended in 2021.[4]

The lesson here is that business risk and commodity price risk are connected. During an economic recession both demand for flights and commodity prices tend to fall. A good risk analysis should take account of these interactions.

8.2.2 Interactions at BHP

BHP is another case that illustrates this point. BHP is a leading global resources company, which is headquartered in Melbourne, Australia but with operations around the world. It is most active in the markets for iron ore, metallurgical coal, copper, petroleum, potash and nickel. These businesses create significant exposures to movements in commodity prices, exchange rates and interest rates. Most commodity prices are set in US dollars but the functional/reporting currency is the Australian dollar.

Until the late 1990s, BHP was a significant user of financial derivatives and hedging was undertaken at the business unit level i.e. risk management was siloed. Derivatives were used to lock in budgetary outcomes and smooth earnings profiles for specific business units. In the Asian crisis the results of this approach were disappointing, resulting in a major review of risk management in 2000.

A key question for BHP was whether the underlying risk exposures offset one another. Could the currency exposure be regarded as a natural hedge against commodity price risks, for example? The quantitative risk unit built a model to analyse cash flows over a three-year horizon. The model took account of the volatility of each individual risk and the correlation between the risks to give a portfolio perspective. One of the advantages of this approach is that when considering changes to the business model (say buying a new mining asset, divesting an existing petroleum asset or adding a hedge) the portfolio effects can be assessed.

In 2000 BHP determined[5] that the aggregate level of market risk it faced (i.e. without hedging or allowing for diversification effects) was $3.1 billion over a one-year horizon. The risk fell to only $1.6 billion, however, on a diversified basis. After taking account of natural hedges within the portfolio, the need for hedging was significantly reduced. Interestingly the analysts found that beyond a certain point, hedging tends to increase portfolio risk because it interrupts the existing natural hedges. A decision was therefore made that any hedging activity must be evaluated in terms of its portfolio effects.

In November 2015, a Brazilian iron ore tailings dam failed causing catastrophic damage (including environmental damage) and loss of life. The dam was owned by Samarco, a joint venture between Vale and BHP. In August 2016 BHP reported a highly unusual full-year loss ($8.3 billion). Revenues were down 31% due to lower commodity prices. Assets write-downs (relating to US shale oil and gas business) were another feature of the results, as were provisions relating to the Samarco disaster. Dividends were cut from US 62 cents per share to US 14 cents per share.

This raises the interesting question of whether there is any interaction between market risk and operational risks. A superficial analysis might say that they are completely independent of one another, and it was just rotten bad luck that BHP suffered both an operational disaster and a commodity price disaster in the same year. But connections between the two may be possible, especially if there is pressure to cut costs when prices are low.

8.2.3 Credit and operational risk interactions in banking

Since the early 2000s many banks have collected operational loss data to assist in determining capital requirements. ORX, an international data consortium, has historically collected this data under the following categories: internal fraud, external fraud, employee related, clients products and business practices, disasters, technology and infrastructure, transactions and processing. The consortium collects not only the number of risk events but their impact expressed in dollars.

Recent analysis has shown that operational losses in the banking sector vary over time, with the variation in losses comes primarily from variation in the category clients, products and business practices (negligence failures).[6] These are losses arising from an unintentional or negligent failure to meet a professional obligation to specific clients (including fiduciary and suitability requirements) or from the nature or design of a product. Operational losses by date of discovery, adjusted for the size of the bank, peak in 2009, with the peak for recognition of losses in 2011. The lag between discovery and recognition results from the fact that for many losses in this category there are protracted legal proceedings before eventual settlement.

Crucially, for banks this pattern suggests that operational losses tend to be high at around the same time or just after the peak in credit losses. This is a time when banks would be most vulnerable to losses, so positive correlation between credit and operational losses is potentially disastrous for bank solvency. The reason for the correlation is a matter for debate. One explanation is the increased scrutiny of banks following a banking crisis. Others have argued that misconduct itself is correlated to the business cycle, tending to increase in periods of high growth, with discovery following in the denouement.[7]

8.3 Managing model risk

As mentioned at the start of Section 8.1, quantitative risk models offer many advantages but create an exposure to model risk. This is the risk that a flawed model may lead to poor decisions. The single most important protection against model risk is understanding of the model. Well educated users of the model will appreciate the underlying assumptions and be able to interpret the outputs appropriately. It's essential that models be treated as a starting point for discussion, triggering informed debate using System 2 thinking. The more people there are in an organisation who understand the risk models, the less likely it is that the model will be applied uncritically. Risk experts with solid grounding in statistical methods are a crucial resource in this regard. Directors who can correctly interpret the output of risk models, questioning as appropriate, are another vital resource.

One of the advantages of quantitative models is the fact that their underlying assumptions are transparent. The conclusions may be very sensitive to these assumptions so it's always a good idea to try different values and see what changes. A risk analyst should always disclose crucial assumptions and highlight key sensitivities to the people that need to interpret the model. Those in positions of oversight should be aware of the potential for bias in the choice of parameters. Is the parameter choice based on the desire to either understate or overstate risk?

Another excellent way of managing model risk is through the use of 'stress tests' as a complement to the 'base case' analysis. In Larry's case, the most crucial parameter is likely to be the assumption regarding the standard deviation of monthly returns. The base case analysis used a standard deviation of 2.7% per month, but it is possible for risk to increase during periods of market turbulence.

In 2008–09, for example, the standard deviation AUD returns relative to the Euro was around 3.5% per month. Larry could repeat the analysis with this higher parameter to test the ability of the company to withstand a period of stress.

8.4 Subjective risk analysis

Quantitative risk analysis is almost always preferred. But what if we have no historical loss data available for analysis or only a handful of loss events? Or what if we believe that the risk environment is changing rapidly so history is of limited value? In such cases there is little choice but to consider a subjective risk analysis.

Subjective analysis is problematic to say the least. There are benefits in bringing together the perspectives of a number of experts who may be able to shed light on the risk being assessed. A common solution is the risk assessment workshop, with 5–10 managers who are subject-matter experts (or SMEs) and a facilitator to guide the discussion. The objective of the workshop is to determine the impact and likelihood of a future risk. For instance, we might consider asking workshop participants to consider the impact and likelihood of a global pandemic or of further significant deterioration in climate.

In this kind of situation where objective information is scarce, it's very easy for various biases to influence the outcome. Consider some of the possibilities, starting with incentives. Often managers are keen to avoid project delays or expenditures that might be needed to reduce risks. Managers in this situation have a natural bias to downplay the risk as much as possible. Alternatively, some managers may have incentives to overstate the risk, because a large risk assessment may lead to a large budget for managing the problem, thus building the manager's prestige and power within the organisation. Being clear about everyone's incentives is often a useful starting point.

Then we need to remember some of the behavioural biases that may be influencing the thinking of the managers participating in the assessment. Optimism bias occurs when people have a tendency to underestimate the probability or impact of negative events. It's a bias that affects some more than others. As explained by Kahneman[8] optimists are cheerful and popular, they are more resilient following setbacks and they are even longer lived. Optimists are hypothesised to be more likely to find themselves in positions of authority where they can make important decisions.

This is closely related to the problem of overconfidence which is prevalent throughout society. For example, 90% of people consider themselves to be above average drivers! This is an example of being overconfident in our abilities. Many people are also overconfident in their knowledge – they know less than they believe they know. This overconfidence in abilities and knowledge leads people to underestimate risk. This is one of the reasons why risk governance is so important; it can temper the hubris of overconfident and overly optimistic senior executives.

Certain risks are taken much too seriously, like the risk of shark attack or the risk of terrorist attack. These so-called dread risks dominate our thinking too much. After the 9/11 terrorist attacks, there was a dip in plane travel with people preferring to drive rather than risk plane travel.[9] The reality is that plane travel is generally far safer than driving, so many people lost their lives or were injured needlessly. Researchers think that our extreme reaction to the dread risks comes from the fact that as passengers we can't control what happens in the aeroplane whereas we feel in control in the car. The car is a very familiar place for most of us so we feel safe there. Also plane accidents tend to have rather catastrophic outcomes whereas many car accidents are not fatal. In the same way many more people are killed driving to the beach than are killed by sharks, yet many people spend much more time worrying about the sharks.

We are increasingly understanding that biases are a major problem for subjective risk assessment. Biases lead us to overlook important risks and to systematically underestimate and undermanage those they do identify. Unfortunately, solutions to these problems are not easy to find because they are so deeply embedded. One thing is clear, however, it's usually easier to see bias in others than in yourself. This suggests we need to work on skills like giving and receiving constructive feedback. One of the most important roles of risk management is to challenge assumptions – to ask the tough questions that might cause people to recognise when they may be overconfident.

While groups can be very useful for capturing a range of perspectives and insights, the dynamics of the group can also produce poor outcomes. Groupthink[10] occurs when team members rush to consensus too quickly, without properly canvassing all possibilities. It is caused by the human desire to avoid conflict and perhaps also just by laziness. A lot of people find it hard to express a dissenting opinion, especially if they have to disagree with the boss or with someone who has high status in the group. Even if people are brave enough to disagree, things don't always play out well. Many senior people find it hard to change their minds publicly due to loss of face.

Is there a way to capture the benefits of groups without being derailed by these problems? Some years ago, the Delphi process[11] was developed with exactly this objective in mind. It's a way of collecting the insights of experts and avoiding problems like groupthink, developed at the beginning of the Cold War. At the time, the military was trying to predict how technology would change the future of warfare – an incredibly difficult problem given the pace of technological change in the second half of the twentieth century. The term Delphi is a reference to the Oracle of Delphi in ancient Greece who answered questions about colonization, religion and power.

Some of the key ideas of the Delphi process are:

Anonymity of the participants

Usually all participants remain anonymous. Their identity is not revealed, even after the completion of the final report. This prevents the authority, personality or reputation of some participants from dominating others in the process.

Arguably, it also frees participants (to some extent) from their personal biases, allowing free expression of opinions, open critique and admission of errors when revising earlier judgments.

Structuring of information flow

The initial contributions from the experts are collected in the form of answers to questionnaires and their comments on these answers. The panel director controls the interaction among the participants by processing the information and filtering out irrelevant content. This avoids the negative effects of face-to-face panel discussions and solves the usual problems of group dynamics.

Regular feedback

Participants comment on their own forecasts, the responses of others and on the progress of the panel as a whole. At any time they can revise their earlier statements. While in regular group meetings participants tend to stick to previously stated opinions and often conform too much to the group leader; the Delphi method prevents it.

Role of the facilitator

The person coordinating the Delphi method is usually known as a *facilitator* or leader and facilitates the responses of their *panel of experts*. The facilitator sends out questionnaires, surveys etc. and if the panel of experts accept, they follow instructions and present their views. Responses are collected and analysed, then common and conflicting viewpoints are identified. If consensus is not reached, the process continues through thesis and antithesis, to gradually work towards synthesis and building consensus.

Even if it is not appropriate to implement a full Delphi process, some elements of it can easily be incorporated in business practices. A simple tactic in meetings is to get everyone present to write down their own prediction or opinion before anyone speaks. This forces people to develop their own ideas before being overwhelmed by the leader or the majority, making it more likely they will speak up to challenge the ideas of others.

Notes

1 The Guardian. (2016). *Death by GPS*. Available at www.theguardian.com/technology/2016/jun/25/gps-horror-stories-driving-satnav-greg-milner
2 The assumption of normality is sometimes criticized. For short-term horizons of a few days, normality tends to understate the true risk whereas for longer horizons of a year or more it is more likely to overstate the true risk. It's possible to incorporate more sophisticated statistical assumptions to reflect the task at hand. For further information see De Mello, L., Sheedy, E., & Storck, S. (2015). A practical guide for non-financial

companies when modeling longer-term currency and commodity exposures. *Journal of Applied Corporate Finance*, *27*(1), 89–100.

3 Meulbroek, L. K. (2002). A senior manager's guide to integrated risk management. *Journal of Applied Corporate Finance*, *14*(4), 56–70.

4 Lay, B. (2020, March 20). *SIA projected losses could total S$1.26 billion in fiscal year 2021*. Available at https://mothership.sg/2020/03/singapore-airlines-losses/

5 BHP: A strategic view of risk. *Risk Magazine* (2001, March), S20–S22.

6 Aldasoro, Iñaki, Gambacorta, Leonardo, Giudici, Paolo, & Leach, Thomas. (2020, February 11). Operational and cyber risks in the financial sector. BIS Working Paper No. 840. Available at SSRN: https://ssrn.com/abstract=3549526

7 Sakalauskaite, I. (2018). *Bank risk-taking and misconduct* (No. 53). Bank of Lithuania.

8 Chapter 24 of Kahneman. (2011). *Thinking, fast and slow*. Allen Lane.

9 Gigerenzer, G. (2004). Dread risk, September 11, and fatal traffic accidents. *Psychological science*, *15*(4), 286–287.

10 Esser, J. K. (1998). Alive and well after 25 years: A review of groupthink research. *Organizational Behavior and Human Decision Processes*, *73*(2–3), 116–141.

11 Hsu, C. C., & Sandford, B. A. (2007). The Delphi technique: Making sense of consensus. *Practical Assessment, Research, and Evaluation*, *12*(1), 10.

Further reading and resources

Alexander, Carol. (2001). *Market models: A guide to financial data analysis*. Wiley Finance.

COSO. (2012). *ERM risk assessment in practice thought paper*. Available at www.coso.org/Documents/COSO-ERM%20Risk%20Assessment%20in%20Practice%20Thought%20Paper%20October%202012.pdf

Riskmetrics Group. (1999). *Corporate metrics technical document*. Available at www.msci.com/documents/10199/8af520af-3e63-44b2-8aab-fd55a989e312

9
RISK TREATMENT

In general, there are six risk treatment options:

- Retain. No action is needed as the risk is acceptable;
- Avoid. Discontinue an activity that creates unacceptable risk;
- Increase. Take additional risk in order to pursue an attractive opportunity;
- Transfer. Share the risk with other parties;
- Reduce the likelihood of an adverse event. This involves preventative controls;
- Mitigate. Mitigant controls reduce the consequences flowing from an adverse event.

The first three are self-explanatory, so this chapter focuses on the last three treatment options. These options tend to be the focus of much risk management activity as organisations seek to find ways of engaging in risky activities without exposing themselves to unacceptable adverse consequences. Skilled risk managers are experts at finding creative solutions that can make risk-taking acceptable. There are usually multiple potential treatments that may be considered, all varying in their effectiveness and cost. The goal is to find the most cost-effective controls that will allow a risky activity to proceed, thus allowing an organisation to meet its objectives.

The bowtie representation of risk in Figure 9.1 is a helpful way of thinking about risk treatments. Preventative controls are those that focus on the source of risk – the hazard – and reduce the likelihood of an adverse event occurring. For example, it might be discovered that accidents in a dangerous workplace are most likely to occur when employees are tired, so a preventative control could be to reduce the length of shifts. In the case of fraud risk, a preventative control might be the use of passwords to limit access to valuable assets.

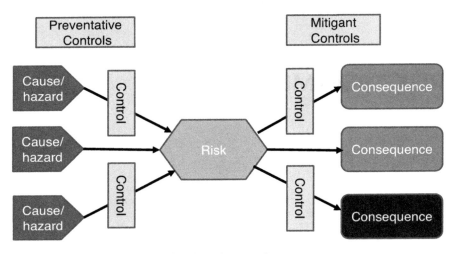

FIGURE 9.1 Bowtie Diagram of Risk and Controls

Directive controls, a subset of preventative controls, are policies and instructions given to employees to reduce risk. Policies could relate to bullying and workplace diversity, thus reducing the possibility of harm to employees, absenteeism, staff turnover and legal costs. In a university there may be policies regarding the conduct of examinations and other assessment tasks to reduce cheating and protect the reputation of the university. Here the policies have a preventative effect because they reduce the source of the risk. The reason they are sometimes considered separately from other preventative controls is that, to be effective, employees must comply with the policies. Achieving high rates of compliance can be challenging, especially when there is a proliferation of policies, and compliance may make it harder to achieve other objectives. In a financial institution, for example, compliance with responsible lending policies may make it more difficult to achieve volume targets for a lender. This creates the need for monitoring of employee behaviour, which creates further costs.

Mitigant controls are those that address the consequences of risk. Assuming that an adverse event occurs, these controls will help to reduce the impact. First aid kits and a workers' compensation scheme would be examples of mitigants in the case of occupational health and safety. They don't stop accidents from occurring, but they limit the impact. On a ship, lifeboats are a mitigant that reduce the risk of loss of life in the event of sinking. For a bank managing credit risk, the security pledged by the borrower, usually property, is an important mitigant. The bank has the right to foreclose on the loan and sell the property to offset its losses.

Detective controls differ in that they identify problems after they have occurred, so they belong on the right-hand side of the diagram. These controls are important for monitoring risk and providing an opportunity for managerial intervention if necessary. Checking trade confirmations, inventory and bank reconciliations are important detective controls for fraud risk. If the inventory check reveals a shortfall, then the cause can and should quickly be identified. This can trigger prompt action to prevent further fraud, such as removing an employee; it might also lead to new preventative controls to prevent theft of inventory. A detective control can be important for triggering a pre-prepared contingency plan.

9.1 Treatments and their (unforeseen) consequences

It turns out that treatments are, themselves, one of the biggest causes of adverse consequences. Surprisingly often, well-intended risk treatments have unforeseen consequences that leave organisations worse off. The old saying 'no good deed goes unpunished' is particularly apt in the realm of risk treatment. So potential consequences of treatments should be carefully considered ahead of time.

One of the obvious consequences of the addition of controls is that they can unduly slow down business processes, making the organisation less able to innovate in a timely fashion. Requirements for staff to comply with directive controls can frustrate employees trying to meet their key performance indicators. Another common problem with controls is that they can create a false sense of security, so less care is taken and people become complacent. It has sometimes been argued that bicycle helmets make some cyclists ride faster and more carelessly, reducing the benefits of helmets as a safety device.[1]

Dowell and Hendershot provide[2] a series of case studies to illustrate that the addition of new safety features can introduce new avenues for failure. Examples are given from manufacturing processes, chemical plants and automobile design. But one of the most relatable examples of this phenomenon comes from the incident at the Academy Awards when the 2016 award for Best Picture was mistakenly given to *Lalaland* rather than *Moonlight*.[3] The presenters, Warren Beatty and Faye Dunaway, had been given the wrong envelope – the one for the previous award of Best Actress -rather than the envelope for Best Picture. The reason for this was that there were two sets of envelopes. Ironically, the second set of envelopes had been introduced as a control to protect against the risk of loss or damage. The lesson here is that adding controls and complexity can go seriously awry.

9.2 Treating 'financial risks'

For many years, courses in financial risk management, such as the one I taught at Macquarie University, were essentially courses in the use of derivative contracts for treating 'financial risks' arising from movements in exchange rates, interest rates and commodity prices. Many hours of class time were devoted to the arcane world of derivatives, including their pricing and application. For companies exposed to foreign exchange risk, interest rate risks and commodity price risks, the solutions offered were futures, forward, swaps and options. While derivative contracts certainly have a place in risk management as mitigant controls, they are no longer seen as the sole or even primary focus.

Even the terminology 'financial risk' and 'non-financial risk' has fallen out of favour in some circles, since risks from virtually any source can have serious financial consequences. Risk managers these days tend to take a more holistic approach, considering risk from all sources and how these may affect the organisation's ability to reach its objectives, whether financial or otherwise.

The trend away from derivatives was partly the result of disastrous outcomes in some of the firms that used them. In the case of Metallgesellschaft,[4] short-term futures hedges were used against long-term oil exposures. This timing mismatch contributed to a cash shortfall of more than $1 billion, threatening the solvency of the organisation.

The complexity of derivatives is arguably one of the underlying reasons why some firms have experienced disappointing outcomes, illustrating the point that risk management treatments can be worse that the risk itself. Surveys of corporate treasurers have indicated that they have a number of concerns about the use of derivatives including: secondary market liquidity, accounting treatment, counterparty credit risk, disclosure requirements, analyst reactions and evaluating hedge results.[5] Another reason for the trend away from derivatives is the growing realisation that there are better solutions. Rather than using derivative contracts to transfer risk, many firms prefer to make operational adjustments within the business itself.

Figure 9.2 shows that firms are increasingly choosing operational treatments over derivatives and financial contracts. This analysis considers only the firms with material risk in six different risk types: interest rates, foreign exchange, energy, commodities, credit risk and geopolitical risk. In all but one case, which is foreign exchange, managers prefer operational strategies over derivatives.

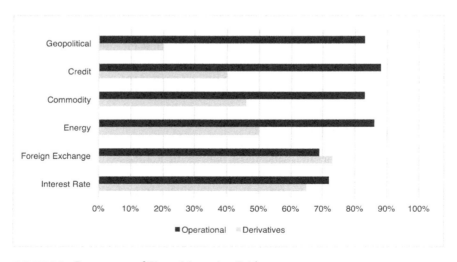

FIGURE 9.2 Percentage of Firms Managing Risk

Source: data sourced from Giambona, Graham, Harvey and Bodnar[6]

Operational strategies are based around the concept of operational flexibility, the ability to adapt practices to changing business conditions. In contrast, derivatives have the opposite effect. They are usually used to fix future input costs or sale prices, so they tend to reduce flexibility in a manner that can have disastrous results. This was illustrated by the case Singapore Airlines case in Section 8.2.1.

For an airline one possible operational solution to the risk of changes in the fuel price is to make adjustments, after the event, to the price of flights. In other words, to pass on cost increases to consumers. This is likely to reduce the demand for flights, but consumers may be sympathetic to the need for cost increases in this context. Normally commodity prices are high during times of economic strength, and this may mean that consumers are willing and able to pay a fuel price surcharge. All of this can be done without the need for complex derivative products and the treasury infrastructure surrounding them.

9.3 Operational treatments and flexibility

The trend to treat financial risks with operational treatments is an important one, consistent with the trend towards integrated risk management. Rather than treating each risk in a siloed fashion, integrated risk management looks at the organisation as a portfolio of risks that interact with one another. If one understands these interactions, effective risk treatments can often be found by making adjustments to business practices. Adapting to the business environment as it unfolds has many advantages, and this was well illustrated in the COVID-19 pandemic of 2020. This section canvases some of the most important operational treatments.

Real options are potential changes in strategy that can be made in response to changing conditions, including the options to delay or abandon a project, to temporarily suspend operations or to expand operations. In contrast to financial options, which are derivative contracts, real options are specific to the organisation's operations and can be exercised at any time, giving important flexibility. Another advantage of real as opposed to financial options is that they are not specific to a particular risk type like fuel or foreign exchange. They are therefore very useful for treating a wide range of risks including those with low probability or emerging and unexpected risks.

The success of this strategy – exercising the option to suspend or cut back operations – relies on the ability to cut costs quickly. Delaying investment projects and reducing discretionary costs like research and exploration for new opportunities is fundamental. In addition, organisations need to be able to cut their operating costs as operations are scaled back.

In this regard it's important to consider *operating leverage*: the relative importance of fixed costs for operations. Lower operating leverage, that is lower reliance on fixed as opposed to variable costs, gives greater financial flexibility. One way of preparing for risk is by reducing the relative importance of fixed costs and increasing variable costs, and this can sometimes be achieved through outsourcing. While greater reliance on fixed costs can lead to higher costs on average, the advantage is that you only pay the high costs when you can afford to do so. Farmers employ this strategy in their use of employees; they employ very few staff on a permanent basis, but they take on seasonal labour at harvest time. Obviously, the farmer will only employ pickers if the product price is high enough to justify the cost. Variable costs can be quickly reduced when problems emerge, such as a drop in demand (for whatever reason) or production problems.

Some other operational responses to financial shocks are as follows:

• *Adjusting product pricing* can be an effective response, especially in the case when the price elasticity of demand is relatively low. An increase in price normally leads to a fall in demand, but the reduction in demand is less severe in cases of low elasticity. Low elasticity, or low sensitivity to changes in price, occurs when there are few good substitutes for the product in question and the product is considered a necessity. Elasticity tends to be lower for goods that make up only a small portion of the total budget. Someone who enjoys eating bananas might be willing to pay double the price, if necessary, because bananas make up a relatively small portion of total expenditure. Elasticity is usually greater in the long-term, relative to the short-term, as consumers are more likely to find substitutes. Understanding the price elasticity of demand in your product markets is therefore a crucial consideration for risk management;

• *Changing production location* can be a good solution for some businesses. Despite the high transition costs, it can be cost effective in some circumstances to move production to a foreign country that has low costs of production or a weak currency;

• *Changing suppliers* might be an option if the supply chain is disrupted or if a supplier becomes too expensive; for overseas suppliers this might result from an adverse exchange rate movement;

• *Changes to inventory* may be an alternative for non-perishable goods, whether they be inputs to the production process or finished goods. Although storage costs must be considered, inventories can be built up when prices are low or when production slows down. The opposite strategy makes sense when prices are high or when production ramps up.

Diversification is another operational risk management strategy that makes sense in some contexts. Expansion into multiple products or markets can help to reduce risk exposure to any single product or market. The fact that the risks in different products/markets are often offsetting or less than perfectly correlated can help to smooth out earnings, reducing the possibility of a cash flow shortage. In other words, diversification can help firms handle an adverse shock as internal capital markets can substitute for external capital markets.

The counterargument is that diversification can lead organisations into products/markets where they lack expertise. Large, diversified firms can be very complex, making management challenging. For listed firms there is an argument that shareholders can form their own diversified portfolios, so they see little value in diversification at the firm level. Shareholders might prefer listed firms to 'stick to the knitting', that is, focus on core strengths despite the possibility of greater earnings variation.

Diversification can work at multiple levels, not just with respect to products and markets. In the airline industry fleet diversity – or diversity in production – is another way of managing risk. When demand for flights is low, perhaps following an increase in fuel costs, airlines can deploy smaller aircraft to maintain load factors. This approach does, however, increase maintenance and staff training costs.

It's very important to realise that all of these so-called solutions will have their own disadvantages. Risk managers must consider those very carefully to figure out if the solution makes sense in the circumstances.

9.4 Financial flexibility as a risk management strategy

Financial flexibility refers to the structure of the balance sheet, particularly the mix of debt and equity capital. The big idea here is that equity capital gives greater capacity to withstand earning variation. The riskier the business, in the sense of earnings variation, the lesser the ability to use debt capital or leverage. Debt capital brings the requirement for regular payments of principal and interest so reliable earnings are essential. In contrast equity capital has no maturity date and dividends can be cut to zero if necessary.

As well as considering the amount of debt needed to fund the business, it's also important to consider its maturity. Having a lot of debt maturing at the same time can be dangerous, exposing the organisation to the risk of having to refinance at a time of adverse trading conditions when lenders may not be willing to provide funds at an acceptable price. Short-term debt is the most problematic of all because of the need for regular refinancing; each refinancing is a period of vulnerability for the business.

Turning to the asset side of the balance sheet, having reserves of cash and liquid (i.e. easy to sell) assets is very helpful. During periods of difficulty, liquid assets can easily be converted to cash and used to meet commitments.

Finally, the existence of undrawn but committed bank loan facilities is the fourth element of financial flexibility. During periods of difficulty, the facility can be drawn down, no questions asked.

Financial flexibility can be defined as the ease with which a firm can fund a cash flow shortfall. A combination of plentiful equity capital, liquid assets, undrawn/committed loan facilities and low reliance on short-term debt provide this flexibility. In the event of an exogenous shock, a firm with financial flexibility can fund its cash flow shortfall, without having to resort to extreme operational measures. There is less need to postpone investment and cut costs, so financial flexibility is particular important for firms with high operating leverage (i.e. high fixed costs) and for those committed to ongoing exploration and research and development.

Having highlighted these advantages, it's also appropriate to discuss the disadvantages and costs associated with financial flexibility. Increasing equity capital involves dilution for existing equity investors, such as the founding investors. New investors will not only share the dividends but will want a say in strategy. Increasing equity relative to debt is also not as tax-effective, since interest on debt is usually deductible. Although, in an era of low corporate tax rates, this issue has become less important.

Another disadvantage of financial flexibility is that it creates 'free cash flow' – cash flows that can be used by self-interested managers to engage in empire building, even investing in negative NPV[7] projects that are not in the interests of shareholders. Higher debt capital can curtail this behaviour because, with higher debt servicing requirements, there are fewer free cash flows. The financial flexibility strategy permits greater managerial discretion and the potential for higher agency costs.[8] Directors may therefore have to engage in more intensive oversight to limit these agency costs.

Other costs of financial flexibility relate to the cost of long-term debt relative to short-term. In a normal yield curve environment, longer-term debt is more expensive. This means that substituting long-term for short-term debt will tend to increase the average cost of debt. Finally maintaining reserves of liquid assets has considerable opportunity cost since less liquid assets generally have much higher yields.

In summary, there are three broad avenues for the treatment of financial risk: financial flexibility, operational flexibility and derivatives. The three can be considered as substitutes for one another. When a business has a high degree of financial and operational flexibility, then there is little need for derivatives and vice versa.

9.4.1 Case study: Larry's Luxury Food and Wine revisited

We revisit the case study from Chapter 8, which considered Larry's Luxury Food and Wine. As an importer, this business was exposed to risk from foreign exchange movements. Larry can consider a number of risk treatment strategies, but we begin by considering debt reduction. One of Larry's biggest challenges is his inability to tolerate variation in earnings on account of his large debt. Debt servicing is a huge monthly commitment and he needs high and stable earnings to meet those commitments. The current debt principal is $20,000,000 with monthly payments of $100,000. If Larry could find another equity investor the funds could be used to reduce debt down to say $10,000,000 and interest payments would be halved. Now the probability of a cash flow catastrophe is significantly lower, at around 1 in 7 (14% chance) rather than 1 in 5 (20% chance).

If leverage is reduced, it may also be possible to renegotiate terms with the bank or to refinance. With less risk from the bank's perspective, it may be possible to reduce the cost of debt, thus bringing further benefits from the strategy.

Another possible treatment for Larry to consider is exercising real options (see the Real Option sheet). Larry considers the possibility of changing his operations given the current weakness of the Australian dollar relative to the Euro. He could cut back the volume of imports from Europe to 5,000 cases a month, focusing on lower-priced European goods on which he can earn a bigger margin. The expected cost would be EUR 190 per case rather than EUR 200 per case. He will make up the shortfall in volumes by also selling Australian sourced luxury food and wine items, at an average cost of $320 per case and a sale price of $400 per case. Unfortunately, the strategy is likely to increase his costs. Variable costs increase to $30 per case and fixed costs increase to $350,000 per month. Modelling suggests that the revised strategy significantly improves Larry's risk profile. While the potential for upside is not as good, the likelihood of cash flow catastrophe is reduced to 1 in 40 (2.5% chance) rather than 1 in 5 (20% chance).

9.4.2 Case study: BHP revisited

In Chapter 8 we examined the risk interactions that were relevant to BHP. Quantitative analysis showed that diversification within the portfolio of commodities and currencies reduced earnings volatility a significant degree. The next issue to consider is whether the residual market risk (after diversification) is acceptable to BHP. In other words, is this risk within appetite? Is further treatment needed?

BHP concluded that it benefitted from high quality assets, meaning that it is one of the lowest cost producers. It's very rare for commodity prices to fall below this level since higher cost producers tend to cut production in such circumstances and consumers of commodities increase their demand. This low-cost position diminishes the need for financial hedges. In addition, BHP knew that extreme market price scenarios could be offset by a variety of business/financial responses, such as temporarily cutting back production.

The residual exposures to market risk did not pose a serious threat to financial security or significantly constrain growth opportunities. The overall conclusion of the review was that BHP would adopt a program of 'conditional self-insurance'. In other words, it would abandon the use of derivatives for risk reduction purposes. The firm did, however, leave open the possibility of using derivatives to exploit market views on an opportunistic basis. Such transactions have a profit-making objective rather than risk mitigation and are managed with stop-loss and VaR limits (similar to a trading portfolio in a financial institution).

One of the factors in the BHP decision was the fact that the firm had a strong balance sheet giving it significant financial flexibility. One of the main benefits of hedging is increased debt capacity due to reduced cash flow volatility. Debt capacity is not, however, a constraint for BHP. An investor profiling exercise revealed that investors were either indifferent to the hedging decision or they viewed unhedged exposures positively.

Another consideration was the cost of financial hedging. Costs include transaction, credit and administrative costs. In some markets (oil, copper, interest rates) the effect of backwardation[9] tends to make hedging less attractive as forward rates are less advantageous than spot on average. BHP concluded that the benefits of financial hedging were not sufficient to justify these costs.

9.5 Treating multiple risks simultaneously

A major benefit of financial flexibility as a risk strategy is that it applies generally to all risks, regardless of whether the problem is an adverse currency movement, a new competitor, production failure, fraud, supply chain disruption, terrorist attack or pandemic. Financial flexibility is effective because it responds to the resultant cash flow shortfall. This is in contrast to treatments that only relate to specific, named risks such as insurance and derivative contracts. This generality is an immense advantage because it takes away the need to foresee specific risk events; it helps to alleviate exposure to the human overconfidence bias.

Fahlenbrach, Rageth and Stulz[10] find that firms with more financial flexibility were less affected by the COVID-19 shock during the collapse period. After controlling for known determinants of stock returns, firms with high financial flexibility experienced a stock price drop that was 26% lower than those with low financial flexibility. The same researchers found that diversified firms had no significant advantage over less diversified firms during the COVID-19 collapse, although there is some evidence that conglomerates performed better during the global financial crisis.[11]

Pandemic protection insurance was available prior to the 2020 COVID-19 outbreak, but few organisations relied on that type of risk transfer. According to Forbes magazine,[12] the All England Lawn Tennis Association was an exception, having taken out a $2 million pandemic insurance contract every year for the past 17 years prior to the outbreak. Following the COVID-19 outbreak, Wimbledon 2020 was cancelled and the association anticipated a pay-out of $141 million, offsetting about half its losses.

Despite the obvious success of insurance in the Wimbledon case, it's unlikely that pandemic insurance would ever become a widespread solution to pandemic risk. By definition, pandemics are global events. It's difficult for insurance companies to diversify pandemic risk in their portfolios, causing pandemic insurance contracts to be relatively expensive. They are expensive and only pay out under very specifically defined events. Add to this the possibility of default by the insurer and legal risk[13] in relation to the insurance contract, and the transfer of risk becomes even less attractive.

Insurance tends to be a less suitable risk treatment when the risk is primarily endogenous as opposed to exogenous. For risks that arise out of problems in the organisation's own business processes, such as internal fraud, it is typically more cost effective to treat the risk by changing the organisation's own business processes and introducing additional controls. Insurance companies will correctly have concerns about moral hazard[14] in cases like this, and this will be reflected in the pricing of the insurance contract.

In contrast, a more realistic response to many non-financial risks is the exercise of real options, a type of adaption strategy. This adaptive response is particularly applicable in relation to strategic risks. In addition to those mentioned in Section 9.3, some real options include: changing suppliers and distribution channels, entering or exiting particular markets, changing production technology, intentionally building up or running down inventories, changing business practices or even switching to different products. As the COVID-19 pandemic emerged, some manufacturing firms were able to repurpose their production facilities to produce test kits, hand sanitiser, face-masks and ventilators – all goods experiencing very high demand. Restaurants shifted to takeaway and home delivery as it became impossible to function in the usual way. Retailers switched to online sales and cashless purchasing to minimise physical contact.

The ability to adapt to a rapidly evolving environment requires flexibility and resilience, which is sometimes inconsistent with efficiency. Just like financial flexibility, operational flexibility comes with a cost. The trade-off between resilience and efficiency is clear in, for example, the management of supply chain risks. A generation of supply chain experts, in an effort to minimise costs, have developed global, interconnected supply chains and worked to reduce inventories. Lean global networks, relying on low-cost but distant suppliers, can be very efficient when everything runs to plan but are highly vulnerable to disruption due to critical dependence on far-flung suppliers. Many businesses learned this to their great cost during the COVID-19 pandemic. To increase operational resilience, many firms are now decentralising and diversifying their supplier network, deploying more inventory close to customers and developing business continuity plans and capabilities for a variety of disruption scenarios. They are willing to incur extra costs in order to build resilience, a strategy sometimes referred to as 'just-in-case', contrasting to the previous 'just-in-time' focus.

9.6 Evaluating expensive risk treatments

Chapter 8 highlighted the benefits of quantitative risk analysis. Risk treatments may also be evaluated quantitatively and this is particularly important when considering treatments that involve significant expenditure.

Suppose there is concern about cyber risk, so you consider investing in new controls to reduce the probability of a breach or to mitigate the impact of a breach. But the cost is high and it's unclear whether the cost can be justified. Another example might be the question of whether to purchase insurance to transfer a particular risk to another party. Again, the cost is substantial so how can you know whether the cost is justified? How can you build a business case for this expenditure? Quantification of risk addresses these problems, helping managers decide whether they can justify expenditure to treat risk. Without this kind of justification, it's often extremely difficult to convince senior leaders to make significant investments in risk management.

Suppose that I have some historical data about a particular risk type as shown in Table 9.1. In this sample the number of risk events per year varies quite a bit from 3 to 13. Across the entire 10 years, the average impact of an event is $35,000 but the largest single event (occurring in year 7) had an impact of $495,000.

On the face of it, it appears that this is a significant risk and some form of treatment may be justified. One of the problems we have is that the data sample is quite small, with only 63 events across 10 years. In statistics we need much larger samples to produce robust inferences. If there were more data, might we observe even more extreme outcomes?

This is another case where Monte Carlo analysis, discussed in Section 8.1, can be very useful. For this kind of operational risk, it is usual to simulate frequency and impact separately. That is, for each simulated scenario, representing say a one-year period, we first randomly simulate the number or frequency of risk events. Across 10,000 simulated years the average number of events might be 6, but in a few simulated years the number of events could be much higher. Then for each one of those events (i.e. some 6x10,000 = 60,000) we simulate the dollar losses or impact, using another statistical distribution. And because the impact of each event varies, the total losses in each simulated year will vary considerably. This analysis gives far greater insight than could be gleaned from history alone, especially for considering more extreme outcomes. Across the 10,000 simulated years we can understand the likely distribution of total losses as shown in Table 9.2.

The Monte Carlo analysis tells us that the expected loss in a typical year is $120,000. The loss with 95% confidence that will be exceeded in only 1/20 years is $778,000. Note that this is similar to the loss experienced in year 7, so

TABLE 9.1 Historical Risk Losses

Year	Number of risk events	Total losses in $'000	Average losses per event in $'000
1	3	68.92	22.97
2	6	93.80	15.63
3	5	23.91	4.78
4	6	122.24	20.37
5	10	323.86	32.39
6	4	322.99	80.75
7	13	787.11	60.54
8	9	298.62	33.18
9	3	59.86	19.95
10	4	134.78	33.70

TABLE 9.2 Estimated Losses

Percentile	50%	90.0%	95.0%	99.0%	99.9%
Losses Estimated from Monte Carlo Simulation in $'000s	120	510	778	1,997	5,311

it does not come as a big surprise. The loss with 99% confidence, which will be exceeded in only 1/100 years, is $1,997,000. Note that a loss of $1,997,000 has never actually occurred historically but is consistent with the dataset we have. The example illustrates a common feature of many risks: there is small probability of very large losses that could potentially be disastrous. It provides insight into the plausible but extreme events that humans tend to underestimate and undermanage.

Let's come back to the issue of equity capital. As explained in Section 9.4, equity capital is a crucial buffer to protect businesses against risk. You could say that capital is the ultimate mitigant control that will protect the firm in the event of serious financial loss. The amount of capital we need for the business will depend on risk appetite. Let's say that the board determines that the risk of insolvency in any year should be no more than 1%. In that case the business will need sufficient capital to cover losses to 99% confidence. For this particular risk type, that equates to $1,997,000. Actually, the amount of risk capital needed for this particular risk type is $1,997,000 − $120,000 or $1,877,000.

We can deduct the expected loss because that part of the loss distribution is handled differently, through provisions and earnings. A resilient business will set its pricing margins to ensure that profits are enough to cover not only costs, but also the expected losses in a typical year. Provisions should be maintained in the balance sheet to cover expected losses in a typical year. Risk capital is needed only to cover the losses **beyond** what occurs in a typical year.

Now for the really important bit – how can we use this information to evaluate the proposed treatment? Let's suppose that it's possible to treat this risk, either with insurance or new controls or systems. But the cost of the treatment is quite expensive, at $200,000 per annum. Based on quantitative modelling we believe that if the treatment were implemented the distribution of losses would be quite different as shown in Table 9.3.

In this example the effect of the treatment is to reduce expected losses by $120,000 − $60,000 = $60,000 p.a. As well as reducing the average loss, the treatment significantly reduces the potential for extreme losses. Before treatment the losses with 99% confidence are $1,997,000 but this comes down to $500,000 after treatment. This means that risk capital (the difference between Losses at 99% confidence and Expected Loss) is also reduced. The reduction in risk capital is $1,877,000 − $440,000 = $1,437,000. With cost of capital assumed to be 10%, this gives an annual saving of $143,700. So, the overall annual saving is $60,000 +

TABLE 9.3 Treatment and Savings in Risk Capital

	Before Treatment	*After Treatment*
Expected Loss	$120,000	$60,000
Risk Capital	$1,877,000	$440,000
Losses at 99% confidence	$1,997,000	$500,000

$143,700 = $203,700. Providing that the treatment costs less than this, investing in the treatment makes good business sense. This analysis will be the basis of a strong argument that is likely to be very influential. The power of risk quantification is clear.

Although many people are discomforted by the statistical assumptions that go into Monte Carlo simulations, statistical distributions confer immense advantages. Historical data is inevitably scarce and doesn't provide sufficient cases of extreme events for robust risk analysis. Monte Carlo addresses this problem and helps managers to assess risk and evaluate risk treatments.

Notes

1 Robinson, D. L. (2006). Do enforced bicycle helmet laws improve public health. *British Medical Journal*, *332*(7543), 722.
2 Dowell, III, A. M., & Hendershot, D. C. (1997). No good deed goes unpunished: Case studies of incidents and potential incidents caused by protective systems. *Process Safety Progress*, *16*(3), 132–139.
3 Cautionary Tales Podcast, episode 3, first broadcast on November 22 2019.
4 Mello, Antonio S., & Parsons, John E. (1995, February). *Maturity structure of a hedge matters: Lessons from the metallgesellschaft debacle*. Available at SSRN: https://ssrn.com/abstract=6104
5 Giambona, E., Graham, J. R., Harvey, C. R., & Bodnar, G. M. (2018). The theory and practice of corporate risk management: Evidence from the field. *Financial Management*, *47*(4), 783–832.
6 Giambona, E., Graham, J. R., Harvey, C. R., & Bodnar, G. M. (2018). The theory and practice of corporate risk management: Evidence from the field. *Financial Management*, *47*(4), 783–832.
7 NPV or 'net present value' is a measure used for valuing investments. Positive NPV projects are attractive to shareholders.
8 Stulz, R. (1990). Managerial discretion and optimal financing policies. *Journal of Financial Economics*, *26*(1), 3–27.
9 Backwardation markets are those where prices for future delivery are lower than spot prices i.e. for immediate delivery. In contango markets the reverse is true i.e. future prices are higher than spot prices.
10 Fahlenbrach, R., Rageth, K., & Stulz, R. M. (2020). How valuable is financial flexibility when revenue stops? Evidence from the COVID-19 crisis. Fisher College of Business Working Paper, (2020–03), 007.
11 Kuppuswamy, Venkat, & Villalonga, Belen. (2016). Does diversification create value in the presence of external financing constraints? Evidence from the 2007–2009 financial crisis. *Management Science*, *62*, 905–923.

12 Forbes. (2020, April 9). *Report: Wimbledon's organizers set for a $141 million payout after taking out pandemic insurance.* Available at www.forbes.com/sites/isabeltogoh/2020/04/09/report-wimbledons-organizers-set-for-a-141-million-payout-after-taking-out-pandemic-insurance/#31ed91b829f6
13 In this context legal risk refers to the possibility that the risk event may fall under an exclusion clause for technical reasons and recoveries do not eventuate.
14 Moral hazard refers to the fact that after purchasing insurance, an insured organisation may make insufficient efforts to prevent risk events from occurring. This behaviour increases the risk to the insurance company.

Further reading and resources

Chance, D. (2019). *Financial risk management: An end user perspective.* World Scientific.
Freund, J., & Jones, J. (2014). *Measuring and managing information risk: A FAIR approach.* Butterworth-Heinemann.
Saunders, A., Cornett, M., & Erhemjamts, O. (2021). *Financial institutions management: A risk management approach.* Tenth Edition McGraw-Hill.

10
REPORT, MONITOR, REVIEW

'If information is power, it must be remembered that too much information is a smokescreen'.
— Sir John Tusa[1]

Risk reports can play a number of different roles, especially in a large organisation. Chapter 6 discussed the communication/consultation process where the goal might be to educate stakeholders about risk or to support a discussion about the need to introduce or significantly upgrade a risk management framework.

This chapter addresses a different challenge. We assume that a risk management framework is operating. How is information about risk reported in the organisation in a 'business as usual' sense and also for the purpose of monitoring and review of the framework? Effective reports aid understanding, encompass all the crucial issues as briefly as possible and support good and timely decisions.

10.1 Link to objectives

Since we define risk as 'uncertainty relative to objectives', a good risk report will be focused on objectives, whether that is ensuring that the organisation can launch a new product, that it grow revenues by 10%, that it remains solvent, that it provides certain customer outcomes or that it reduces emissions to a specified level.

The organisation should report on the risk criteria that relate to the chosen objectives, focusing on any criteria where risk may be out of appetite or in danger of being out of appetite. Good risk reporting often analyses trends in key metrics over time. This helps leaders understand the risk trajectory of the organisation.

For these reasons, the popular 'heat map' approach to risk reporting is not recommended. A heat map is a graphical representation with likelihood normally on the x-axis and impact normally on the y-axis. Various risks are then represented by points on the graph. The intention of this approach is to focus attention on the risks in the top right of the of the graph – those with both high impact and high likelihood.

Some problems with the heat map approach are that a) it represents a point in time and doesn't show time trends b) it doesn't highlight which risks are out of appetite and therefore require attention c) often the assessment of likelihood and impact is done in a subjective way and d) it doesn't relate to the objectives of the organisation.

For a small-medium-sized enterprise, a crucial objective is normally to retain adequate liquidity for survival. There are numerous risk criteria that could cause a cash flow catastrophe e.g. a change in the exchange rate that adversely affects either exports or imports, a new competitor that takes market share, loss of key staff etc. Each one of those risk criteria might individually be tracking reasonably well but in aggregate, the possibility of disaster might be excessively large.

Say, for example, that there are eight different risk criteria that might all be relevant to the liquidity objective. For each one the probability of exceeding appetite and causing a liquidity catastrophe may be only 10%. But the aggregate risk, that is the chance that one or more of the eight criteria becomes problematic, is much higher. This is why enterprise level risk reporting linked to objectives is so important.

10.2 Reporting to line 1

In many risk management frameworks there is a designated 'risk owner'. Here the focus is line one of the three lines model, so the owner will typically be a senior executive with responsibility for a particular product or market. (S)he owns the risks that are connected to that business or to the achievement of particular objectives. The risk owner will need information to support business decisions and ensure that objectives are achieved.

Importantly, business managers must monitor detective controls (as discussed in chapter 9) and key risk indicators (KRIs). These can trigger contingency plans or additional management attention. A KRI is simply a measurable quantity that relevant subject matter experts believe is sensitive to the underlying operational risk exposure.

Because of the uncertainty in that belief, a single KRI is rarely useful on its own, and instead a business normally tries to construct several KRIs for each distinct risk. KRIs are also generally not used as absolute indicators of risk but rather as flags that change in value in response to increasing or decreasing risk exposure and then collectively act as prompts for further investigation.

Desirable characteristics of a KRI:

* Relevance to underlying risk – can it move because of other things;
* Ease of measurement;
* Responsiveness/forward-looking.

As an example, an organisation might decide it is experiencing a rising risk of internal fraud if it finds that the number of expense reports being submitted without proper receipts is rising or if several key employees in the markets division have not taken their mandated two consecutive weeks of vacation for several years. An organisation concerned about project risk might monitor the turnover of project staff as a KRI. In relation to mistakes and omissions, increased transaction volume and staff turnover are often used as KRIs. The age of a firm's IT system could be predictive of system failure.

Relatedly, line one will be interested in information about the effectiveness of its controls, since controls are used to mitigate risk. Many organisations now collect key control indicators (KCI's). These are metrics that indicate the potential for a control to fail within an organisation. For example, annual testing of the disaster recovery plan might be a control in relation to operational risk. Failure to conduct the annual testing would then show up as a KCI. Meeting project milestones would be a detective control in project risk management, so failure to meet a project milestone would be a KCI.

10.3 Board risk reporting

Poor reporting of risk to the executive and to the board has proven to be a factor in many risk governance scandals, notably the Commonwealth Bank of Australia scandal discussed in Chapter 12. Non-executive directors rely on what is reported to them, but they also have an obligation to ensure that reports cover all the relevant issues and that information is presented in a meaningful way. Some important issues to consider are as follows:

- Are significant matters escalated promptly?
- Is data accompanied by useful narrative and analysis to aid interpretation?
- Has assurance been sought on the accuracy and completeness of reports?
- Are 'best practice' reporting practices for the industry being applied?

One of the most common complaints from directors is that they receive voluminous reports and it is often difficult to identify what is important. Aggregate measures of risk information, combined with trend analysis, is important for getting the big picture. But directors also must be able to see more granular/specific metrics for issues that are emerging as potentially damaging for the future.

10.4 Monitoring and review

Risk management maturity requires a commitment to continuous improvement of the risk management framework. For this to succeed, the existing system needs ongoing monitoring and review. This is one of the key roles of the third line of defence: internal audit. Internal audit reviews the work of the first and second lines, providing independent assurance to the board that the framework is operating as intended.

When reviewing the risk framework one should consider:

• Were the actual outcomes for our objectives and risk criteria in line with expectations, and if not, why?
• How effective was the risk analysis for predicting possible outcomes? If not, why?
• Did the treatments operate in the manner expected, and if not, why?
• Do we need to review the objectives and risk criteria to better address the needs of stakeholders?
• Are risk reports providing useful, accurate and complete information to the key stakeholders?

Serious, adverse risk outcomes present a wonderful opportunity to reflect upon and hopefully improve a risk management framework. Techniques such as root cause analysis help to tease out the underlying causes and guide efforts to avoid any repetition.

Note

1 The Economist. (2020, November 21). *How to play the board game.* Available at www.economist.com/business/2020/11/21/how-to-play-the-board-game

PART C

Case studies

11

VOLKSWAGEN DIESELGATE CASE

Volkswagen, or 'peoples' car', is a German car manufacturer that was established in 1937. As well as selling VW branded cars, the group also produces Audi, Porsche and Skoda vehicles, making it one of the largest car manufacturers worldwide. VW traded on its reputation for German engineering and innovation.

Volkswagen AG is a listed company, owned 31.5% by the Porsche and Piëch families. In addition one of the German states, Lower Saxony, holds 12.4%, and Qatar Holdings owns 15.4%.[1] The presence of significant and active block holders is often considered to be a favourable governance feature as the block holders have the resources and the incentives to closely monitor the executive. As is typical for German companies, there is a dual-board structure with the supervisory board overseeing the management board. Under the German principle of co-determination, the supervisory board has both shareholder and employee representatives. Martin Winterkorn had taken over as CEO or chair of the management board in 2007.

Winterkorn was architect of the 'Strategy 2018', which had been designed to establish VW as the pre-eminent worldwide car manufacturer. His ambition was to triple sales over a ten-year period, overtaking General Motors and Toyota, all based on innovation.[2] Part of this innovation was the investment in 'clean diesel' technology, aiming to capture the performance and energy efficiency of diesel while minimising the release of toxic Nitrogen Oxide (NOx) emissions. Producing clean diesel is an enormous technological challenge because the methods for reducing NOx also reduce fuel economy and performance, as well as taking up space and increasing cost. Nevertheless, this strategy produced some apparent successes, with Volkswagen awarded 'Green Car of the Year' in 2009 for the Jetta TDI Clean Diesel and in 2010 for the Audi A3 TDI Clean Diesel. Previously only electric and hybrid models had won this award.

The company publicly espoused a commitment to environmentally sound products, as highlighted in its Code of Conduct. The same Code espoused several ideals deemed essential for becoming the world's number one car manufacturer, including: acting responsibly for the benefit of customers, shareholders and employees; complying with international conventions and laws; acting in accordance with statements and accepting responsibility for actions.

> 'A sustainable supply chain and environmentally compatible transportation solutions form an indispensable part of demonstrating comprehensive responsibility for human rights, as well as a commitment to the environment and to the battle against corruption'.
>
> *Volkswagen Sustainability Report 2014, page U3*

The US had always been a difficult market for Volkswagen because of its demanding NOx emissions standards. American regulations permit only about one-sixth of the NOx emissions permitted in Europe. Historically Europe has focused more on reducing carbon emissions than reducing NOx emissions and has offered subsidies for diesel cars due to their fuel economy. Why do we care about NOx emissions? According to the US Environment Protection Agency (EPA), diesel exhaust contains tiny particles known as fine particulate matter and toxic air pollutants. Exposure causes lung damage and aggravates conditions such as asthma. In the US, diesel exhaust causes 15,000 premature deaths every year.[3]

In this context it is not surprising that Volkswagen, with its diesel focus, struggled to achieve high sales in the United States. Toyota, with its successful hybrid models, was a strong competitor. But by the end of 2014, Volkswagen was close to achieving its sales goals, exceeded only by Toyota in terms of the number of units sold worldwide. VW's worldwide market share was 13% and 4.5% in North America.

In 2014 reports started to emerge that the clean diesel models were not as clean as claimed. Independent evaluation of vehicles tested on the open road showed that emissions were much higher than those observed in the testing laboratory and the EPA was informed. Initially Volkswagen denied any wrongdoing. In September 2015, following enquiries from the EPA, Volkswagen admitted that some models had been fitted with a 'defeat device' intended to bypass the vehicle's emission control system during testing. But on the road, the vehicles exceeded US emissions standards many times over.

Within days, CEO Martin Winterkorn had resigned and German authorities opened a fraud investigation. Initially the company claimed that knowledge of the fraud was limited to engineers and the senior executives knew nothing about it. More recently, Volkswagen has admitted that Winterkorn received a memo detailing the cheating in May 2014, although he claims he may not have read it.[4] As at the time of writing, the matter had not gone to trial but Winterkorn, along with other executives, has been charged with fraud in Germany and could face up to 10 years in prison. His bonus payments of €11 million, boosted by the fraud, may also be confiscated. Prosecutors now claim that more than 40 people were involved in the fraud, working for 3 different Volkswagen brands across at least 4 cities, as well as supplier Robert Bosch.[5]

The health consequences of the fraud are alarming. Particulates from diesel exhaust contribute to deaths through cancer, chronic respiratory diseases and cardiovascular diseases. According to Oldenkamp, Van Zelm and Huijbregts (2016)[6] the excess emissions resulting from the fraud cost 45,000 disability adjusted life years, valued at approximately US$39 billion.

Volkswagen has had to spend billions on rectifying and refitting affected vehicles as part of a recall campaign. The legal and regulatory consequences for Volkswagen were also considerable. In the US alone, Volkswagen has paid $25 billion in fines, penalties, civil damages and restitution in relation to 580,000 affected vehicles.[7]

And this does not include the effects on reputation and subsequently on car sales. Media interest in the story was intense, as shown in Figure 11.1.

Social media posts provide another window into reputational effects, as shown in Figure 11.2. Semantic analysis of the tweets during the period of interest shows positive sentiment fall away after the September 2015 announcement and a corresponding spike in negative sentiment.

These reputational effects were reflected both in car sales and the share price. Indeed, the Volkswagen share price has never fully recovered. Following the

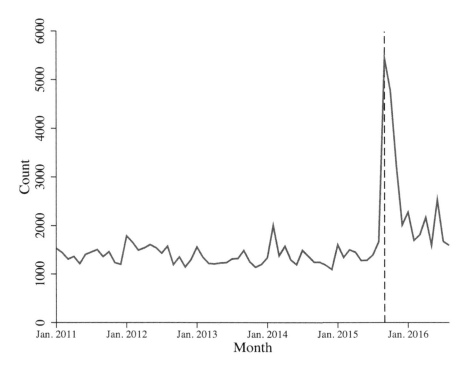

FIGURE 11.1 Monthly Print Media Mentions of 'Volkswagen' in the United States

Source: Bachman Ehrlich and Ruzic (2017)[8] Used with permission

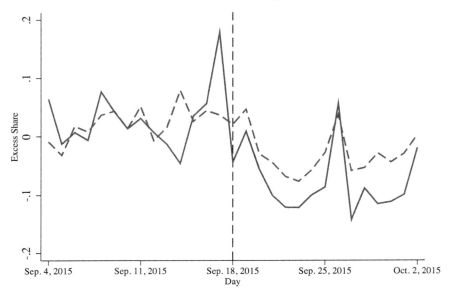

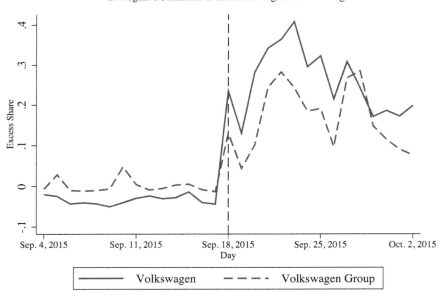

FIGURE 11.2 Daily Twitter Sentiment Towards Volkswagen

Source: Bachmann, Ehrlich and Ruzic (2017) Used with permission

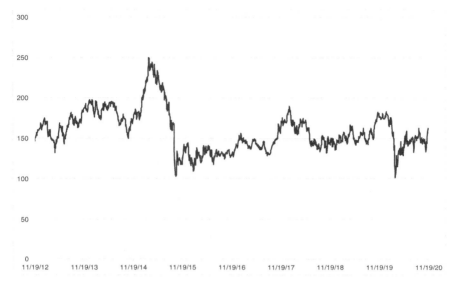

FIGURE 11.3 Volkswagen Share Price in Euro

scandal, Volkswagen's share of US light vehicle sales collapsed.[9] Figure 11.3 shows that the share price has not, as at 2020, ever recovered its 2014 value. Not only was Volkswagen harmed, but other German car manufacturers suffered loss of sales following the scandal. This can be attributed to damage to the reputation of the German automotive industry generally.

For outsiders, it seems extraordinary that a fraudulent scheme, known to so many individuals, could have flourished in a well-respected company like Volkswagen. How could so many people accept such an egregious wrongdoing as an acceptable strategy for boosting sales? There are a number of possible explanations.

1 Lax European regulations. It has since emerged that cheating on NOx emissions was endemic across Europe. This was a result of lax oversight of emissions standards by regulators in Germany and 6 other EU nations. Other European car manufacturers have also come under scrutiny for similar irregularities.[10] These regulatory failures created an environment where NOx emissions were perhaps not seen as an important issue; there were no consequences for cheating the standards in Europe so the practice of cheating flourished. This can be seen in the context that German environmental policy favoured the production of diesel cars and the car manufacturing industry has enormous economic importance for Germany and for Europe more broadly

2 Culture and leadership. The culture of Volkswagen was based on engineering excellence. The ability to solve technical problems quickly was highly

prized, and success had bred a degree of arrogance. Winterkorn was a PhD qualified engineer, known for being a perfectionist with extraordinary attention to detail. He always carried a micrometre, for example, for checking gaps between body panels to an accuracy of a hundredth of a millimetre.[11] He was known as a martinet – a disciplinarian who demanded complete obedience and would not tolerate failure. This authoritarian management style created a culture of fear, where employees would not have felt able to raise concerns about practices.[12] The pressure on engineers to overcome the insurmountable technical challenge of clean diesel was immense, and admitting failure would have been unthinkable. The consequences of failure were likely to be first anger from Winterkorn and then dismissal. According to one executive

> There was always a distance, a fear and a respect. . . . If he would come and visit or you had to go to him, your pulse would go up. If you presented bad news, those were the moments that it could become quite unpleasant and loud and quite demeaning.[13]

The combination of aggressive goals that were probably unachievable technically speaking and a culture of fear had devastating consequences

3   Poor governance. Winterkorn had been the protégé of Ferdinand Piëch, the chairman of the supervisory board and a former CEO. Arguably this close relationship worked against true independence of the supervisory board to monitor and challenge the management board. In addition, Piëch himself had been a tyrannical leader of Volkswagen, who terrorised and intimidated subordinates.[14] So it's unlikely that he would have questioned Winterkorn's authoritarian style. Indeed, under Piëch's chairmanship of the supervisory board, the culture of fear probably developed even further. While block holders are often seen as positive for good governance, in this particular case the block holders were not effective in their scrutiny of managers. The state of Lower Saxony, with 20% of the voting stock and economically reliant on the automotive industry, had a cosy relationship with executives, allowing them free reign. Some have criticised the practice of co-determination, where both shareholder and employee representatives sit on the supervisory board, as a contributing factor in the scandal. Under co-determination it is common to have large, unwieldy boards that may encourage free-riding. Volkswagen had a supervisory board with some 20 members during the relevant period.

Notes

1   Elson, C. M., Ferrere, C., & Goossen, N. J. (2015). The bug at Volkswagen: Lessons in co-determination, ownership, and board structure. *Journal of Applied Corporate Finance, 27*(4).
2   Blackwelder, B., Coleman, K., Colunga-Santoyo, S., Harrison, J. S., & Wozniak, D. (2016). *The Volkswagen Scandal.* Case Study. University of Richmond: Robins School of Business.

3 Environmental Protection Agency. *Diesel exhaust in the United States.* Available at https:// nepis.epa.gov/Exe/ZyPDF.cgi/P1001T82.PDF?Dockey=P1001T82.PDF
4 The Guardian. (2019, April 16). Former head of Volkswagen could face 10 years in prison. Available at www.theguardian.com/business/2019/apr/15/former-head-of-volks wagen-could-face-10-years-in-prison#:~:text=The%20former%20boss%20of%20 Volkswagen,emissions%20tests%20on%20diesel%20vehicles
5 Fortune. (2018, February 6). How VW paid $25 billion for dieselgate: And got off easy. Available at https://fortune.com/2018/02/06/volkswagen-vw-emissions-scandal- penalties/#:~:text=U.S.%20authorities%20have%20extracted%20%2425,that%20 Oliver%20Schmidt%20was%20guilty
6 Oldenkamp, R., van Zelm, R., & Huijbregts, M. A. (2016). Valuing the human health damage caused by the fraud of Volkswagen. *Environmental Pollution, 212,* 121–127.
7 Fortune. (2018, February 6). How VW paid $25 billion for dieselgate: And got off easy. Available at https://fortune.com/2018/02/06/volkswagen-vw-emissions-scandal- penalties/#:~:text=U.S.%20authorities%20have%20extracted%20%2425,that%20 Oliver%20Schmidt%20was%20guilty
8 Bachmann, R., Ehrlich, G., & Ruzic, D. (2017). Firms and collective reputation: The Volkswagen emission scandal as a case study (No. 6805). CESifo Working Paper.
9 Bachmann, R., Ehrlich, G., & Ruzic, D. (2017). Firms and collective reputation: The Volkswagen emission scandal as a case study (No. 6805). CESifo Working Paper.
10 Fortune. (2018, February 6). How VW paid $25 billion for dieselgate: And got off easy. Available at https://fortune.com/2018/02/06/volkswagen-vw-emissions-scandal- penalties/#:~:text=U.S.%20authorities%20have%20extracted%20%2425,that%20 Oliver%20Schmidt%20was%20guilty
11 Fortune. (2018, February 6). How VW paid $25 billion for dieselgate: And got off easy. Available at https://fortune.com/2018/02/06/volkswagen-vw-emissions-scandal- penalties/#:~:text=U.S.%20authorities%20have%20extracted%20%2425,that%20 Oliver%20Schmidt%20was%20guilty
12 The Guardian. (2015, October 11). Volkswagen executives describe authoritarian cul- ture under former CEO. Available at www.theguardian.com/business/2015/oct/10/ volkswagen-executives-martin-winterkorn-company-culture#:~:text=Volkswagen%20 executives%20describe%20authoritarian%20culture%20under%20former%20C EO,-VW%20Group%20of&text=Like%20many%20chief%20executives%2C%20 Martin,who%20didn't%20like%20failure.&text=Volkswagen%20has%20declined%20 to%20comment,a%20factor%20in%20the%20cheating
13 Reuters. (2015, October 11). Fear and respect: VW's culture under winterkorn. Available at www.reuters.com/article/us-volkswagen-emissions-culture/fear-and-respect- vws-culture-under-winterkorn-idUSKCN0S40MT20151010
14 Road and Track. (2015, November, 4). One man established the culture that led to VW's emission scandal. Available at www.roadandtrack.com/car-culture/a27197/bob- lutz-vw-diesel-fiasco/

12

CBA/CONDUCT RISK CASE STUDY

The Commonwealth Bank of Australia (CBA) case study of conduct risk offers some rich governance lessons. The case covers a series of misconduct scandals that gripped the bank from 2010–18, leading to the Prudential Inquiry into the CBA by the Australian Prudential Regulation Authority (APRA). The Royal Commission into Misconduct in the Banking, Superannuation and Financial Services Industry[1] (Royal Commission) revealed similar practices in many other Australian financial institutions during this period.

Founded in 1911, the CBA was a government-owned commercial bank until privatisation in the 1990s. The CBA is the largest Australian bank both by assets and market capitalisation and it ranks in the top 50 banks worldwide by assets.[2] The CBA is one of four major commercial banks in Australia that dominate the banking industry, with more than 70% of banking assets between them.[3]

The CBA, like the other four major Australian banks, performed relatively well during the global financial crisis of 2007–09, remaining profitable throughout.[4] This was due to the primarily domestic focus of the bank and the fact that Australia did not experience an economic recession. For the financial year ended June 2010 the bank's return on equity was 18.7% and the bank maintained a ROE above 18% through the 2010s until 2016. This remarkable profitability relative to global peers made the bank a darling of the stock market. Asset and balance sheet quality were exemplary, and to this day, the bank is one of the few in the world to retain a AA- credit rating from Standard and Poors.

Some of the scandalous events that occurred within the CBA group are presented in Table 12.1.

There are two important environmental factors that contributed to this pattern of behaviour.

1   Regulatory failure. One of the findings of the Royal Commission[5] was that regulators had not sufficiently held institutions to account for wrongdoing.

TABLE 12.1 CBA Scandals

Misconduct by financial advisers in CBA's wealth business (2010/11)	A group of financial advisers in a CBA subsidiary put client money into risky investments, without their permission, by forging documents. The motivation was increased commissions for the planners and high profits for the firm. Misconduct was enabled by a reckless, sales-based culture and negligent management, with little regard for compliance with the law.[6]
Fees for no service in financial advice (2012–15)	The CBA's wealth business charged clients regular fees for services that were never provided, such as annual portfolio reviews. This continued over a number of years despite customer complaints and the fact that external auditors highlighted the issue.[7]
Life insurance products sold by CommInsure (2016)	Through CommInsure, the CBA provided trauma insurance. The scandal related to systematic denial of claims by persons who had suffered heart attack or other illness, based on, for example, outdated medical definitions.[8]
Anti-money laundering (AML) breaches (2012–17)	In 2012 the CBA introduced 'intelligent deposit machines' that facilitated cash deposits by immediately counting bank notes and crediting CBA accounts. Prior to 2017 there was no limit on the size of deposits, so drug dealers and other criminals were able to create CBA accounts with false identities and launder large volumes of cash. CBA eventually admitted to numerous breaches of the AML and counter-terrorist financing act. On more than 53,000 occasions the bank failed to provide the regulator, Austrac, with threshold transaction reports within the required timeframe and failed to comply with its own compliance framework between 2012–15. CBA agreed to a $700 million civil penalty.[9]
Mis-selling of credit card insurance (2011–18)	CBA customers were encouraged to purchase this profitable (to CBA) insurance product, even those who were ineligible ever to claim on account of being unemployed or students.[10] These practices continued for years despite concerns being raised both by the regulator and auditors.
Superannuation (pension fund) products (2013–18)	The CBA Group offered superannuation funds via trustee companies. A trustee must act in the best interests of members and prefer their interests over the interests of anyone else. Trustee companies in the CBA group failed to act in the best interest of members in a number of respects, instead acting to maximise its own fees. Notoriously, fees continued to be charged to deceased estates even after notification of death.[11]

Misconduct was often not detected and when it was, penalties were insufficient to provide a strong deterrent effect. They were regarded more as a cost of doing business in the sector, a mere slap on the wrist

2   Industry characteristics/norms. Usually when a firm treats its customers poorly it suffers the natural consequences of dissatisfied customers and loss of market share. These forces tend to prevent or reduce any mistreatment of customers. The market for financial services is somewhat unusual in the sense that financial products are often opaque and complex, while consumers are often disengaged and lack financial literacy. This means that customers may be unaware that they have been exploited. Even when a customer becomes dissatisfied, they may not take their business elsewhere because of high switching costs or a perception that all providers are much the same. Indeed, misconduct was present in much of the industry so this perception was well-founded at the time. As a result of this, the reputational costs normally associated with misconduct to customers were low in this industry.

12.1 Governance, culture and accountability at the CBA

While external factors were relevant, the CBA case is ultimately about three interconnected issues: governance, culture and accountability. These three underlying elements are explained in detail in the report of the Prudential Inquiry into the CBA (Inquiry).[12]

The Inquiry found that a behavioural bias, overconfidence, was one of the fundamental causes: 'CBA's continued financial success dulled the senses of the institution' at p. 3. This misplaced confidence papered over significant weaknesses in the management of so-called operational risks, defined as: 'the risk of loss resulting from inadequate or failed internal processes, people and systems or from external events'.[13] In financial services, the Basel Committee's operational risk taxonomy, with 7 broad categories, is often used.[14] The Achilles heel for the CBA was the category known as Clients, Products and Business Practices. This category captures 'losses arising from a negligent failure to meet a professional obligation to specific clients (including fiduciary and suitability requirements), or from the nature or design of a product'. Some would refer to this as conduct risk.

Interestingly this category has proven problematic for many global financial institutions, contributing more than any other to the value of operational losses. A number of banks worldwide have experienced AML scandals e.g. Deutsche Bank, HSBC, Standard Chartered, Danske Bank and many have experienced mis-selling scandals e.g. Lloyds, Barclays, RBS. This category would also include the well-known scandal at Wells Fargo involving unauthorised account opening and also LIBOR rigging (UBS, Barclays, RBS, Deutsche Bank, JP Morgan).[15] It is a category with low velocity in the sense that the impacts (fines, customer remediation, reputational damage) occur long after the problematic business practices. This time lag tends to aggravate the well-known biases related to discounting events well in the future.

Due to overconfidence and complacency, the operational risk framework at CBA was cumbersome, immature and incomplete. Issues, incidents and risks were not effectively escalated through the organisation, and resolution was slow and bureaucratic with a lack of urgency. There was a focus on process over outcomes. The compliance function was immature and under-resourced. The voice of the risk function was weak in relation to operational risks and customer complaints were inadequately addressed. The organisation was reactive, failing to learn lessons from past incidents and operated in reactive mode. An undue emphasis on collegiality meant that accountability was lacking.

Another fundamental problem at CBA was the use of short-term incentives based on sales or revenues, often paid out as annual cash bonuses. Bank employees could boost short-term bank profits – and their own bonuses – by exploiting customers and violating both company policies and national laws. In this way misconduct was rewarded, and if it were later discovered, poor conduct was often ignored by management provided that profits were good. The bonus culture contributed to a classic 'avoidance trap' as discussed in Section 3.2. Table 12.2 presents the culture issues at CBA using the four-factor Macquarie University Risk Culture framework from Table 3.4:

TABLE 12.2 Risk Culture Issues at the CBA

Risk Culture Dimension	Risk Culture Issues
Valued	• Credibility, authority and respect for the risk/compliance function was inconsistent, with weakness especially relating to operational risk (as opposed to credit risk). This was likely linked to lack of capability and expertise within line 2 of the 3 lines model.
	• Risk management was seen by many as an administrative brake on short-term success, not an enabler for sustainable success.
	• Rather than a desirable sense of 'chronic unease' to continuously improve risk management, the CBA exhibited a sense of 'chronic ease' or complacency regarding risk management.
Proactive	• Risk management was fundamentally reactive, responding in an ad hoc manner to issues as they arose.
	• While issues and concerns were often raised, follow-up and resolution lacked urgency. Resolution deadlines were repeatedly extended.
	• Lessons were not learned effectively from past problems.
	• Customer complaints were not systematically analysed and used as a learning opportunity.
	• First line staff did not consistently understand what was expected of them in a risk management sense.

(Continued)

TABLE 12.2 (Continued)

Risk Culture Dimension	Risk Culture Issues
Avoidance	• Complacency and overconfidence exacerbated a 'tick-the-box' approach to risk management, focusing on process rather than outcomes.
	• Known risk issues (e.g. red audit reports relating to anti-money laundering) were not resolved effectively.
	• Reward and status flowed to people who generated high short-term profits, even if risk outcomes were bad or even if they violated policies
	• Unclear accountabilities for risk. The Three Lines Model was not functioning well in the sense that primary first line responsibility was not well established. Responsibility for key risks at the executive level was vague.
	• Important information about risk did not flow all the way to the most senior leaders; bad news was downplayed or excluded from reports.
	• Lack of investment in risk/compliance was another sign that it was not a priority. In 2017, the CRO had a list of 27 projects considered important that had not been funded or progressed.
	• Leaders spoke in lofty terms about values in formal settings, but their behaviour suggested that these espoused values were empty words. An example of this is the continuation of products and practices that blatantly exploited customers for the benefit of CBA, despite the obvious risks. Upon raising concerns, the head of retail was told by the CEO to 'temper his sense of justice'.
Managers and Leaders	• Leaders and managers did not consistently model good risk management behaviour. Constructive debate among directors – and challenge of the executive – was inadequate.
	• The 'should we?' question, in relation to business practices, was not sufficiently debated by managers.
	• Through their lack of urgency in resolving issues, leaders indicated that risk management was a low priority.
	• Leaders and managers did not adequately incorporate risk and compliance into the performance management system (financial rewards, promotions, sanctions).

This avoidance trap was sustained by the incentives and accountability failures in the senior executive. The remuneration framework provided no meaningful sanctions for senior executives who presided over poor risk and customer outcomes. This was partly due to the lack of ownership of key risks by individuals in the executive, that is, unclear accountabilities. Instead, executives tended to hide behind ignorance and group decision making. With a heavy focus on short-term incentives, executives focused on short-term profits and failed adequately to consider the negative consequences of strategies that might take years to emerge. Indeed, the long-time span between misconduct and adverse consequences is one of the characteristics of this type of operational risk.

BOX 12.1 MISCONDUCT AND CULTURE

Since the Global Financial Crisis many firms have tried to inculcate risk culture – an organisational culture that focuses on risk management and ensuring that the organisation meets its objectives. Despite this, we continue to see misconduct towards customers, causing them significant detriment. This has caused some to question whether risk culture, alone, can address misconduct. The respective roles of risk and ethical culture in relation to misconduct are summarized in Figure 12.1.

Often misconduct is motivated by the fact that it produces short-term benefits for the organisation and hence the managers/employees. These benefits could take the form of bonuses, promotion or high status.

But in the long-term the organisation suffers as well as customers. In some organisations, risk culture is only indirectly concerned about customer outcomes. Poor customer outcomes may not be a concern for their own sake but rather because they may result in losses to the organisation via fines, legal costs, customer remediation programs and reputational damage.

Ethical culture, on the other hand, considers customer outcomes for their own sake. If a customer is harmed by the organisation then that is a problem in its own right, not just because of the possibility of consequential losses to the organisation. Perhaps ethical culture is more effective for producing good customer outcomes?

A recent Macquarie research project[16] investigated these questions. We surveyed staff in large Australian superannuation funds to identify the type of organisational culture that is most helpful for addressing misconduct towards customers. We found that risk culture alone is not the best way forward. Firms also need to promote a culture that is more ethical and less

FIGURE 12.1   Culture and Misconduct

self-interest, to care about outcomes for stakeholders beyond just share-holders and managers.

When the culture is self-interested, misconduct flourishes. The mentality is: 'what's in it for me?'. Employees perceive that the organisation implic-itly condones self-interested behaviour, even if it harms customers or other stakeholders. These perceptions are usually picked up from the informal statements and actions of managers and respected peers, even though there may be formal policies and statements to the contrary. Employees will prioritise profits over customer outcomes because they are thinking about bonuses, promotions etc.

We demonstrated that the combination of favourable risk culture with an ethical, low self-interest culture results in optimum workplace conditions for reducing misconduct. Practitioners should be aware that both risk and ethical cultures matter.

The rationale for short-term incentives in the senior executive is to reward good behaviour and to sanction poor behaviour. At the CBA – and many other institutions – executive bonuses had become an entitlement and were not truly 'at risk'. For financial year 2016, then–chief-executive Ian Narev recommended all executives receive at least 100% of their short-term incentives. Despite mul-tiple scandals having been aired in the press, only one executive lost any bonus, and that was a discount of only 5%. At the board remuneration committee, the directors allocated only 10 minutes to discuss the matter, granting millions of dollars in rewards at the stroke of a pen.

The board and its committees play an important role in setting the tone for risk management, through both words and actions. The inquiry identified a number of shortcomings in the operation of the board and its committees as follows:

- Length of committee meetings was not sufficient to allow adequate cover-age of risk and audit issues;
- Insufficient rigour and urgency. The board and its committees did not suf-ficiently hold executives to account in the way they responded to issues that had been identified by auditors and others. There was too much trust in the executive and insufficient challenge. This was particularly true in the response of the board audit committee to 'red' audit reports.[17] There were three red internal audit reports on the topic of anti-money laundering and counter-terrorism financing matters in 2013, 2015 and 2016. Repeat red issues ought to be treated with particular urgency, with issue owners and the relevant executive held to account for failure to close these out, yet this did not occur at the CBA;
- Weaknesses in reporting. The governance of non-financial risks was ham-pered by a lack of useful board reports in these risk areas. Reports did not have the right balance of both summarised and detailed reporting. For

example, the reporting of unsatisfactory controls did not include any trend analysis that may have helped the board risk committee glean insights. The board did not receive any analysis of customer complaints; information that would have been extremely valuable for highlighting systemic problems. Instead board reports focused on the Net Promotor Scores, which gave a misleadingly favourable impression of the customer experience. The board audit committee (BAC) did not receive metrics on the status of the highest rated audit issues and the timetable for remediation;

- Heavy reliance on key individuals. For example, the chair of the board audit committee was highly regarded and other committee members tended to defer to his expertise. More discussion and challenge within the committee may have helped. In the board risk committee the Chair and the CRO collaborated closely, but again there was insufficient debate of issues across the entire committee. Both individuals had a particular interest in the management of credit and market risks, with less interest in operational risks;
- Inadequate communication between board committees. Gaps in the flow of information between committees was an issue;
- Candour of messaging to the board and its committees. Reports tended to focus on the positive and downplay negative information;
- Overconfidence of the board in itself and lack of benchmarking to best practice governance;
- Board assessment of culture. The inquiry observed immaturity in this regard and also in the identification of necessary actions to further enhance risk culture. CBA aspired to be a values-led institution but there was an overreliance on good intent. Focus on customer outcomes was not consistent.

BOX 12.2 THE BOARD AND CONDUCT RISK

Conduct risk has brought considerable shame to many organisations and their boards. The Dieselgate and CBA cases in this book are well-known but unfortunately there are numerous examples.

An innovative supervision program has been introduced by the UK's Finance and Conduct Authority (FCA) based around five questions. This set of questions is useful for boards wanting to ensure that conduct risk within their organisations is well-managed. The questions highlight the complexity of the issue and the need to ensure that all aspects of the organisation are consistently aligned to both support good behaviour and discourage misconduct. This supervision program has brought a wealth of insight that is relevant to the topic, as shown in the 2020 report.[18]

The FCA's 5 conduct questions:

1   What proactive steps do you take as a firm to identify the conduct risks inherent within your business?

2 How do you encourage the individuals who work in front, middle, back office, control and support functions to feel and be responsible for managing the conduct of their business?

3 What support (broadly defined) does the firm put in place to enable those who work for it to improve the conduct of their business or function?

4 How does the Board and Executive Committee gain oversight of the conduct of business within their organisation and, equally importantly, how does the Board or Executive Committee consider the conduct implications of the strategic decisions that they make?

5 Has the firm assessed whether there are any other activities that it undertakes that could undermine strategies put in place to improve conduct?

Notes

1 A Royal Commission is a formal inquiry funded by – but independent of – the Australian government, with broad powers to collect evidence and hear submissions. This particular inquiry was led by Kenneth Hayne AC QC, former Justice of the High Court of Australia, the highest court in the Australian court hierarchy. It commenced in late 2017 and presented its final report in 2019.

2 S&P Global. (2020). The world's 100 largest banks. Available at www.spglobal.com/marketintelligence/en/news-insights/latest-news-headlines/the-world-s-100-largest-banks-2020-57854079

3 APRA. (2020, June). *Quarterly authorised deposit-taking institution performance statistics*. Available at https://www.apra.gov.au/quarterly-authorised-deposit-taking-institution-statistics

4 APRA. (2010, March). *Financial stability review*. Available at www.rba.gov.au/publications/fsr/2010/mar/pdf/0310.pdf

5 Financial Services Royal Commission. (2019). *Final report*, Volume 1. Available at www.royalcommission.gov.au/sites/default/files/2019-02/fsrc-volume-1-final-report.pdf

6 Centre for Law, Markets and Regulation. (2014). *ASIC, the CBA, business cultures and the giving of financial wisdom*. Available at https://clmr.unsw.edu.au/article/market-conduct-regulation/asic%2C-the-commonwealth-bank-of-australia%2C-business-cultures-and-the-giving-of-financial-wisdom

7 Financial Services Royal Commission. (2018). *Interim report*, Volume 2. Available at https://financialservices.royalcommission.gov.au/Documents/interim-report/interim-report-volume-2.pdf

8 Financial Services Royal Commission. (2019). *Final report*, Volume 2. Available at https://treasury.gov.au/sites/default/files/2019-03/fsrc-volume-2.pdf

9 Australian Financial Review. (2018). Money laundering scandal: What CBA admitted to and why it happened. Available at www.afr.com/companies/financial-services/money-laundering-scandal-what-cba-admitted-to-and-why-it-happened-20180604-h10xm3

10 ABC News. (2018). *CBA CEO Matt Comyn blames predecessor Ian Narev for dodgy credit insurance*. Available at www.abc.net.au/news/2018-11-20/cba-ceo-matt-comyn-blames-predecessor-ian-narev/10513836#:~:text=The%20Commonwealth%20Bank's%20relatively%20new,of%20his%20predecessor%2C%20Ian%20Narev

11 Financial Services Royal Commission. (2019). *Final report*, Volume 2. Available at https://treasury.gov.au/sites/default/files/2019-03/fsrc-volume-2.pdf

12 APRA. (2018). *Prudential inquiry into the commonwealth bank of Australia*. Available at www.apra.gov.au/sites/default/files/CBA-Prudential-Inquiry_Final-Report_30042018.pdf

13 Basel Committee. (2001). *QIS 2 operational risk loss data.* Available at www.bis.org/bcbs/qisoprisknote.pdf
14 The other categories are: Internal fraud, External fraud, Employee practices and workplace safety, Execution, delivery and process management, Damage to physical assets, Business disruptions and systems failures.
15 McConnell, P. (2013). Systemic operational risk: The LIBOR manipulation scandal. *Journal of Operational Risk, 8*(3), 59–99.
16 Sheedy, E., Garcia, P., & Jepsen, D. (2019). The role of risk climate and ethical self-interest climate in predicting unethical pro-organisational behaviour. *Journal of Business Ethics,* 1–20.
17 A red audit report from internal audit is intended to convey that a serious risk weakness has been identified.
18 Financial Conduct Authority. (2020). *Message from the engine room: 5 conduct questions.* Available at www.fca.org.uk/publication/market-studies/5-conduct-questions-industry-feedback-2019-20.pdf

Further reading and resources

APRA. (2018). *Prudential inquiry into the commonwealth Bank of Australia.* Available at www.apra.gov.au/sites/default/files/CBA-Prudential-Inquiry_Final-Report_30042018.pdf
Financial Conduct Authority. (2020). *Message from the engine room: 5 conduct questions.* Available at www.fca.org.uk/publication/market-studies/5-conduct-questions-industry-feedback-2019-20.pdf
Grimwade, M. (2021). *Operational risk: Ten fundamental laws.* London: Risk Books.

13

STRATEGIC RISK MANAGEMENT

Strategic risk deserves special mention because of its criticality for the successful governance of an organisation. Arguably strategic risk management has never been more challenging because the environment exhibits turbulence, uncertainty, novelty and ambiguity or 'TUNA' conditions. This chapter describes the principles of strategic risk management, with further discussion of strategic risks in Chapter 14 (climate risk), Chapter 15 (cyber risk) and Chapter 16 (COVID-19 pandemic).

Examples of organisational failure due to strategic risk abound, but Table 13.1 highlights some notable examples.

Strategic risks are risks related to strategy, defined here as the set of resource allocation decisions that help a firm create and sustain a competitive advantage over its rivals in the pursuit of its strategic ambitions.[1] Setting strategy involves answering the following questions: what unique value will we offer customers? How will we create that unique value? Where will we compete? What would prevent competitors imitating us or creating a substitute for our competitive advantage?

The case of Volkswagen illustrates a strategy that was flawed at the outset due to technological constraints. Other cases, such as Blockbuster Video, illustrate how a successful strategy can be derailed over time due to changes in the external environment and the agility of competitors. Other cases, such as NAB and HBOS, are arguably related more to incompetence in the execution of strategy.

In the most recent edition of the OECD Corporate Governance Principles, greater emphasis is placed on strategy. Notably, strategy is seen as the foremost responsibility of the board of directors.

> The corporate governance framework should ensure the *strategic guidance* of the company, the effective monitoring of management by the board, and the board's accountability to the company and the shareholders.
>
> *OECD Principles 2015, p. 45, emphasis added*[2]

TABLE 13.1 Strategic Risk Examples

National Australia Bank (NAB)	The bank made a series of international acquisitions including Clydesdale Bank, the Northern Bank in Northern Ireland and the National Irish Bank in the Republic of Ireland, Yorkshire Bank in the UK, Bank of New Zealand, Michigan National Corporation, HomeSide and Great Western Bancorp in the US.[3] In most cases these acquisitions failed to meet their objectives and significant loss of shareholder value ensued.
Halifax/Bank of Scotland (HBOS)	The UK parliamentary inquiry into the failure of HBOS concluded that the collapse was due to an incompetent and reckless strategy. The strategy was focused on revenue growth and market share, growth that outpaced the ability of the firm to control risks.[4]
Blockbuster Video	In the early 1990s Blockbuster Video had an enviable position in the large market for video rentals. In the late 1990s Netflix launched an online, mail-delivery DVD service. Over time this evolved to a monthly subscription service with unlimited access to DVDs. Ultimately Netflix offered live online streaming and began creating original content. Blockbuster was slow to respond to technological innovations, handicapped by concerns that sales through its brick-and-mortar stores would be cannibalised. From 2008, Blockbuster's revenues steadily fell, resulting in bankruptcy in 2010.[5]
Volkswagen and Dieselgate	As discussed in Chapter 11, Volkswagen's strategic objective was to become the world's largest automobile producer based on 'clean diesel' technology. The strategy proved fundamentally flawed as diesel engines, while very efficient in some respects, produce high levels of emissions. This meant that Volkswagen's vehicles were not able to pass strict emissions standards in the US. Dominance of the global market was not possible without significant US sales. Attempts to beat the US emissions standards by fraudulent means led to the 'dieselgate' scandal with significant fines and reputational damage.

Similarly, strategy has been featured more heavily in recent revisions to international risk management standards such as ISO31000. This suggests that in the past, strategic risk was not adequately addressed. In the 2018 revision of ISO31000, strategy and risk management are seen as fundamentally entwined, with strategy setting and risk management being an iterative process.

These developments suggest that strategic risk should be a board concern in a way that other risks are not, since the board takes ultimate responsibility for approving if not setting strategy. Adequate time and resources must be devoted to exploring strategic options and the risks associated with them. The chosen strategy must take account of risk appetite, having regard for the resources and objectives of the organisation. Independent review should be incorporated through consultation with stakeholders, especially institutional investors. Having approved a strategy, the board should also regularly review it, monitoring the progress of execution and key risks associated with it.[6]

Strategic risk management is one of the most challenging areas of risk governance so it is appropriate to consider some of the principles and analytical approaches that are relevant to this crucial risk.

13.1 Strategic risk identification with the PESTLE

The underlying sources of strategic risk are often examined with the 'PESTLE' model, an acronym standing for political, economic, societal, technological, legal and environmental forces.[7] Strategic risk often results from changes in one of these six domains, so it provides a useful checklist for scanning the business environment.

13.2 Evaluating strategic risk through scenario analysis

The future is inherently unpredictable; even the best forecasters struggle to make sense of the TUNA environment. This fundamental truth means that strategists must be prepared for a range of possible futures. Scenario analysis is a methodology for identifying plausible future scenarios, then exploring their implications. It was pioneered by the Rand Corporation and the military after World War Two, to address the complexities of the cold war era.[8] The method was further popularised when Shell used it with some success to adapt to the oil shock of the 1970s.

BOX 13.1 FORECASTING AND SUPERFORECASTING

Scenario analysis is about evaluating possible future states of the world that have a high enough probability to be considered plausible. Scenarios are inevitably based on forecasts of future conditions – forecasts of the economy, the political environment, consumer preferences and technological advances. All of these are 'low validity' domains[9] where even experts are often wrong. The average expert in these domains does about as well as random guessing, as shown by the well-known work of Phillip Tetlock.[10]

Experts often display overconfidence. For example, events they predict with 80% confidence typically happen only 60% of the time, events they predict with 99% confidence happen only about 80% of the time. On average, experts underperform people with good general knowledge but with no particular expertise relevant to the topic at hand (sophisticated dilettantes).

But some experts do better than the average and have significant predictive ability, although their ability to predict in low-validity environments wanes for horizons beyond about one year. The Good Judgment Project[11] is a network of 'superforecasters', individuals who have proven their predictive ability and contribute their insights, and it is led by Professors Tetlock and Mellers at the University of Pennsylvania. The crowdsourced forecasts are published online and its track record continuously monitored. It came to international renown following a forecasting tournament conducted by the US Intelligence Advanced Research Projects Activity (IARPA).

In this tournament, five teams competed to generate forecasts on the questions of interest to intelligence analysts. They submitted forecasts daily from September 2011 to June 2015, gathering over one million separate future projections. The Good Judgment Project beat the official control group by 60% in the first year and by 78% in the second. It beat all other teams by convincing margins, including professional intelligence analysts with access to classified data.

The remarkable aspect of the Good Judgment Project is that it has contributed so much to our scientific understanding of what makes a 'superforecaster', as explained in the 2015 book *Superforecasting*. Some of the characteristics of superforecasters are as follows:

- Good numeracy/intelligence and general knowledge;
- Understanding of probability and inclined to probabilistic thinking (as opposed to belief in fate, determinism);
- Open-minded, willing to consider evidence that goes against their beliefs and willing to change their minds;
- Curious and interested in puzzles or mental challenges;
- Self-critical and committed to improvement, accepting feedback;
- Aware of cognitive and emotional biases.

Another crucial insight of the Good Judgment Project was that teams of superforecasters are more accurate than individuals, by a factor of 23%. This was achieved by actively working against the risk of groupthink and creating a culture where people were encouraged to respectfully disagree. The best teams had good cognitive diversity and were also good at sharing information.

Further Reading

Schoemaker, P. J., & Tetlock, P. E. (2016). Superforecasting: How to upgrade your company's judgment. *Harvard Business Review, 94*, 72–78.

Tetlock, P. E., & Gardner, D. (2016). *Superforecasting: The art and science of prediction*. Random House.

In her excellent book 'Uncharted', Margaret Heffernan explains the benefits of this methodology for illuminating the contingencies and contradictions of the real world, for confronting complexity and the need for adaptation and shifting to a long-term focus.[12] It's unlikely that even one of the scenarios will play out in the future exactly as predicted, but that is not really the point of scenario analysis. Scenario analysis helps those involved to develop a capacity for imagining future possibilities and appropriate responses. Practising these skills makes it easier to respond to shocks when they actually occur. A typical result of scenario analysis is that leaders will be more inclined to build in the operational and financial flexibility that makes the organisation resilient to a range of possible future states (see Section 13.3).

Designing appropriate scenarios is the key to success. According to the literature,[13] some principles to consider are as follows: internal consistency, plausibility, relevance to the risks/issues facing the organisation and challenging. Availability bias means that many organisations will be too timid in imagining a future world very different from the present. There are numerous government resources that can be used to assist with scenario design. The Intergovernmental Panel on Climate Change, for example, publishes climate scenarios.

'Wargaming' – or management simulation – can be used to help strategists tease out the implications of specific scenarios and formulate responses. The participants role-play a dynamic situation, often split into opposing teams. The simulation can last a full day or more, with multiple decision rounds, followed by debriefings to capture learning.[14]

One of the advantages of this method is the ability to identify key risks associated with the scenario and suitable responses. The simulation helps managers to 'experience' the risk, making it more salient and overcoming the apathy, overconfidence, confirmation and inertia biases that too often prevail. Management simulation helps the participants discover weaknesses in their strategies, test strategic alternatives and prepare for a future that is very different from the present.

13.3 Treating strategic risk: flexibility and preparedness

Strategic risks often involve major political, economic, social, technological, legal and environmental forces. Think of some of the events and trends of the last 10 years: the Arab spring, populist politics leading to Brexit and the election of Donald Trump, online commerce, social media, falling interest rates, the sharing economy, online streaming, cloud computing, legalisation of same-sex marriage in many western countries, the #MeToo movement, the Black Lives Matter movement, numerous catastrophic weather events and growing awareness of climate risk, the rise of Environmental Social and Governance (ESG) investing and, most recently, the COVID-19 global pandemic. Few of these events and trends could have been accurately predicted, and to the extent they were predictable, their implications were not fully appreciated in advance.

From this flows an important lesson: that preparedness and adaptability are of the utmost importance for strategic risk management. Strategic flexibility refers to the ability of an organisation to respond to change in the environment and also to act on opportunities in a timely manner. In a review of the literature on strategic flexibility, Brozovic[15] identifies the following enablers: market orientation, maintaining strategic options, having flexible and slack resources, access to technology, capability in strategic planning and contingency planning.

Learnings from the COVID-19 pandemic have highlighted the importance of 'just-in-case' thinking as opposed to 'just-in-time' thinking. The latter focuses on efficiency and removing any slack resources – an approach that makes organisations and their supply chains vulnerable to unexpected strategic shocks. In contrast, 'just-in-case' thinking intentionally builds in slack and retains strategic options (see Section 9.3). One example would be to maintain a wide network of possible suppliers that can be called upon in need, despite the costs of establishing and maintaining these relationships. It invests in 'insurance strategies', in the broad sense, that may create short-term cost but will produce substantial benefit in certain future scenarios.

Not just operational flexibility but also financial flexibility should be considered (Section 9.4). Having healthy levels of equity capital and liquid assets, diverse sources of debt capital, undrawn but committed debt facilities, all provide strategic flexibility to respond to unexpected strategic threats and proactively exploit new opportunities.

13.4 Monitoring and reviewing strategic risk

Monitoring and review, while essential for all risks, have particular importance for strategic risk. Broadly speaking, there are two aspects to this. First, leaders must regularly review whether past strategy choices remain valid. New information materialises over time, so the organisation should identify a set of signals to determine which scenario(s) are emerging as the most likely. The second aspect is more operational. Leaders must regularly review whether strategic choices are being executed effectively. McConnell[16] provides excellent advice for managing strategic execution risks using, for example, strategic key risk indicators.

Notes

1 Godfrey, P. C., Lauria, E., Bugalla, J., & Narvaez, K. (2020). *Strategic risk management: New tools for competitive advantage in an uncertain age.* Berrett-Koehler Publishers, Chapter 1.
2 G20/OECD. (2018). *The G20/OECD principles of corporate governance.* Available at www. oecd.org/corporate/principles-corporate-governance/#:~:text=%E2%80%8CThe%20 G20%2FOECD%20Principles%20of,sustainable%20growth%20and%20financial%20 stability
3 McConnell, P. (2016). *National Australia Bank 30 years of strategy failure.* Available at https:// theconversation.com/national-australia-bank-30-years-of-strategy-failure-55159
4 McConnell, P. J. (2016). Strategic risk management: The failure of HBOS and its regulators. *Journal of Risk Management in Financial Institutions, 9*(2), 147–162.

5 Voigt, K. I., Buliga, O., & Michl, K. (2017). Entertainment on demand: The case of netflix. In *Business model pioneers: Management for professionals*. Springer, Cham. https://doi.org/10.1007/978-3-319-38845-8_11

6 McConnell, P. (2013). Strategic risk: The beanstalk syndrome. *Journal of Risk Management in Financial Institutions, 6*(3), 229–252.

7 This acronym has evolved over time but the original concept is due to Francis Aguilar in his 1967 book *Scanning the business environment* published by Macmillan. For more detail see Godfrey, P. C., Lauria, E., Bugalla, J., & Narvaez, K. (2020). *Strategic risk management: New tools for competitive advantage in an uncertain age*. Berrett-Koehler Publishers, Chapter 2.

8 Amer, M., Daim, T. U., & Jetter, A. (2013). A review of scenario planning. *Futures, 46*, 23–40.

9 By contrast examples of high validity domains are: predicting the times of day when traffic will be busy, predicting the weather over a one-day horizon, predicting the time of sunset on a particular day in a particular location. These are all domains where good models have been developed over time and can be improved as new information comes to light.

10 Tetlock, P. E. (2017). *Expert political judgment: How good is it? How can we know?* (New ed.). Princeton University Press.

11 For information about the Good Judgment Project, see www.goodjudgment.com

12 Heffernan, M. (2020). *Uncharted: How to map the future together*. Simon & Schuster, Chapter 5.

13 Amer, M., Daim, T. U., & Jetter, A. (2013). A review of scenario planning. *Futures, 46*, 23–40.

14 Godfrey, P. C., Lauria, E., Bugalla, J., & Narvaez, K. (2020). *Strategic risk management: new tools for competitive advantage in an uncertain age*. Berrett-Koehler Publishers, Chapter 6.

15 Brozovic, D. (2018). Strategic flexibility: A review of the literature. *International Journal of Management Reviews, 20*(1), 3–31.

16 McConnell, P. (2016). *Strategic risk management*. Risk Books, Chapter 15.

Further reading and resources

Godfrey, P. C., Lauria, E., Bugalla, J., & Narvaez, K. (2020). *Strategic risk management: New tools for competitive advantage in an uncertain age*. Berrett-Koehler Publishers.

Heffernan, M. (2020). *Uncharted: How to map the future together*. Simon & Schuster.

McConnell, P. (2016). *Strategic risk management*. London: Risk Books.

Ramirez, R., & Wilkinson, A. (2016). *Strategic reframing: The Oxford scenario planning approach*. Oxford University Press.

Schoemaker, P. J. (1995). Scenario planning: A tool for strategic thinking. *Sloan Management Review, 36*(2), 25–50.

Tetlock, P. E., & Gardner, D. (2016). *Superforecasting: The art and science of prediction*. New York: Broadway Books.

14

CLIMATE RISK MANAGEMENT

Climate risk is arguably the ultimate risk governance challenge. Not only are the impacts of climate change likely to be experienced over a very long-time horizon, but the exact path of climate change is ambiguous, along with future responses by government, consumers and investors. For many organisations it is a strategic risk, with the capacity to derail existing strategies and to create new strategic opportunities. But too often the risk is undermanaged, through a combination of myopia, inertia, availability and optimism biases.

> Global warming is precisely the kind of threat humans are awful at dealing with: a problem with enormous consequences over the long term, but little that is sharply visible . . . in the short term. Humans are hard-wired for quick fight-or-flight reactions in the face of an imminent threat, but not highly motivated to act against slow-moving and somewhat abstract problems.
>
> New York Times *(March 21, 2017)*

The problems associated with climate change are both chronic and acute. The gradual increase in the average temperature of the sea and air means, for example, that sea levels are rising and we experience more droughts and heatwaves. We also experience more extreme weather events creating acute problems such as cyclones, severe storms, floods and bushfires. So what does that mean for businesses? Some examples of direct and indirect effects are shown in Tables 14.1 and 14.2.

Hugon and Law[1] conducted a major study examining the impact of increased temperature on thousands of firms based in the United States, from 1970 to 2016. The researchers examined regional temperature variation around the corporate headquarters. They found that for an average-sized firm, an increase in temperature

TABLE 14.1 Direct Effects of Climate Change

Agriculture in Australia – heat and drought	By 2030 the average temperature is expected to increase by between 0.6 and 1.5 degrees Celsius. This will lead to higher intensity and incidence of severe weather and an increase in the number of dry days in southern regions. For agricultural producers, risks will be higher with reduced predictability of seasons, more prevalent and severe pest and disease outbreaks, higher losses from flood and drought and heat stress and changes in the suitability of some production systems.[2] Heat stress can harm the health and productivity of crops, animals and agricultural workers.[3]
Hurricane Maria in Puerto Rico 2017	High winds destroyed an unknown number of structures, including 95% of cell phone towers and the electrical grid. Between 380–500 mm of rain caused rivers to flood, inflicting further damage. One month after the hurricane, less than 8% of roads were open. Five months after, one quarter of the residents of Puerto Rico still did not have electricity. Not surprisingly, many residents fled for the mainland US.[4] The hurricane destroyed around 80% of the island's agricultural crop. The effects on agriculture were long lasting since coffee and banana plantations take years to regrow. One third of the island's hotels and 20% of firms in general were still closed 6 months after the disaster and tourists deserted Puerto Rico as a destination. Even the local fishery suffered on account of damage to the reef.[5]
Kincade fire (northern California) of 2019	In late 2019 the Kincade fire destroyed 374 structures and forced more than 200,000 people to evacuate.[6] Preventative power outages were implemented to limit the spread of fire and these meant that many businesses were forced to close; restaurants and shops lost inventory. The tourism sector was also impacted with many travellers choosing to cancel their travel plans.
Stranded assets	Stranded assets are defined as 'assets that have suffered from unanticipated or premature write-downs, devaluations, or conversion to liabilities'.[7] Climate change will cause some assets to significantly fall in value or become worthless because adaptation is not viable in all cases. An example might be a farm or a ski resort in a region where temperatures are rising and precipitation is reduced, such that operations can no longer continue. Another would be infrastructure in a coastal area that is destroyed by rising sea level. The issue of stranding is particularly acute for fossil fuels. Stranding might occur if technological breakthroughs in the renewables sector make fossil fuels uncompetitive.

TABLE 14.2 Indirect Effects of Climate Change

Impact through customers and the supply chain	Many organisations will experience the impact of climate change indirectly through their customers and their supply chains. Financial institutions fall into this category because they experience losses when the firms they lend to suffer losses and cannot repay their debts or the firms they insure make large insurance claims.
	The Port of Rotterdam is located in the mouth of the Rhine-Meuse Delta on the north sea. Coastal flooding in the area has the potential for massive flow-on effects via supply chains, since the Port of Rotterdam is the largest in Europe and one of Europe's largest industrial and electricity hubs. From here, cargo is sent to roughly 500 million consumers in Europe, while the industrial cluster contains five oil refineries and its power plants power a quarter of the Netherlands.[8]
More stranded assets through policy change	In order to meet temperature targets under the Paris Agreement, significant fossil fuel reserves will have to remain unused, causing a massive write-down in asset values. According to a study published in Nature,[9] this issue applies to around one third of oil reserves, half of gas reserves and more than 80% of known coal reserves. This could come about because of changes in government policy i.e. phase-out of coal-fired power stations, or the introduction of carbon pricing making fossil fuels uncompetitive with renewables.
Cost of capital and insurance premiums	Since the 2015 Paris Agreement, greater susceptibility to climate risk is associated with lower firm leverage, suggesting that firms with greater exposure to climate risk have difficulty accessing debt markets.[10] Such firms also pay a premium for debt capital.[11]
	Equity investors demand compensation for investing in firms with high carbon intensity.[12] This is related to the phenomenal growth in ESG (Environmental, Social, Governance) investing,[13] with many organisations now publicly declaring a commitment to the principles for responsible investment. Sautner et. al. 2020[14] find that institutional ownership is negatively related to climate change exposure, especially in recent years.
Legal costs	Since 2015, climate litigation against major fossil fuel companies has become much more common.[15] Litigants claim, for example, that companies have not adequately assessed the environmental impact of projects or have engaged in greenwashing.
	PG&E, a Californian utility, declared bankruptcy in 2019 due to liabilities arising from its role in causing bushfires. Deadly fires started when trees fell on power lines during dry conditions, and plaintiffs accused PG&E of failing to adequately adapt to the changing conditions.[16]
	Lawsuits result in legal and administrative costs, fines and awards of damages. They can also lead to higher liability insurance premiums, higher cost of capital and lower market value.

of 1°C in that region, relative to the long-run regional average, was associated with a decrease in earnings that year of $1.6 million. Reduced sales, higher operating expenses and higher extraordinary expense items all contributed to the earnings reduction.

Cross-sectional analysis showed that firms vary significantly in their sensitivity to warming, with around one-third benefitting from higher temperature. Health-care firms are an example of organisations in this category whereas utilities are more likely to suffer negative effects from warming. Firms with greater diversification (both product and market) experience substantially reduced impact from warming. Firms that are both large and well-diversified are the most likely to mitigate the impact of warming.

14.1 Potential strategic responses

14.1.1 Accept

Accepting the risk of climate change may be a reasonable strategic response, especially in cases where the expected negative impact is not significant or if the impact is expected to be favourable. As explained earlier, some firms benefit from climate change.

14.1.2 Operational adaptation

Adaptation refers to adjustments that are undertaken both in response to and in expectation of environmental changes. This includes both taking advantage of new opportunities and reducing or avoiding harm. Adaptation could be either preventative (reducing the likelihood of risk events) or mitigating (reducing the impact of risk events).

Linnenluecke et. al (2013)[17] review climate adaptation studies in the field of business. While surprisingly few studies of this type have been conducted, a literature already exists on adaptation to changes in the external environment broadly speaking. According to the 'environmental determinism' school, firms have limited capacity to adapt to a changing external environment and some will be selected out.

According to Busch,[18] successful adapters need to be able to absorb information about climate change as it emerges. They must conduct forward-looking analyses of vulnerabilities and risks from climate change, gathering information from the climate-science community regarding impacts in particular regions. Research in the sugarcane industry[19] has shown that impacts − and therefore adaptation strategies − can vary significantly according to the specific location of operations and can be non-linear.

In addition, successful adapters must demonstrate both short-term operational flexibility and the capability to engage in long-term innovation. The challenge is for firms to strengthen their competitive position and ensure survival in a changing environment. They must consider not only the change in mean conditions but also increased variation leading to more extreme events.

Often adaptation involves incurring short-term costs for longer-term benefit. Examples might include building slack into the supply chain or building firm infrastructure with greater capacity to withstand storms and cyclones. A wine producing company might purchase land in cooler regions or invest in more efficient water management practices. A utility might clear vegetation around power lines or install high-definition cameras in areas at high risk of fires to quickly identify new ignitions. A ski resort might expand its slopes to higher elevations where snowfall is more reliable or might invest in snowmaking equipment. Analysis to consider these adaptations has traditionally been based on net present value (NPV) analysis, whereby future cash flows are discounted at an appropriate risk-adjusted rate to determine whether the investment can be justified. When considering these costs of adaptation, it is important to also weigh up the benefits of adaptation, but these are typically more difficult to predict.

The agricultural sector provides many interesting adaptation case studies, such as the example of macadamia production. Macadamia trees only start to bear fruit after 4–5 years and fully mature after 12–16 years, so switching to cultivars that are more resistant to heat and humidity is expensive.[20] Many growers choose to convert their orchards gradually so that they can continue to earn income from existing trees during the conversion process.

Traditional NPV methods ignore the value of embedded options that are inherent in a long-term conversion process such as in the macadamia case. Embedded options include the option to vary the rate of conversion over time depending on the evolution of macadamia prices, economic conditions and local weather conditions or the option to switch to other land uses. Adopting a contingent-claims (or real options) methodology helps to capture the value in these sequential adaptation decisions, making it more likely that producers will invest in gradual adaptation (see Further Reading).

In some instances there are constraints on operational adaptation because the impact of climate change is too severe. Rivera and Clement[21] find evidence that organisations most severely impacted by climate change are less likely to pursue adaptation strategies. Some ski resorts, for example, may not have sufficient elevation or distance from the equator to be able to successfully adapt. They must therefore consider more radical solutions such as those considered in the following sections: diversification and transition, divestment and managed decline.

14.1.3 Diversification and transition

Diversification can take a variety of forms from adding new markets and new products, to new production processes, suppliers and distribution channels. For example a ski resort could diversify by developing summer recreational activities such as hiking. As demonstrated in the study by Hogan and Law quoted earlier, diversification can help make organisations more robust to climate change.

As existing markets/products/processes/suppliers/distribution channels become less effective, the new ones may fill a gap, allowing the firm to remain viable. Testing a new market/product etc., without abandoning the old, allows companies to explore opportunities in a relatively low-risk manner. What was initially designed as a short-term diversification strategy may evolve, if successful, into a longer-term strategy shift as demonstrated by Denmark's Orsted.[22]

The firm, previously known as Dong Energy, previously operated coal and gas-fired power plants and produced oil. It started to operate wind farms in the early 2000s, initially just as a small part of its business portfolio in the power sector. By 2018, wind accounted for 90% of its gross operating profit. The strategic shift began in earnest in 2013 when the firm began selling fossil fuel assets and using the funds to further invest in wind. The name change in 2016 served to emphasise the metamorphosis from fossil fuels to renewables.

The strategic conversion of Dong Energy to Orsted, starting initially with diversification, is analogous to the conversion of macadamia plantations from old to new cultivars as discussed previously. The crucial idea is that the company exploits the value of embedded options to vary the rate of conversion over time, as conditions evolve and opportunities come along. The value of these embedded options is significant and not always considered by companies considering their strategic options.

While diversification has its merits, it has its problems and requires intensive oversight. One obvious problem is the possibility of empire building, as managers seek expansion for its own sake in order to enhance their own status and remuneration. Shareholders of listed firms will often argue that they can diversify their own portfolios more efficiently and do not necessarily value the efforts of companies to diversify their business portfolios.

The greatest risk of diversification/translation is that the expertise and resources of the firm do not translate well to the new business model, causing it to fail. In the worst case, the new business model experiences problems and distracts managers from the existing business, causing both the new and old parts of the business to suffer. This is where diversification can cause significant loss in shareholder value.

The diversification and transition strategies that are most plausible are those that make use of existing expertise and resources. For example, do the skills of oil and gas extraction transfer easily to renewables? Could the skills of coal-mining transfer to mining lithium, copper and nickel for battery production? Interestingly, a coal-miner does not necessarily have what it takes to exploit lithium resources due to its technical challenges.[23] Unlike a coal or iron ore deposit, the mineral deposits containing lithium and nickel are complex, making both mining and processing much more difficult.

A number of large oil companies are attempting transition strategies, relying on the fact that their engineering, construction, management and energy trading functions can be put to other uses in a green future. If governments decide to back hydrogen as a future low-carbon fuel, then their expertise in managing gas infrastructure may prove useful.[24]

14.1.4 Divestment

A firm with assets likely to become stranded could consider selling those assets. This is a strategy currently being pursued by many fossil-fuel companies, of which BP is a notable example.[25] In 2020 BP sold its Alaskan oilfields for US$5.6 billion. But finding buyers is becoming harder as institutional investors increasingly eschew fossil fuels, and the risks of stranded assets are both better understood and priced in the market.

The valuation of fossil fuel deposits is challenging in its own right.[26] The likelihood and size of potential losses from stranding depends on different scenarios about the future for government policy. They also depend on technical breakthroughs that might change the relative competitiveness of fossil fuels relative to renewable energy sources. Scenario Analysis[27] is therefore essential.

For example, a 2020 study looked at the impact of the phase-out of coal-fired power stations on the German coal industry.[28] The approach taken was to use Monte Carlo simulation to value the assets in multiple regulatory scenarios. In the scenario considered most likely (phase-out by 2038) the value of stranded assets was estimated at €0.4 billion. This value increased by €14.3 billion, however, if the phase-out was brought forward by 8 years.

Having established a suitable valuation for the assets, the goal of divestment is to find a party that values the assets more. This might be because they have greater skill for managing the asset through the decline phase.

One argument is that private capital may be a more suitable home for fossil fuel assets than a listed firm because of the difficulty of communicating and consulting with a large and dispersed group of shareholders.

14.1.5 Managed decline

While the term 'managed decline' sounds unappetising, it may be a sensible strategy in an environment where divestment of assets becomes increasingly difficult. The goal is to extract as much value as possible for stakeholders prior to the asset becoming stranded. In other words, exercise the 'option to close' as efficiently as possible, returning capital to investors over time for other uses. The strategy requires close consultation with stakeholders including shareholders, lenders, employees and the local community.

The strategy also requires a detailed understanding of the assets. The lowest-cost, lowest-emissions resources are least susceptible to the risk of stranding, so it's important to closely analyse the cost structure and emissions intensity of the assets relative to competitive sources of energy. How large is the resource and how long will it take to exhaust? What are the technical challenges in production? Are there benefits in ramping up production in advance of possible changes in government policy? What ethical challenges relating to higher emissions might this raise and how are key stakeholders likely to respond to these ethical concerns?

For assets facing possible stranding, further investments must be carefully scrutinised. An investment to reduce costs or increase production is most easily justified if there is a short pay-back period, reducing the possibility that the investment will be derailed by a change in government policy or new technological developments. If the pay-back period is long, then a high return on capital will be needed to compensate for these risks.

14.1.6 Insurance and other contractual solutions

Insurance can be used to protect against short-term weather events and business disruption linked to climate change. As climate change is long-run and non-diversifiable in nature, it is an imperfect solution and premiums are increasing as the risks grow. It's difficult for insurers to provide a credible guarantee against long-term losses in a climate disaster, as multiple claims might be payable simultaneously.

Long-term contracts with major customers are another possible solution to protect future revenues and provide some certainty. This is worth exploring but it may be difficult to find customers willing to sign long-term contracts given the risk of changes to government policy and technological breakthroughs. And if they are willing to sign, they would probably insist on clauses that allow them to break the contract in certain circumstances, so the risk of stranding may not be resolved.

14.1.7 Financial flexibility

As explained in Chapter 9, organisations can become more resilient to withstand shocks, including climate shocks, by building financial resilience. This means funding assets with a greater proportion of equity capital as opposed to debt capital, ensuring that the firm has adequate liquid assets and access to undrawn, committed debt facilities.

14.2 Governance of climate risk

The principles of climate risk governance are no different to other risks, so the standard governance structures discussed in Chapter 2 apply. The very long time horizons and the ambiguous yet strategic nature of the risk, however, demand particular attention.

14.2.1 Board focus

As climate risk is a strategic risk for many organisations, it should command significant attention at board level. The board must allocate sufficient time and resources for the development and review of strategy, having regard for climate change.

14.2.2 Disclosure

Stakeholders are increasingly demanding more detailed disclosure of climate risks; firms that fail to provide this are penalised by capital markets.[29] This is because investors may assume that lack of disclosure implies lack of preparedness.

A task force on climate-related financial disclosures was established by the Financial Stability Board. Recommendations[30] relate to four main themes of governance, strategy, risk management, metrics and targets. Specifically, an organisation should:

- Disclose the governance systems relating to climate risks and opportunities;
- Disclose the actual/potential impact of climate change on operations, strategy and resilience to different scenarios;
- Disclose how it identifies, assesses and manages climate-related risks;
- Disclose the metrics and targets used to assess and manage climate-related risks and opportunities. For example, it should disclose Scope 1, 2 and 3 greenhouse gas emissions.[31]

14.2.3 Communication

Special attention to communication of risk is needed for risks that are evolving over long horizons. A solution, recommended by Meyer and Kunreuther[32] is to use longer timeframes for communicating the risks. If the risk of flood in a single year is only 2%, the risk of a flood over a twenty-year period rises to 33%.[33] Given the human tendency to downplay low-probability events, the latter figure is far more likely to produce action.

The human tendency is to quickly forget the lessons of past disasters. If we have no recent/salient experience of risk events such as flood, fire or storm we tend to undermanage the risk. A solution to apathy is to use communication strategies with strong emotional hooks e.g. dramatized cases and testimonials, vivid visuals and lively language. A great example of this is the 2020 Netflix documentary 'A Life on Our Planet'. The presenter, Sir David Attenborough, opened with scenes shot in what remains of Chernobyl – still desolate and abandoned following the 1986 nuclear disaster. The bleak images served as a metaphor for the harm being inflicted on the planet through climate changes, making it increasingly uninhabitable.

14.2.4 Incentives

Due to the long-term nature of climate risk, performance measures and reward systems need to be adjusted accordingly. Many so-called long-term incentive plans for senior executives cover only the next 3–5 years. As argued in Chapter 4, there is a case for much longer deferrals of cash bonuses and vesting periods for shares and options if long-term risks are to be managed effectively. Malus/

clawback clauses for risk management lapses, including climate risk, are essential in this context.

Building environmental measures into short-term incentives is another possible approach.[34] Some firms have incorporated environmental indicators into the balanced scorecard systems that determine executive bonuses. This is most likely to succeed if meaningful and objective environmental indicators can be found that cannot easily be manipulated by executives.

14.2.5 Analysis

The challenge of climate risk demands a variety of analytical methods. These include scenario analysis (Section 13.2), Monte Carlo analysis (Section 8.1) and real options analysis (See Further Resources). To determine the appropriate assumptions for these analyses it's important to engage with climate-science experts, customers, suppliers and other business partners. The Delphi process (Section 8.4) may be useful for helping address some common problems such as groupthink.

Notes

1 Hugon, Artur, & Law, Kelvin. (2019, January 24). *Impact of climate change on firm earnings: Evidence from temperature anomalies.* Available at SRN: https://ssrn.com/abstract=3271386

2 Australian Government Department of Agriculture, Water and the Environment. *Adapting to a changing climate.* Available at www.agriculture.gov.au/ag-farm-food/climatechange/australias-farming-future/adapting-to-a-changing-climate#:~:text=Adapting%20wheat%20and%20sorghum%20cropping,crop%20growth%20and%20grain%20yield

3 Beggs, P. J., Zhang, Y., Bambrick, H., Berry, H. L., Linnenluecke, M. K., Trueck, S., . . . Hanigan, I. C. (2019). The 2019 report of the MJA: Lancet countdown on health and climate change: A turbulent year with mixed progress. *Medical Journal of Australia, 211*(11), 490–491.

4 National Oceanic and Atmospheric Administration. *Hurricane Maria's devastation of Puerto Rico.* Available at www.climate.gov/news-features/understanding-climate/hurricane-marias-devastation-puerto-rico

5 The Economist. (2018, April 14). American has let down its Puerto Rican citizens. Available at www.economist.com/briefing/2018/04/14/america-has-let-down-its-puerto-rican-citizens

6 The Economics Review at New York University. (2019, December 6). *The economic cost of Northern California wildfires.* Available at https://theeconreview.com/2019/12/06/the-economic-cost-of-northern-california-wildfires/

7 Caldecott, B., Howarth, N., & McSharry, P. (2013). *Stranded assets in agriculture: Protecting value from environment-related risks.* Available at https://ora.ox.ac.uk/objects/uuid:4496ac03-5132-4a64-aa54-7695bfc7be9d/download_file?safe_filename=2013.08.09_SA_in_Ag.pdf&file_format=application%2Fpdf&type_of_work=Report

8 Enhance Project. *Flood risk management Port of Rotterdam.* Available at http://euaffairs.brussels/enhance/flood-risk-management.php#read

9 McGlade, C., & Ekins, P. (2015). The geographical distribution of fossil fuels unused when limiting global warming to 2 C. *Nature, 517*(7533), 187–190.

10 Ginglinger, E., & Moreau, Q. (2019). Climate risk and capital structure. Université Paris-Dauphine Research Paper (3327185).

11 Delis, M. D., de Greiff, K., & Ongena, S. (2019, April 21). Being stranded with fossil fuel reserves? Climate policy risk and the pricing of bank loans. Climate Policy Risk and the Pricing of Bank Loans. Swiss Finance Institute Research Paper (18–10).
12 Bolton, P., & Kacperczyk, M. (2020). Do investors care about carbon risk? (No. w26968). National Bureau of Economic Research.
13 Daugaard, D. (2020). Emerging new themes in environmental, social and governance investing: A systematic literature review. *Accounting & Finance*, *60*(2), 1501–1530.
14 Sautner, Zacharias, van Lent, Laurence, Vilkov, Grigory, & Zhang, Ruishen. (2020, July 3). Firm-level climate change exposure. European Corporate Governance Institute: Finance Working Paper (No. 686/2020). Available at SSRN: https://ssrn.com/abstract=3642508 or http://dx.doi.org/10.2139/ssrn.3642508
15 Setzer, J., & Byrnes, R. (2020). Global trends in climate change litigation: 2020 snapshot. *Policy Report*. Available at www.lse.ac.uk/GranthamInstitute
16 The Economist. (2019, January 10). California's biggest utility is in deep trouble. Available at www.economist.com/business/2019/01/10/californias-biggest-utility-is-in-deep-trouble
17 Linnenluecke, M. K., Griffiths, A., & Winn, M. I. (2013). Firm and industry adaptation to climate change: A review of climate adaptation studies in the business and management field. *Wiley Interdisciplinary Reviews: Climate Change*, *4*(5), 397–416.
18 Busch, T. (2011). Organizational adaptation to disruptions in the natural environment: The case of climate change. *Scandinavian Journal of Management*, *27*(4), 389–404.
19 Linnenluecke, M. K., Zhou, C., Smith, T., Thompson, N., & Nucifora, N. (2020). The impact of climate change on the Australian sugarcane industry. *Journal of Cleaner Production*, *246*, 118974.
20 West, J. (2018). Optimising adaptation decisions in macadamia production using contingent claim valuation. *Australian Journal of Agricultural and Resource Economics*, *62*(4), 527–547.
21 Rivera, J., & Clement, V. (2019). Business adaptation to climate change: American ski resorts and warmer temperatures. *Business Strategy and the Environment*, *28*(7), 1285–1301.
22 The Economist. (2018, August 31). Orsted has helped boost the prospects of offshore windpower. Available at www.economist.com/business/2019/08/31/orsted-has-helped-boost-the-prospects-of-offshore-windpower
23 AFR article 31/8. *Mining's next super cycle will be low carbon*. Available at www.afr.com/companies/mining/geologists-turned-fundies-hunt-mining-s-next-super-cycle-20200825-p55p7m
24 The FT View. (2020, June 16). *Big oil faces up to a future beyond petroleum* www.ft.com/content/590b1fec-af0d-11ea-a4b6-31f1eedf762e
25 The Economist. (2020, July 18). Oil giants want to own only the cheapest, cleanest hydrocarbons. Available at www.economist.com/business/2020/07/18/oil-giants-want-to-own-only-the-cheapest-cleanest-hydrocarbons
26 Grantham Institute. (2018, January). *What are stranded assets?*. Available at www.lse.ac.uk/granthaminstitute/explainers/what-are-stranded-assets/
27 Task Force on Climate-related Financial Disclosures. (2017, June) *Technical supplement: The use of scenario analysis in disclosure of climate-related risks and opportunities*. Available at www.fsb-tcfd.org/wp-content/uploads/2017/06/FINAL-TCFD-Technical-Supplement-062917.pdf
28 Breitenstein, M., Anke, C. P., Nguyen, D. K., & Walther, T. (2020). *Stranded asset risk and political uncertainty: The impact of the coal phase-out on the German Coal Industry*. Available at SSRN: 3604984.
29 Borghei, Zahra. (2021). Carbon disclosure: A systematic literature review. *Accounting and Finance*, http://dx.doi.org/10.1111/acfi.12757; Düsterhöft, Maximilian, Schiemann, Frank, & Walther, Thomas. (2020, September 14). *Let's talk about risk! The firm value effect of risk disclosure for European energy utilities*. Available at SSRN: https://ssrn.com/abstract=3692372 or http://dx.doi.org/10.2139/ssrn.3692372

30 Task force on Climate-related Financial Disclosures. *Overview*. Available at www.fsb-tcfd. org/wp-content/uploads/2020/03/TCFD_Booklet_FNL_Digital_March-2020.pdf

31 Emissions are broken down into three categories by the Greenhouse Gas Protocol in order to better understand the source. **Scope 1 – All Direct Emissions** from the activities of an organisation or under their control, including fuel combustion on site such as gas boilers, fleet vehicles and air-conditioning leaks. **Scope 2 – Indirect Emissions** from electricity purchased and used by the organisation. **Scope 3 – All Other Indirect Emissions** from activities of the organisation, occurring from sources that they do not own or control.

32 Meyer, R., & Kunreuther, H. (2017). *The ostrich paradox: Why we underprepare for disasters.* Wharton School Press, see p. 81.

33 The probability of at least one flood in 20 years is 1 minus the probability that no flood will occur over the course of 20 years, that is $1 - 0.98^{20} = 0.332$.

34 Monteiro, S., & Ribeiro, V. (2017). The balanced scorecard as a tool for environmental management. *Management of Environmental Quality: An International Journal, 28*(3), 332–349.

Further reading and resources

For more guidance on decision-making for adaption, including discussion of various analytical approaches: Linnenluecke, M. K., & Griffiths, A. (2015). *The climate resilient organization: Adaptation and resilience to climate change and weather extremes.* Edward Elgar Publishing, Chapter 6.

For guidance on the use of scenario analysis: Taskforce on Climate-Related Financial Disclosures. (2017). *Technical supplement: The use of scenario analysis in disclosure of climate-related risks and opportunities.* Available at www.fsb-tcfd.org/wp-content/uploads/2017/06/FINAL-TCFD-Technical-Supplement-062917.pdf

For guidance on climate-related reporting: European Reporting Lab. (2020). *How to improve climate-related reporting.* Available at www.efrag.org/Assets/Download?assetUrl=/sites/webpublishing/SiteAssets/European%20Lab%20PTF-CRR%20%28Main%20Report%29.pdf&AspxAutoDetectCookieSupport=1

For guidance on real options analysis: Shockley, R. (2006). *An applied course in real options valuation: Thomson*; Kodukula, P., & Papudesu, C. (2006). *Project valuation using real options: A practitioner's guide.* J. Ross Publishing.

15
CYBER RISK

Very few organisations can operate effectively these days without digital technology; the ability to interact with customers, suppliers and other stakeholder electronically is vital. While electronic interactions bring enormous benefits, they also bring susceptibility to cyber threats, defined as:

> Any circumstance or event with the potential to adversely impact organizational operations (including mission, functions, image, or reputation), organizational assets, or individuals through an information system via unauthorized access, destruction, disclosure, modification of information, and/or denial of service. Also, the potential for a threat-source to successfully exploit a particular information system vulnerability.
>
> *National Institute of Standards and Technology*[1]

Cyber risk should be considered by many organisations as a strategic risk, as cyber events can threaten the ability to function and survive. Table 15.1 illustrates some well-known recent cyber events.

The 2020 Verizon Data Breach Investigations Report[2] covers 30,000 incidents and 3,950 breaches across 81 countries. Organised criminal groups were behind 55% of breaches and 86% were financially motivated with espionage a much less common motivation. In the Asia Pacific region, however, espionage is relatively more important (39% of cases). While these are the most common motivations, some attacks are conceived by 'hactivists' pursuing political or social agendas or even by bored teenagers and social misfits who enjoy the challenge of breaking in for its own sake.

The most common tactic utilised is 'hacking', that is, gaining entry via stolen or weak password credentials. Denial of service (DOS)[3] attacks remain a significant issue, motivated by activism, revenge or blackmail. Phishing was involved

TABLE 15.1 Recent Cyber Attacks – Causes and Consequences

Bank of Bangladesh, 2016	Fraudulent instructions were issued by security hackers through the SWIFT network to illegally transfer funds from an account belonging to Bangladesh Bank with the Federal Reserve Bank of New York.[4] Perpetrators, suspected to be linked to the government of North Korea, may have been assisted by insiders at Bangladesh Bank. Losses were around US$100 million.
NotPetya attack in 2017	This attack was an act of war – instigated by Russian military intelligence to cripple Ukrainian critical infrastructure. Malware[5] was released through accounting software used by Ukrainian firms. This spread into global firms (such as Maersk, Merck and FedEx) through their Ukrainian subsidiaries. Many businesses had to shut down, and this affected their customers through supply chains, especially those reliant on particular suppliers. The supply chain impact alone is conservatively estimated at US$15 billion.[6]
Wannacry attack in 2017	This hacking attack exploited a Microsoft vulnerability. Many companies had not installed the recommended patch and affected computers had all their data encrypted by criminals who demanded a ransom payment in bitcoin. In a few days, WannaCry encrypted data on at least 350,000 computers in 99 countries and did damage costing in the billions. A number of countries have claimed that the North Korean government was behind the attack.[7]
Equifax, US credit-reporting agency 2017	Hackers gained access to sensitive customer data including social security numbers, which can be used by criminals in identity theft. This affected some 143 million people making it one of the most serious cyber-incidents ever.[8] Hackers accessed the data through a consumer complaint web portal, taking advantage of a well-known vulnerability that should have been patched.[9] The Equifax response was mishandled in a way that further damaged its reputation. For example, customers were not notified until 6 weeks after the firm became aware of the breach. The company estimates that it spent $1.4 billion to address data security issues after the attack and $1.38 billion to resolve consumer claims. The data were never released on the dark web, raising suspicions that the attack was motivated by espionage, rather than criminal activity. In early 2020 the US Justice Department charged 4 members of the Chinese military over the attack.
Travelex, UK foreign exchange company in late 2019	A criminal gang was behind a ransomware attack in late 2019. The gang was able to access sensitive customer data and threatened to release it on the dark web. Reports suggest that Travelex agreed to pay US$2.3 million in bitcoin as ransom for the data. This event contributed to the firm entering administration in 2020.[10]

in 22% of breaches and can be defined as attempts to obtain sensitive information (such as login credentials) through deceptive emails and text messages, falsely claiming to be from a trusted entity or individual. Using so-called social engineering, the attacks are often cleverly devised to prey on biases and vulnerabilities such as busy times of day or the month.

According to Verizon, some 30% of breaches can be blamed on internal rather than external actors. It's important to note, however, that this is mostly due to error rather than malicious intent. Sometimes information is made public because system administrators erroneously configure the data for public access. Malicious insiders could be financially motivated or could be acting out of a sense of grievance.

There is often a perception that smaller businesses are less likely to be attacked but the threat is still real. In small organisations phishing accounts for over 30% of breaches, followed by stolen credentials at 27%.

15.1 Nature of impact

When firms suffer a cyber-event, the impact is felt in a number of ways.[11] First we can consider the direct costs of the incident such as restoring data and damaged systems, theft of money or digital assets, loss of business income, extortion payments and forensic investigations to detect evidence of an attack. Then there are some indirect costs such as fines, costs to notify and service affected customers and public relations costs. Finally, there are the so-called third-party liability costs whereby the organisation is sued, for example by customers. These liabilities could relate to compromised data, unintended propagation of malware and even business interruption.

15.2 Why is cyber risk so challenging?

Cyber risk creates unique challenges for risk governance. An obvious reason for this is the fact that it is linked to new technologies that are often not well understood by boards and senior executives. Jargon terms add to the mystery and fear surrounding this risk. It is also an evolving risk because the nature of the threat is evolving as technology changes, users and criminals alike adapt to those changes and the geopolitical situation changes. Another challenge is the fact that cyber risk touches many parts of the organisation but is often perceived as an 'information technology' (IT) responsibility. Lack of clarity about accountability for cyber risk is therefore common.

The 'human' dimension of cyber risk is arguably the greatest challenge of all. Preventing cyber events relies on the vigilance of many individuals throughout an organisation, but consistent vigilance is difficult to maintain. Employees are expected, for example, to report suspicious emails and avoid clicking on the links contained within them. Behaviour changes are difficult for a range of reasons, especially if employees do not fully understand the risks or the behaviour that is expected of them. Employees working under pressure are particularly vulnerable if cyber-compliance is an obstacle preventing them for carrying out their regular duties.

While some industries, notably financial services, have accumulated considerable experience with cyber-events, other industries have much less experience. For those who have had few attacks, there is the danger of overconfidence and apathy. Organisations that are part of critical infrastructure or with lots of sensitive data may be obvious targets, but in reality no organisation is safe. Many cyber-criminals and hackers are opportunistic, looking for vulnerabilities they can exploit. Unfortunately it's often the case that senior leaders only become engaged with cyber risk after a breach.

Cyber risk will only be well handled when senior leaders are engaged with cyber risk and are adequately prioritising it. One senior executive should have clear accountability for cyber risk as joint accountabilities rarely work effectively. As a strategic risk, cyber risk should feature in board discussions. An excellent way to activate engagement is through a breach simulation exercise. This helps to make cyber risk more salient and highlights possible strategic responses.

Applying the four-factor risk culture model from Chapter 3:

- *Leaders and managers* must demonstrate that cyber risk is a priority, both in their words and deeds. Informal comments are even more important that formal statements documents for public consumption. They must be active and visible in cyber risk-management, for example by supporting effective policies and systems for cyber risk management;
- *Proactive* behavioural norms related to cyber risk should be established through training, modelling and reinforcement. These include reporting and learning from cyber events, identifying emerging cyber threats and responding in a timely fashion, considering cyber risk in all business decisions as a matter of course;
- *Cyber-avoidance* or complacency is not observed. That is, poor cyber behaviour has appropriate consequences, cyber issues are not swept under the carpet.
- Cyber risk management is *valued* as a business enabler and not an impediment to doing business. Cyber-controls have been designed in such a way that cyber security is consistent with other organisational objectives. Cyber experts are respected and enjoy status.

Table 15.2 presents the management process from Chapter 5 to the cyber context.

15.3 Cyber security frameworks

A number of cyber security frameworks are available to help organisations guide cyber security initiatives. Two of the most important are NIST and ISO/IEC as explained here:

National Institute of Standards and Technology (NIST)[12] This US agency has adopted a practical, risk-management approach based around 5 functions:

TABLE 15.2 The Risk Management Process Applied to Cyber Risk

Risk Management Process Stage	Examples and issues for cyber risk
Communication and Consultation	• Cyber, along with other risks, should be adequately disclosed to stakeholders in an understandable manner. Depending on the jurisdiction, many organisations have legal obligations to publicly disclose cyber events and the way in which cyber risk is managed.
	• IT people need training in how to communicate the risk in plain English. Their influencing skills should be developed so that they can attract adequate resources to address cyber risk.
	• Fear is often used as an emotional hook to engage executives. While fear appeals are generally effective for changing behaviour,[13] there is a danger of mishandling this. Failing to also highlight the availability of effective, viable solutions can mean that executives become overwhelmed by fear and fail to act. Many cyber-attacks can be prevented by enacting relatively small changes.
Scope, Context, Criteria	• What are the 'crown jewels' in a cyber-security sense? That is, what are the assets that are critical for achieving organisational objectives but vulnerable to cyber-attack? Examples could be the customer database, systems for controlling crucial business processes or critical intellectual property. This understanding will guide the choice of cyber risk criteria.
	• In collaboration with suppliers, customers and other stakeholders, identify your risk appetite along the key cyber criteria.
	• With the help of experts, understand how the cyber threat landscape is evolving e.g. new actors, new technologies. How are cyber-criminals adapting to changes in the environment? The COVID-19 pandemic, for example, proved to be a bonanza for cyber-criminals who exploited the trend to working from home.
Risk Assessment	• Identify all the possible avenues for cyber-attack including physical devices, software applications and suppliers. Many large firms have been infected by smaller firms in their supply chain with weak cyber-security.
	• Consider joining a data consortium for sharing information with similar organisations about cyber-attacks. An example of this is the ORX (Operational Risk Exchange),[14] which is a consortium used by financial institutions.

(Continued)

TABLE 15.2 (Continued)

Risk Management Process Stage	Examples and issues for cyber risk
	• Quantitative cyber risk modelling, based either on consortium or own historical data, is recommended for organisations considering large expenditures in the area. This analysis helps firms determine whether expenditure can be justified. To build a business case, organisations should consider how the expenditure might reduce expected losses in a typical year and also the potential for extreme losses. Reducing extreme losses is vital for survival with an appropriate capital structure. For more information on this see Section 9.5 and also the FAIR Institute.[15] • One of the challenges of cyber risk is its dynamic nature, meaning that historic losses are not necessarily a guide to the future. To supplement historically based analysis, simulations should also be run to explore possible future scenarios (see Section 13.2). These could be based on emerging threats such as internet-of-things[16] and working from home.
Risk Treatment	• High quality, engaging training programs are needed that employ the principles of adult learning.[17] This is essential to address the human element of cyber risk, boosting compliance with good cyber-hygiene practices. Ideally training should be followed up with simulated phishing attacks so that participants can practice the skills they have learned and receive reinforcement. Those people who perform poorly in the simulation can be offered additional training. • Preventive controls include basics like patching system and software vulnerabilities as soon as they are known or configuring the system to ensure that access to sensitive data is accessible only by approved users. The 'Essential Eight' is a set of useful controls.[18] • Detective controls identify when the systems have been breached. For example, they might detect when encryption has started to occur in a ransomware attack. • Mitigant controls include containment solutions. As soon as a breach is detected, the device or server is isolated to contain the damage and prevent it from becoming widespread. Other mitigants include daily backups – so that data and systems can be quickly restored – and insurance. • Business continuity planning[19] is another important mitigant. A well thought out incident response plan can help reduce the impact of a cyber-event. • Financial flexibility is another mitigant strategy as explained in Section 9.4. Organisations with plentiful equity capital often choose to self-insure, especially in light of the challenges of cyber insurance. This is another reason why quantitative cyber risk modelling is useful to determine how much equity capital is needed as a buffer against cyber risk.

Monitoring and Review

- Internal audit can be used to check on the effectiveness of controls such as the system to grant access to critical data.
- An independent review of cyber risk systems should be carried out periodically against an established cyber risk framework (see discussion of NIST and ISO/IEC frameworks in the following section).
- Penetration testing, also known as ethical hacking, is an authorized simulated cyberattack on a computer system. The aim is to check the security of the system.
- The incident response plan should be tested in simulation.
- Actual cyber-events create a great opportunity for further assessment of cyber resilience and thorough root cause analysis.
- The cyber-resilience of suppliers and third-party partners should also be evaluated relative to contractual obligations.

Recording and Reporting

- Incidents, near-misses and unplanned outages are reported and categorised consistent with established criteria. Records should include information about impacts.
- Other key risk indicators might be: proportion of staff who have completed the cyber-security awareness training, proportion of IT staff with cyber risk certification, click rates in simulated phishing attacks, transaction volume (since attacks are often more successful when people are very busy).

identify, protect, detect, respond and recover. This general use framework works well for even small businesses and was updated in 2018.

ISO/IEC 27000 series[20] This is a series of frameworks set by the International Organisation of Standardisation and the International Electrotechnical Commission. For example, ISO/IEC 27000:2018 provides an overview of information security management systems (ISMS). It also provides terms and definitions commonly used across the family of standards.

15.4 Insurance

Insurance – or risk transfer – is used by a growing number of firms to treat cyber risk. The firms most likely to adopt cyber cover are those holding large volumes of sensitive data or those relying on digitalised technology processes. Policies can be procured for both first-party and third-party losses[21] with firms tending to distinguish between the two types of loss (see discussion under 'Nature of Impact').

But the use of insurance is hampered by the challenge faced by insurers in pricing this risk and obtaining reinsurance, given the rapid evolution of this risk and variation in data protection laws globally.[22] In this risk type, as for many others, information asymmetry is important. That is, the insurer has less information about the quality of controls within the insured organisation than the insured company itself. Another challenge is the fact that cyber risk events can be widespread events affecting multiple organisations simultaneously, meaning that the claims are not independent and the risk is difficult to diversify.

According to Zeller and Scherer,[23] companies choose not to insure for a variety of reasons. These include the perceived high cost, concerns that the policies may fail to deliver due to exclusions and restrictions, lack of understanding of the risks they face due to rapid changes in exposure, lack of policy availability and a preference to self-insure.

Romanosky et. al.[24] provide detailed analysis of cyber policies in the United States, with a number of fascinating insights. First, there is variation in both the types of losses covered and exclusions but particularly the latter. Exclusions relating to extortion or ransom and acts of war were among the most common. Second, some carriers require the insured to complete a security questionnaire to aid understanding of the risk and potentially adjust pricing. The most common questions related to the amount and type of data collected, but there was surprisingly little attention to technical and business infrastructure. Third the pricing of policies appears to be surprisingly simplistic. The most common approach is 'base rate' pricing with the cost of the policy based primarily on company size (either by assets or revenues), with adjustments for limits on policy pay-outs and the size of the excess (also known as the deductible).[25] Adjustments may also apply for history of claims, history of litigation against the insured, whether co-insurance is present and the industry of the insured, although practices vary considerably according to the insurer. Policies for small firms tend to be very simple. Overall this study points to the need to shop around and to study the fine print carefully.

Notes

1 National Institute of Standards and Technology. (2018). *Framework for improving critical infrastructure cybersecurity*, Appendix B. Available at www.nist.gov/cyberframework/framework
2 Verizon. (2020). *Data breach investigations report*. Available at www.verizon.com/about/news/verizon-2020-data-breach-investigations-report
3 A Denial-of-Service (DoS) attack is an attack meant to shut down a machine or network, making it inaccessible to its intended users. DoS attacks accomplish this by flooding the target with traffic or sending it information that triggers a crash.
4 KPMG. (2016). *Bangladesh hack highlights increasing sophistication of attacks*. Available at https://assets.kpmg/content/dam/kpmg/xx/pdf/2016/08/swift-it.pdf
5 Malware is software that is designed to disrupt, damage or gain unauthorized access to a computer system.
6 Crosignani, M., Macchiavelli, M., & Silva, A. F. (2020). Pirates without borders: The propagation of cyberattacks through firms' supply chains. FRB of New York Staff Report (937).
7 Pascariu, C., Barbu, I. D., & Bacivarov, I. C. (2017). Investigative analysis and technical overview of ransomware based attacks: Case study: WannaCry. *International Journal of Information Security and Cybercrime, 6*, 57–35.
8 The Economist. (2017, September 16). Once more into the breach: The big data breach suffered by Equifax has alarming implications. Available at www.economist.com/finance-and-economics/2017/09/16/the-big-data-breach-suffered-by-equifax-has-alarming-implications
9 CSO Online. (2020). *Equifax data breach FAQ*. Available at www.csoonline.com/article/3444488/equifax-data-breach-faq-what-happened-who-was-affected-what-was-the-impact.html
10 IFSEC Global. (2020, August). *Travelex: Company cites cyber attack as key factor in administration announcement*. Available at www.ifsecglobal.com/cyber-security/travelex-hit-by-cyber-attack/
11 Romanosky, S., Ablon, L., Kuehn, A., & Jones, T. (2019). Content analysis of cyber insurance policies: how do carriers price cyber risk? *Journal of Cybersecurity, 5*(1).
12 NIST Framework is available at www.nist.gov/cyberframework/framework
13 Tannenbaum, M. B., Hepler, J., Zimmerman, R. S., Saul, L., Jacobs, S., Wilson, K., & Albarracín, D. (2015). Appealing to fear: A meta-analysis of fear appeal effectiveness and theories. *Psychological Bulletin, 141*(6), 1178.
14 The advantage of data sharing is that it's possible to access a much large pool of data, allowing for more sophisticated quantitative analysis. For information about ORX see https://managingrisktogether.orx.org/about
15 The Factor Analysis of Information Risk (FAIR) Institute provides information risk, cybersecurity and business executives with the standards and best practices to help organisations measure, manage and report on information risk from the business perspective. According to its website, the FAIR™ Institute and its community focus on innovation, education and sharing of best practices to advance the FAIR™ cyber risk framework and the information risk management profession. www.fairinstitute.org/
16 Internet-of-things or IoT refers to the network of physical objects –'things' – that are embedded with sensors, software and other technologies for the purpose of connecting and exchanging data over the Internet. These days even refrigerators can be connected. A case has been reported of a successful hack to a casino through the fishpond in the lobby that was connected to the internet.

17 Galbraith, D. D., & Fouch, S. E. (2007). Principles of adult learning application to safety training. *Professional Safety, 52*(9). See also Manke and Winkler. (2012). *The habits of highly successful security awareness programs: A cross-company comparison.* Available at www.securementem.com/wp-content/uploads/2013/07/Habits_white_paper.pdf

18 Australian Signals Directorate. (2020). *Essential eight maturity model.* Available at www.cyber.gov.au/sites/default/files/2020-06/PROTECT%20-%20Essential%20Eight%20Maturity%20Model%20%28June%202020%29.pdf

19 Alsmadi, I. (2019). Continuity planning and disaster recovery. In *The NICE cyber security framework* (pp. 41–51). Springer, Cham.

20 Information about the ISO 27000 family may be found at www.iso.org/isoiec-27001-information-security.html

21 Romanosky, S., Ablon, L., Kuehn, A., & Jones, T. (2019). Content analysis of cyber insurance policies: How do carriers price cyber risk? *Journal of Cybersecurity, 5*(1), tyz002.

22 Zeller, G., & Scherer, M. A. (2020). *A comprehensive model for cyber risk based on marked point processes and its application to insurance.* Available at SSRN: 3668228.

23 Zeller, G., & Scherer, M. A. (2020). *A comprehensive model for cyber risk based on marked point processes and its application to insurance.* Available at SSRN: 3668228.

24 Romanosky, S., Ablon, L., Kuehn, A., & Jones, T. (2019). Content analysis of cyber insurance policies: How do carriers price cyber risk? *Journal of Cybersecurity, 5*(1), tyz002.

25 The 'excess' or deductible refers to the amount paid by the insured before the insurance kicks in, so a higher excess would tend to reduce the cost of the policy.

Further reading and resources

Australian Signals Directorate. (2020). *Essential eight maturity model.* Available at www.cyber.gov.au/sites/default/files/2020-06/PROTECT%20-%20Essential%20Eight%20Maturity%20Model%20%28June%202020%29.pdf

National Cyber Security Centre. (2019). *Cyber security toolkit for boards.* Available at www.ncsc.gov.uk/collection/board-toolkit

National Institute for Security and Technology. (2018). *Framework for improving critical infrastructure cybersecurity.* https://nvlpubs.nist.gov/nistpubs/CSWP/NIST.CSWP.04162018.pdf

16
COVID-19 PANDEMIC

'There's almost no chance of a recession this year'.

(Barron's Roundtable, January 2020)

'Making predictions is difficult, especially about the future'.

Yogi Berra

The arrival of COVID-19 in early 2020 has prompted much re-evaluation of risk management thinking and practices. Businesses, economies and societies have suffered such an upheaval that it remains doubtful that things can ever or should ever return to their pre-pandemic state.[1] While the pandemic has brought about some changes that are likely to be permanent, such as greater use of video-conferencing to replace business travel, it remains to be seen whether risk governance and attitudes to risk will be permanently transformed. The power of behavioural biases is hard to defy.

Initially labelled a 'black swan', it soon became apparent that a pandemic was always inevitable and had been foreseen by many. A famous TED-talk by Bill Gates in 2015,[2] not long after the Ebola outbreak, had warned of the dangers of infectious pathogens and urged world leaders to prepare. The Global Preparedness Monitoring Board,[3] for example, wrote in September 2019 that:

> There is a very real threat of a rapidly moving, highly lethal pandemic of a respiratory pathogen killing 50 to 80 million people and wiping out nearly 5% of the world's economy. A global pandemic on that scale would be catastrophic, creating widespread havoc, instability and insecurity. The world is not prepared.

The widespread failure to prepare for a pandemic has greatly contributed to its consequences. At the time of writing this in late 2020 recorded cases stood at more than 64 million worldwide with around 1.5 million deaths. The OECD was projecting the global economy to contract in 2020 by 4.2%.

Failure adequately to prepare for a pandemic is a perfect illustration of the phenomena discussed in Chapter 1: availability bias, overconfidence, short-termism, ambiguity. Preparing for a pandemic is costly, and few organisations or countries were willing to incur those costs ahead of an event they hadn't themselves experienced, one with such ambiguous consequences. Predicting the likely consequences of an event such as a pandemic is extraordinarily difficult given the unpredictability of human behaviour and the complexity of inter-relationships in an interconnected world.

While the pandemic itself cannot be considered a true 'black swan', the response by many governments to close borders and lock down communities and economies for extended periods was truly unprecedented. Nothing like it has ever been attempted, except perhaps in time of war. In an interconnected and complex world, even the best analysts could never foresee the cascade of consequences unleashed by a global event such as this, where numerous actors respond in unpredictable ways. Many of the consequences of the pandemic were therefore unforeseen even by those who understood the gravity of the pandemic risk.

16.1 Behaviour changes and dread risk

When considering the impact of an exogenous shock like a pandemic, we need to somehow account for the way that human behaviour shifts in response to a shock. The initial news about a strange virus in western China had surprisingly little impact on behaviour at first; people and governments outside of China continued life as normal. The lack of any early reaction is hard to explain rationally, especially as it confirmed so many previous warnings that a catastrophic pandemic was inevitable and that Chinese wet markets were a possible point of origin. For a time, much of the world was in a state of denial, preferring not to think about the unimaginable.

One possible explanation is psychological inertia, which is related to the status quo bias. Inertia inhibits any action that might be needed, causing us to instead maintain the status quo. It has been observed in other situations, such as the case of New Orleans, which is situated in a hurricane prone area.[4] After Hurricane Ivan hit in 2004, the extent of the risk facing New Orleans and the inadequacy of its infrastructure were laid bare. Clearly there was much to be done to prepare for future hurricane seasons, but this meant making difficult choices and facing into enormous challenges. In the end, nothing at all was done, and when Hurricane Katrina hit in 2005 there was a humanitarian disaster. This illustrates that humans are prone to inertia; we look for easy default options rather than choosing laborious system 2 thinking and costly action.

Another possible explanation lies in the herding bias or the tendency to follow social norms. In uncertain situations we look to others for direction; we use the behaviour of others as a signal to guide us. If others are doing nothing, then the natural tendency is to do nothing oneself. Social norms have been shown to play a big part in risk management behaviour, such as the purchase of flood insurance.[5] A Queensland study of households showed that the decision to purchase insurance was closely linked to the extent to which people believed that others had insurance. Similarly, social norms are important for vaccination behaviour, with the anti-vaccination movement now creating norms that inhibit some parents from vaccinating their children.[6]

But eventually the mood shifted. A society can move rapidly from complacency to panic, and fear is undoubtedly one of the strongest motivators once it takes hold. Horrific images of people struggling to breathe, relying on ventilators, started to dominate the news. Social media disseminated stories of besieged hospitals unable to cope with the demand and temporary morgues being erected to cope with bodies. The exponential climb in case numbers, illustrated by charts of 'the curve', invoked a 'dread risk' response. That is, many people felt overwhelmed by this potentially catastrophic, strange and unfamiliar threat and the fear arguably became disproportionate to the actual risk. The fact that it originated from a foreign country only added to the sense of alarm, producing some unfortunate xenophobia.

Dread risks are particularly prone to social amplification. The more a message is passed on, via social media for example, the more negative it becomes and likely to contain false information that further increases the dread and panic response.[7] In 2020 we observed an 'infodemic': the spread of rumours and misinformation that contributed further damage.[8]

One of the most noticeable early behavioural responses was panic-buying of pantry items and toilet paper, which, together with existing supply-chain disruptions, caused unnecessary shortages. Research into the panic buying phenomenon[9] has found that it is a coping behaviour used by consumers in response to negative emotions and uncertainty. Panic buying helps to relieve anxiety as it brings a sense of control. It is also associated with social distrust, that is, the belief that people are acting in their own individual interests rather than for the greater good. When images of empty shelves and stacked trolleys are being disseminated through social media, this kind of social distrust proliferates. Hoarding behaviour is a logical response due to the fear of missing out on scarce but necessary goods.

As the extent and the degree of danger started to become obvious, further extraordinary behavioural changes ensued. To avoid infection people avoided public gatherings and stayed home, stopped using cash[10] and public transport, started working from home and withdrew their children from school. While these decisions were spontaneous to some extent, organisations and governments also imposed these decisions on their members and citizens. As workplaces, factories and borders closed, stocks ran short, supply chains were disrupted and revenues dried up. Businesses in sectors such as arts/entertainment and travel/ accommodation were devastated.

In combination with social media, financial markets were another mechanism that amplified fear.[11] Fund managers located in COVID-19 hotspots sold more shares than fund managers in areas with fewer infections.[12] The sell-off in the hotspots was triggered by social connections, and since those same shares subsequently rebounded, it appears that the fear and sell-off in the first quarter of 2020 was excessive.

Gyrating share prices (Figures 16.1 and 16.2) added to the uncertainty and created a new dimension to the panic, as investors focused on the economic implications of the pandemic and what that might mean for their personal solvency. The collapse in share prices from the February peak to the 23rd of March was 34%, sharper than anything experienced in the early stages of past bear markets. On the 16 March 2020, the S&P500 index fell by nearly 13%, the third largest one-day price move ever recorded.[13] Bond markets also reflected the panic as investors deserted risky high-yield (below investment grade) bonds. The yield required to attract investors to buy such bonds more than doubled (Figure 16.3), and the market mayhem prompted significant central bank intervention from late March 2020.

Earnings conference calls in the US started mentioning the virus from late January 2020 and by mid-March, it was unusual for an earnings call not to

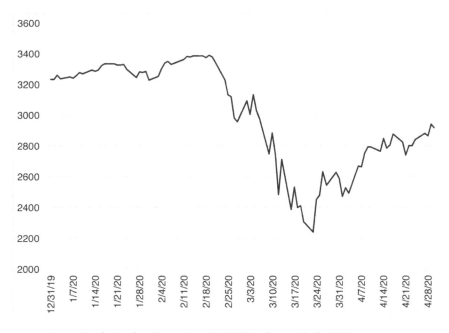

FIGURE 16.1 Stock Market Reaction: S&P500 Index in Early 2020

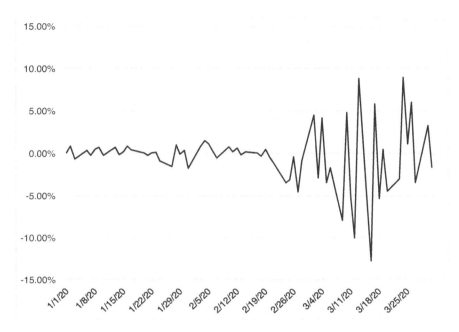

FIGURE 16.2 Daily Returns in S&P500 Index in Early 2020

Source: (Data source for figures: Thomson Reuters Datastream)

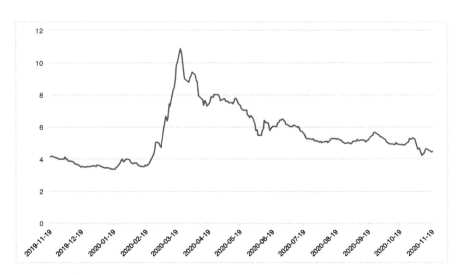

FIGURE 16.3 ICE BofA US High-yield Corporate Bond Spread Over Treasuries, Percentage Points

Source: Data sourced from Federal Reserve Bank of St Louis

include discussion of COVID-19. These developments in the financial markets coincided with and arguably contributed to the panic, evidenced by a surge in internet searches related to the disease.

Central banks responded with new lending programs to support the flow of credit to households and firms in distress. Some established programs that would provide attractive long-term funding to banks, conditional on the banks in turn supporting small and medium-sized enterprises (SMEs). To support liquidity, central banks extended or inaugurated asset purchase programs and some also cut interest rates.[14]

16.2 Financial and operational adaptation

As explained in Chapter 9, there are two broad avenues by which organisations and individuals can address unforeseen events: financial and operational. Financial flexibility refers to the ease with which an organisation or individual can fund a cash flow shortfall; it's about the use of the balance sheet to respond to unforeseen events. Operational flexibility refers to the ability to adapt to new circumstances through changes to behaviour and business practices. Tables 16.1 and 16.2 apply these concepts to the COVID-19 pandemic.

Notice that while the financial strategies described previously help to guarantee the solvency of an organisation, they can be harmful to the providers of capital. As an example, shareholders who rely on dividends to fund their retirement suffer when dividends are cut. Similarly, the operational strategies described later can harm external stakeholders e.g. standing down workers, raising the prices of goods in high demand. Organisations must therefore weigh up the significant consequences of these strategies and their longer-term impact on reputation. On the other hand, if the organisation does not survive, then reputation becomes a moot point.

16.3 Rethinking risk management: resilience and adaptability

The pandemic experience of 2020 has had a profound impact on risk management thinking. COVID-19 has powerfully illustrated the human inability to predict and prepare for shocks, suggesting that a different approach may be needed. If we can't foresee what lies ahead, then the key is resilience, that is, the ability to respond and adapt to new situations. The new paradigm replaces the 'just in time' thinking of the past, with 'just in case' thinking. While efficiency is the key to success in a stable environment, adaptability triumphs in an unpredictable and volatile world.

Operational resilience can be defined as the ability to deliver critical operations through disruption. Similarly, financial resilience can be defined as the ability to fund operations through disruption. Both elements are necessary to ensure that the organisation survives and achieves its objectives. They must be prioritised despite the loss in efficiency usually entailed.

TABLE 16.1 Financial Flexibility and COVID-19

Dimension of Financial Flexibility	Examples
Strong preference for liquid assets (over illiquid assets) since these can be utilised in an emergency.	• Households prefer to conserve cash, with many choosing to save rather than to spend stimulus payments.[15] Households build up cash buffers where they can.[16] • The pandemic has less impact on the stock prices of firms with larger cash holdings.[17] • Early in the crisis there is a 'run' on bank credit lines as firms rush to accumulate cash.[18] This is especially true for BBB and non-investment grade firms. • AAA–A rated firms instead raise cash by issuing bonds in public debt markets. • Central banks introduce new measures to enhance liquidity from the end of March 2020. Asset purchase programs allow the private sector to sell risky assets and instead hold cash.
More equity capital and less debt capital reduces the need for debt servicing (payments of principal and interest) and creates free cash flow.	• Firms with higher leverage (more debt capital) suffer significantly larger losses in their stock prices.[19] • Personal credit growth plunges as consumers avoid additional debt. • Firms rush to the equity capital markets in the first half of 2020 to shore up their balance sheets.[20] This is particularly true for firms suffering significant earnings shocks. The capacity of the market to meet this demand is somewhat unusual for a crisis period.[21]
Reduce or eliminate dividends to conserve precious cash.	• Numerous firms cut dividends and in some countries banks are required to cut dividends for reasons of prudential safety.
Avoid reliance on short-term debt, with the need for frequent refinancing.	• Firms with more short-term debt experience significantly larger losses in their share prices.[22] • Noticeable trend to raising longer-term debt capital (versus short-term debt).[23]
Insurance	• The Wimbledon tennis tournament took out pandemic insurance for 17 years and received a significant pay-out in relation to the 2020 event.[24] Pandemics are, however, in a class of risks that are extremely difficult to insure through private markets. This is because a pandemic event is, by definition, worldwide and claims cannot be diversified easily.[25]

TABLE 16.2 Operational Flexibility and COVID-19

Dimension of Operational Flexibility	Examples/Issues
Inventory and supply chain adaptation.	• Firms with greater exposure to global supply chains suffer more significant falls in stock price during the pandemic.[26] • Households purchase survival necessities e.g. food, medicines, other household basics. US toilet paper purchases rise 845% in mid–March following lockdown announcements in several states.[27] • Closure of factories and borders mean that stocks run low. Organisations are forced to find new local suppliers.[28] • Retailers place purchase limits on essential items to protect vulnerable customers.
Exercise real options in order to reduce costs and conserve cash. This is most effective when operational leverage is high i.e. low proportion of fixed costs relative to variable.	• Households cut discretionary spending, such as eating out, to conserve cash.[29] • Organisations temporarily suspend or cut back operations reducing variable costs. • Companies stand down employees, cut salaries, enforce annual leave. • Organisations defer projects that no longer make sense in the pandemic context.
Exercise real options to adapt and repurpose operations and exploit pandemic opportunities.	• Increase sales through online platforms to replace sales through bricks and mortar outlets. • Where possible, allow employees to work from home, while simultaneously addressing the other risks that this strategy produces.[30] • Adapt sit–down restaurants to takeaway. • Repurpose existing manufacturing to produce ventilators and hand sanitizer. • Expand production of health-related goods such as face-masks, personal protective equipment and ventilators. • Expand production of work-from-home equipment such as monitors, video–conferencing software.
Price changes. Increase prices of goods in high demand, especially if price elasticity of demand is low. Decrease prices of goods in low demand, especially if price elasticity of demand is high.	• As shortages become obvious early in the pandemic, the prices of face-masks, sanitiser and toilet paper sky-rocket. The benefit is that it encourages new suppliers to enter the market and discourages hoarding. But at a certain point it can be seen price-gouging behaviour.

One example of this is the shift to shorter and more flexible supply chains.[31] For many years, the dominant trend in supply chain management was to minimise the cost of individual components. Often this meant relying on a single, offshore supplier for critical materials. This critical reliance made organisations highly vulnerable to disruption either in the production process used by that sole supplier or in the transport system linking the two organisations. Following the pandemic there is now a trend to 'multishoring' or fostering relationships with multiple suppliers, as well as onshoring (preferring local suppliers). Instead of optimising for cost, the new paradigm optimises for resilience and speed.

Some characteristics of resilient organisations:

- Management agility to respond to circumstances as they change;
- Low financial leverage (less reliant on debt capital and more reliant on equity capital);
- Generous buffers of liquid assets;
- Committed credit lines for emergencies;
- Less reliant on short-term debt;
- Use of insurance where cost-effective;
- Business continuity plans developed and tested for a range of severe but plausible disaster scenarios;
- Shorter and more diverse supply chains;
- Good understanding of suppliers and their risk management practices;
- Low operational leverage (proportion of fixed costs relatively low);
- Lots of real options (ability to change the use of assets to another purpose, to change production inputs, production schedules, transport modes, suppliers, distributors);
- Redundancy in production capacity, labour force and inventory;
- Adequate detective controls so that contingency plans can be quickly activated;
- Risk-aware managers and employees to identify new and emerging risks.

The COVID-19 pandemic has opened the eyes of society to other systemic dangers. Not only is it possible for other infectious diseases to emerge, but the earth is becoming increasingly vulnerable to the threat of climate change bringing with it extreme weather events and food/water scarcity in some regions. The threats facing the organisations and peoples of our planet are very real and in the current environment there is much greater willingness to confront those risks.

So has the pandemic shifted the dial on risk governance? Yes it has for now, but based on our knowledge of human biases it would be unrealistic to think that the change will last indefinitely. Availability biases mean that as memories fade, humans will tend to revert to their more typical ways of operating – unduly short-term focused, optimistic and overconfident. It will be difficult to maintain the current focus on resilience because the mechanisms of resilience are costly with benefits only observed in the long-term. But for now, there is a window of opportunity to address some major risk challenges such as climate change. By applying the principles of risk governance outlined in this book, choices now could potentially make a difference for tackling the biggest threats to humans and organisations.

Notes

1 Brammer, S., Branicki, L., & Linnenluecke, M. (2020). COVID-19, societalization and the future of business in society. *Academy of Management Perspectives*, (ja); also Australian Financial Review. (2020, November 4) *Ten ways coronavirus will shape world in the long term*. Available at www.afr.com/policy/economy/ten-ways-coronavirus-crisis-will-shape-world-in-long-term-20201104-p56bc5

2 Bill Gates' TED Talk. (2015). *The next outbreak: We're not ready*. Available at www.ted.com/talks/bill_gates_the_next_outbreak_we_re_not_ready?language=en#t-46888

3 Global Preparedness Monitoring Board. (2019). *The world at risk*. Available at https://apps.who.int/gpmb/assets/annual_report/GPMB_annualreport_2019.pdf

4 Meyer, R., & Kunreuther, H. (2017). *The ostrich paradox: Why we underprepare for disasters*. Wharton School Press, Chapter 5.

5 Lo, A. Y. (2013). The role of social norms in climate adaptation: Mediating risk perception and flood insurance purchase. *Global Environmental Change*, *23*(5), 1249–1257.

6 Okuhara, T., Ishikawa, H., Okada, H., Ueno, H., & Kiuchi, T. (2020). Dual-process theories to counter the anti-vaccination movement. *Preventive Medicine Reports*, *20*, 101205.

7 Jagiello, R. D., & Hills, T. T. (2018). Bad news has wings: Dread risk mediates social amplification in risk communication. *Risk Analysis*, *38*(10), 2193–2207.

8 The Guardian. (2020). Fake news about the COVID 19 can be as dangerous as the virus. Available at www.theguardian.com/commentisfree/2020/mar/14/fake-news-about-covid-19-can-be-as-dangerous-as-the-virus

9 Yuen, K. F., Wang, X., Ma, F., & Li, K. X. (2020). The psychological causes of panic buying following a health crisis. *International Journal of Environmental Research and Public Health*, *17*(10), 3513.

10 Cevik, S. (2020). Dirty money: Does the risk of infectious disease lower demand for cash? *International Finance*. https://doi.org/10.1111/infi.12383

11 Ramelli, Stefano, & Wagner, Alexander F. (2020, March). Feverish stock price reactions to COVID-19. CEPR Discussion Paper No. DP14511. Available at SSRN: https://ssrn.com/abstract=3560319

12 Au, Shiu-Yik, Dong, Ming, & Zhou, Xinyao. (2020, October 27). Does social interaction spread fear among institutional investors? Evidence from COVID-19. Available at SSRN: https://ssrn.com/abstract=3720117 or http://dx.doi.org/10.2139/ssrn.3720117

13 Exceeded only by moves on 19 October 1987 (which is the largest) and 28 October 2929 (the second largest).

14 Bank for International Settlements. (2020). *BIS bulletin no. 21: Central banks' response to Covid-19 in advanced economies*. Available at www.bis.org/publ/bisbull21.pdf

15 Baker, Scott R., Farrokhnia, R., Meyer, Steffen, Pagel, Michaela, & Yannelis. (2020, September 15). Constantine, income, liquidity, and the consumption response to the 2020 economic stimulus payments. University of Chicago, Becker Friedman Institute for Economics Working Paper (No. 2020-55). Available at SSRN: https://ssrn.com/abstract=3587894 or http://dx.doi.org/10.2139/ssrn.3587894

16 Reserve Bank of Australia. (2020, October). *Financial stability review*. Available at www.rba.gov.au/publications/fsr/2020/oct/pdf/financial-stability-review-2020-10.pdf

17 Ramelli, Stefano, & Wagner, Alexander F. (2020, March). Feverish stock price reactions to Covid-19. CEPR Discussion Paper No. DP14511. Available at SSRN: https://ssrn.com/abstract=3560319

18 Acharya, V. V., & Steffen, S. (2020). The risk of being a fallen angel and the corporate dash for cash in the midst of COVID. *CEPR COVID Economics, 10.*

19 Ramelli, Stefano, & Wagner, Alexander F. (2020, March). Feverish stock price reactions to COVID-19. CEPR Discussion Paper No. DP14511. Available at SSRN: https://ssrn.com/abstract=3560319

20 National Australia Bank. (2020). *A big year for equity capital raisings on the ASX.* Available at https://business.nab.com.au/a-big-year-for-equity-capital-raisings-on-the-asx-41548/

21 Hotchkiss, Edith S., Nini, Gregory, & Smith, David Carl. (2020, November 1). *Corporate capital raising during the COVID crisis.* Available at SRN: https://ssrn.com/abstract=3723001

22 Ding, Wenzhi, Levine, Ross Eric, Lin, Chen, & Xie, Wensi. (2020, August 10). Corporate immunity to the COVID-19 pandemic. *Journal of Financial Economics (JFE),* Forthcoming, Available at SSRN: https://ssrn.com/abstract=3578585

23 Hotchkiss, Edith S., Nini, Gregory, & Smith, David Carl. (2020, November 1). *Corporate capital raising during the COVID crisis.* Available at SRN: https://ssrn.com/abstract=3723001

24 Forbes. (2020, April 9). Wimbledon's organizers set for a $141 million payout. Available at www.forbes.com/sites/isabeltogoh/2020/04/09/report-wimbledons-organizers-set-for-a-141-million-payout-after-taking-out-pandemic-insurance/?sh=3b2562d629f6

25 A possible way forward is through the use of catastrophe bonds. See Schwarcz, Steven L., & Bonds, Catastrophe. (2020, October 15). *Pandemics, and risk securitization.* Available at SSRN: https://ssrn.com/abstract=3712534 or http://dx.doi.org/10.2139/ssrn.3712534

26 Ding, Wenzhi, Levine, Ross Eric, Lin, Chen, & Xie, Wensi. (2020, August 10). Corporate immunity to the COVID-19 pandemic. *Journal of Financial Economics (JFE),* Forthcoming. Available at SSRN: https://ssrn.com/abstract=3578585

27 Loxton, M., Truskett, R., Scarf, B., Sindone, L., Baldry, G., & Zhao, Y. (2020). Consumer behaviour during crises: Preliminary research on how coronavirus has manifested consumer panic buying, herd mentality, changing discretionary spending and the role of the media in influencing behaviour. *Journal of Risk and Financial Management, 13*(8), 166.

28 McKinsey. (2020). *Jump-starting resilient and reimagined operations.* Available at www.mckinsey.com/business-functions/operations/our-insights/jump-starting-resilient-and-reimagined-operations#

29 Loxton, M., Truskett, R., Scarf, B., Sindone, L., Baldry, G., & Zhao, Y. (2020). Consumer behaviour during crises: Preliminary research on how coronavirus has manifested consumer panic buying, herd mentality, changing discretionary spending and the role of the media in influencing behaviour. *Journal of Risk and Financial Management, 13*(8), 166.

30 As many people started working from home, using unfamiliar technology such as video conferencing software, cyber risk rose. They were more likely to be experiencing anxiety and more likely to be using less secure devices in the home office. All of these factors meant that home workers were more vulnerable to phishing scams, as criminals also adapted to the new environment. Attackers increased their success rate by using fraudulent health updates and offers of government support. See Australian Financial Review. (2020, May 18). *Recent cyber attacks just the tip of the iceberg for Australia.* Available at www.afr.com/technology/recent-cyber-attacks-just-the-tip-of-the-iceberg-for-australia-20200515-p54thf

31 McKinsey. (2020). *From thinking about the next normal to making it work.* Available at www.mckinsey.com/featured-insights/leadership/from-thinking-about-the-next-normal-to-making-it-work-what-to-stop-start-and-accelerate

Further reading and resources

Basel Committee on Banking Supervision (2020, August). *Consultative Document: Principles for operational resilience.* Available at: https://www.bis.org/bcbs/publ/d509.pdf

McKinsey. (2020, May). *Is your supply chain risk blind: Or risk resilient?* Available at www.mckinsey.com/business-functions/operations/our-insights/is-your-supply-chain-risk-blind-or-risk-resilient

Melnyk, S. A., Closs, D. J., Griffis, S. E., Zobel, C. W., & Macdonald, J. R. (2014). Understanding supply chain resilience. *Supply Chain Management Review, 18*(1), 34–41.

Sheffi, Y. (2015). *The power of resilience: How the best companies manage the unexpected.* MIT Press.

RISK GOVERNANCE GLOSSARY

3 Lines Model   See Three Lines Model.

Accountability   Perceived expectation that one's decisions or actions will be evaluated by a salient audience; rewards/sanctions will be contingent on this evaluation.

Accounting risk
a)   Failure to file accounting statements according to the appropriate accounting standards or with due care and attention, or
b)   The risk that accounting reports will present information in a manner that fails to accurately reflect the true economic situation, resulting in inefficient management decisions.

Activist investor   An individual or group that purchases large numbers of a public company's shares and/or tries to obtain seats on the company's board with the goal of effecting a major change in the company. A company can become a target for activist investors if it is mismanaged, has excessive costs, could be run more profitably as a private company or has another problem that the activist investor believes it can fix to make the company more valuable. Alternatively, activist investors may be motivated by social issues e.g. to effect change that will benefit the environment or other social policies.

Agency risk   The risk that an agent, appointed by the principal, will act out of self-interest rather than in the interests of the principal. Often associated with incentive conflicts and information asymmetry.

Audit committee   The Audit Committee is a sub-committee of the main board, usually comprising independent directors and chaired by an independent director. While the full board is responsible for ensuring the integrity of the financial statements, the Audit Committee brings focused attention on the integrity of the corporation's accounting and financial reporting systems, including the independent audit, ensuring that appropriate systems of control are in place, in particular, systems for financial and operational control and compliance with the law and relevant standards.

Assurance   See Internal Audit

Availability bias   Availability bias refers to the ease with which people can bring to mind a certain adverse event. The more frequently an event occurs, the more likely that salient examples will come to mind. If people have not had any recent, impactful experience of such an occurrence, they are prone to underestimate the risk.

Block holders   A shareholder that owns a significant percentage of company shares. The existence of block holders is often considered beneficial for protecting shareholder rights as the block holder is more likely than a small shareholder to have resources for monitoring the activities of the company. In addition, a block holder is more likely to be able to influence the board and the executive than a small shareholder.

Chief risk officer (CRO)   A CRO is accountable for ensuring that there is robust, independent oversight and challenge of risk-taking activities across the organisation.

Claw-back provisions   In the context of deferred bonus payments, these are mechanisms to return funds to the company in the light of poor performance or fraud. See also malus.

Cognitive diversity   Cognitive diversity refers to differences in thinking styles and perspectives. It is not predicted by factors such as gender or race.

Compliance (function)   Compliance can refer to conformity both with external laws and regulations and internal policies. The compliance function is an organisational function that helps the organisation achieve its compliance objectives by (for example) identifying changing laws and regulations, educating/advising managers.

Compliance risk   Exposure to legal penalties, financial forfeiture and material loss an organisation faces when it fails to act in accordance with industry laws and regulations, internal policies or prescribed best practices.

Conduct risk   The risk of inappropriate, unethical or unlawful behaviour by the management or employees of an organisation. That conduct can be caused by deliberate actions or may be inadvertent, because of inadequacies in an organisation's practices, frameworks or education programs.

Corporate social responsibility (CSR)   Corporate initiatives to assess and take responsibility for the company's effects on the environment and impact on social welfare. The term generally applies to company efforts that go beyond what may be required by regulators or consideration of shareholder interests alone (adapted from Investopedia).

Country risk   Risks arising from cross-border transactions or investment into a specific country. May include devaluation of currency, imposition of currency controls or debt servicing moratoria, regulatory changes, political risk etc.

Credit risk   The possibility of a loss resulting from a borrower's failure to repay a loan or meet contractual obligations. Traditionally, it refers to the **risk** that a lender may not receive the owed principal and interest, which results in an interruption of cash flows and increased costs for collection.

May also refer to loss as a result of a decline in market value stemming from a credit downgrade of an issuer or counterparty or a change in the market's perception of the probability of default.

CRO   See Chief Risk Officer

Cronyism   Unfair partiality shown, especially in political or business appointments, for one's friends (adapted from Macquarie Dictionary).

Diversity   Board/executive diversity is often viewed as the extent to which there are directors or executives of different gender or race. See cognitive diversity.

Dread risk   Dread risks are risks that produce disproportionate fear and induce suboptimal responses. The dread risk response is associated with threats that are unfamiliar, over which the one has little control and in cases where the potential adverse consequence is very severe and images are graphic. Shark and terrorist attacks are examples.

Empire building   The act of attempting to increase the size and scope of an individual or organisation's power and influence. In the corporate world, this is seen when managers or executives are more concerned with expanding their business units, their staffing levels and the dollar value of assets under their control than they are with developing and implementing ways to benefit shareholders. Managers often engage in empire building in order to gain status or to earn more since managers of larger businesses are typically paid more.

Entrenchment   Originally related to digging trenches around oneself for defensive purposes in a military sense. In the context of governance, this refers to strategies used by managers to secure their own jobs and make a change of management difficult. It may, however, be in the best interests of other stakeholders to bring in a new manager. Managers can entrench their position by (for example) choosing investments that make them difficult to replace. Entrenchment can also be achieved by changes to the corporate constitution making a hostile takeover more difficult e.g. poison pill provisions.

Escalation   An increase in the intensity or seriousness of something. In the management context, typically involves getting more senior management to address issues that are not able to be resolved at lower levels of the organisation.

Fiduciary duty   A fiduciary is a person or a company in a legal relationship of trust and confidence e.g. trustee and beneficiary, advisor and client, director and company. Fiduciary duties include: acting in the interests of the beneficiary, not placing oneself in a position where conflicts of interest arise and not profiting from the relationship unless informed consent is given.

Fiduciary risk
   a) The risk of breach of the fiduciary relationship (potentially leading to claims against the fiduciary) or
   b) the risk that a fiduciary relationship is deemed to exist by a (potential) beneficiary when the (potential) fiduciary does not recognise such a relationship.

Free-rider A **free rider** is someone who benefits from resources, goods or services without paying for the full cost of the benefit. (Wikipedia) Where people work in teams, it refers to the fact that some people tend to shirk yet still benefit from the hard work of other team members.

Gaming behaviour Attempting to make one's performance appear better than it is in actuality. For example, exploiting the properties of a performance measurement system to create a misleading impression.

Grey director Director who is neither an executive nor truly independent. See Independent Director.

Groupthink Groupthink occurs when team members rush to consensus too quickly, without properly canvassing all possibilities. It is caused by the human desire to avoid conflict and perhaps also just by laziness.

Herding behaviour The tendency to follow social norms. That is, to base one's own decisions and behaviour on beliefs about what others are doing. It is a common response to uncertainty.

Hostile takeover The acquisition of one company (called the target company) by another (called the acquirer) that is accomplished not by coming to an agreement with the target company's management but by going directly to the company's shareholders or fighting to replace management in order to get the acquisition approved. A hostile takeover can be accomplished through either a tender offer or a proxy fight.

Independent director An independent director is a non-executive director who is not a member of management and who is free of any business or other relationship that could materially interfere with – or could reasonably be perceived to materially interfere with – the independent exercise of their judgement (ASX Corporate Governance Principles).

Inefficient risk bearing Forcing risk-taking by parties who are risk averse and therefore require a high risk premium when risk could instead be taken more efficiently by less risk averse parties. Leads to greater costs overall.

Inertia bias The tendency to do nothing – despite evidence that action is necessary to avoid disastrous outcomes – and instead maintain the status quo.

Internal audit (aka assurance) The internal audit function aims to help protect the assets, reputation and sustainability of the organisation by providing independent assurance to both the board audit and risk committees.

Investor activism See Activist Investor.

ISO31000 An international standard for risk management, updated in 2018.

Key risk indicator (KRI) A measure used by managers to predict changes in the risk environment or that may indicate the riskiness of an activity. For example, a downturn in economic activity might predict a future reduction in sales and hence liquidity pressures.

Legal risk   The risk to a party to a contract that the obligation(s) arising from the contract:

(1) may be legally unenforceable, in whole or in part;
(2) may give rise to an unanticipated liability or
(3) may result in the imposition of a duty or obligation to conduct oneself in a particular manner (in each case different from that anticipated at the time the transaction was entered into).

Liquidity risk   The risk of inability to fund current obligations or of being forced to fund obligations at penalty rates. Inability to fund obligations might arise because access to external sources of funding is inadequate or is withdrawn. Alternatively, asset sales may be ineffective to meet obligations due to depressed prices or delayed timing. See also Market Liquidity Risk.

Malus provisions   Malus provisions apply to benefits that have been awarded but not yet paid. If misconduct emerges during the deferral period, the benefit can be reduced or withdrawn entirely. See also Clawback provisions.

Managerial expropriation   Expropriating or taking company assets for personal use of management.

Managerial self-dealing   A situation in which a manager or fiduciary acts to advance his/her own interests rather than acting in the best interest of stakeholders or of clients. A fiduciary is legally obligated to act in the best interest of his clients. If he breaches this obligation, the wronged party can sue the fiduciary for monetary damages.

Market liquidity risk   Market Liquidity – also known as asset liquidity – refers to the ability *quickly* to convert an asset to cash (or vice versa) with minimal costs of trading including spreads, commission and market impact. Consequently, market liquidity *risk* refers to the potential for an increase in the costs of trading or the inability to transact within the timeframe expected. Market Liquidity risk may arise because a given position is very large relative to typical trading volumes, or because market conditions are unsettled. Market Liquidity risk is usually reflected in a wide bid-ask spread and large price movements in response to any attempt to buy or sell. See Funding Liquidity risk.

Market risk   The risk of movements in the market price of an asset. Usually discussed in reference to liquid or heavily traded assets such as commodity price, interest rate, stock price or exchange rate.

Model risk   The risk that a model will provide information that misleads and results in poor decisions e.g. model may provide an inaccurate assessment of value (relative to market price).

Moral hazard   A situation in which a person has an incentive to take unwarranted risks because others will bear the consequences of negative outcomes.

Myopia bias The tendency to focus on the short-term at the expense of the long-term.

NED or non-executive director A director who is not an executive of the company.

Nepotism Unfair partiality shown, especially in political or business appointments, for one's family members.

Operational risk The risk of direct or indirect loss resulting from inadequate or failed internal processes, people and systems or from external events (Basel Committee on Banking Standards).

This 'catch-all' category captures many sub-categories such as cyber, fraud, legal, natural disasters, pandemic etc.

Opacity Opaque or unclear in meaning.

Outsourcing risk Outsourcing is the contracting out of business processes to a third party, usually to reduce costs. Outsourcing risk is the risk that the third party does not perform these services to expectations or that risks associated with those services are not adequately managed.

Overconfidence Overconfidence can relate to both knowledge and ability. An overconfident person knows less than they think they know and is less able to manage a bad outcome than they think they are. The consequence of misplaced confidence is that individuals do not do enough to prevent or avoid the bad outcomes.

Optimism bias The tendency to believe that one is immune to threats.

Perquisite An incidental benefit, fee or profit over and above salary or wages e.g. business or first class travel paid for by the firm when an executive travels on company business, opportunities to attend sporting/cultural events as part of corporate entertaining.

Political risk The risk that there will be policy shifts either by the incumbent government or by an incoming government that affect the financial viability of an entity e.g. a change in policy regarding mergers between banks.

Poison pill A strategy used by corporations to discourage hostile takeovers and is often used as part of an entrenchment strategy. With a poison pill, the target company attempts to make its stock less attractive to the acquirer. There are two types of poison pills:

1   A 'flip-in' allows existing shareholders (except the acquirer) to buy more shares at a discount.

2   A 'flip-over' allows stockholders to buy the acquirer's shares at a discounted price after the merger (Investopedia).

Price elasticity of demand The percentage change in quantity demanded by consumers following a percentage change in price. Necessities (versus luxuries) tend to have lower price elasticity i.e. people will often still purchase necessities even if the price rises.

Proxy fight Shareholders often have the right to appoint a proxy – or substitute – to vote on their behalf at a meeting. A proxy fight occurs when a group of shareholders join forces and gather enough shareholder proxies to win a corporate vote. This term is used mainly in the context of takeovers. The acquirer will persuade existing shareholders to vote out company management so that the company will be easier to take over (Investopedia).

Regulatory risk   The risk of losses due to changes in regulations or failure to comply with regulations. Losses could arise due to investigations, fines, regulatory sanctions or changes to business operations.

Rent-seeking   Cutting yourself a bigger slice of the cake rather than making the cake bigger. Trying to make more money without producing more for customers or shareholders. Classic examples of rent-seeking, a phrase coined by an economist, Gordon Tullock, include: a protection racket, in which the gang takes a cut from the shopkeeper's profit; a cartel of firms agreeing to raise prices; a union or other group of staff demanding higher wages without offering any increase in productivity; lobbying the government for tax, spending or regulatory policies that benefit the lobbyists at the expense of taxpayers or consumers or some other rivals. Whether legal or illegal, as they do not create any value, rent-seeking activities can impose large costs on an economy (The Economist).

Residual risk   The risk that remains after controls have been used to mitigate the natural or inherent risk.

Restricted shares   Restricted shares are often awarded to executives in order to align the incentives of the executives with external shareholders. They are restricted in the sense that they may not be sold until certain conditions are met. Most commonly, this means that a certain period of time must elapse, usually several years until the shares 'vest' to the executive.

Risk appetite   The degree of risk an organisation is prepared to accept in the pursuit of its strategic objectives and business plan.

Risk   The effect of uncertainty on objectives.

Risk culture   Risk culture, an aspect of the overall culture, refers to the norms of behaviour shared by a group of people in relation to risk management. These norms, linked to regulatory practices as well as underlying values and assumptions, determine the collective ability to identify, understand, openly discuss and act on current and future risk. For risk management to be seen as the true priority of the group, it must prevail over other competing priorities such as short-term profits.

Risk management   Activities that direct and control an organisation in terms of risk, including the identification, analysis, treatment and monitoring of risk.

Risk management framework   According to ISO 31000, a *risk management framework* is a set of foundations and arrangements that support and sustain risk management throughout an organisation. *Foundations* include the risk management policy, objectives, mandate, and commitment. A*rrangements* include the plans, relationships, accountabilities, resources, processes, and activities used to manage risk.

Risk shifting   The transfer of risk to another party. Risk shifting has many connotations, the most common being the tendency of a company or financial institution facing financial distress to take on excessive risk. This high-risk behaviour is generally undertaken with the objective of generating high rewards to equity owners – who face little additional downside risk but may garner significant extra return – and has the effect of shifting risk from shareholders to debt holders. Risk shifting also occurs when a company goes from offering a defined benefit plan to its employees, to a defined contribution plan. In this case, the risk associated with pensions has shifted from the company to its employees (Investopedia).

Shareholder activism   See activist investor.

Shirking   Neglecting responsibilities, usually to an employer or a party to whom you owe certain duties.

Short-termism   Acting to boost short-term results at the expense of long-term results.

Stakeholder   Someone who is affected by, is concerned with etc. an issue or enterprise.

Strategic risk   Strategic risks are risks related to strategy, defined here as the set of resource allocation decisions that help a firm create and sustain a competitive advantage. The risk covers both the choice of strategy and its execution.

Systemic risk   Risk associated with an entire financial system, such as the clearing house system in commodity markets or the international system of commercial banks. Usually refers to the system's ability to handle large quantities of market or credit risk. In particular, the risk that the failure of one or more institutions will trigger a domino effect, causing further and often extensive failures.

Takeover   In business, a **takeover** is the purchase of one company (the *target*) by another (the *acquirer* or *bidder*). Management of the target company may or may not agree with a proposed takeover and so takeovers are often classified as either friendly or hostile. A *friendly takeover* is an acquisition that is approved by the management of the target company. Before a bidder makes an offer for another company, it usually first informs the company's board of directors. In an ideal world, if the board feels that accepting the offer serves the shareholders better than rejecting it, it recommends the offer be accepted by the shareholders. A *hostile takeover* allows a bidder to take over a target company whose management is unwilling to agree to a merger or takeover. A takeover is considered *hostile* if the target company's board rejects the offer and if the bidder continues to pursue it or the bidder makes the offer directly after having announced its firm intention to make an offer.

Tax risk
(1)   The risk that the returns to a transaction will be different from those expected due to a change in taxation law or practice or an error in assessing the relevant tax treatment under constant taxation law and practice.

(2) The risk that a new tax provision will frustrate an otherwise attractive transaction, either directly or by injecting significant tax uncertainty.

Three Lines Model (aka Three Lines of Defence) Under the three lines model, the business unit is the first line of defence, with risk/compliance functions being the second line and internal audit being the third line.

Vesting Process by which authority, benefit or privilege or rights to or interest in an asset or property, passes unconditionally to a particular person or entity (www.businessdictionary.com).

Whistle-blowing A person, usually an employee or member of an organisation, who alerts the public or appropriate authorities to some scandalous practice or evidence of corruption of that organisation.

INDEX

Page numbers in *italics* indicate a figure and page numbers in **bold** indicate a table on the corresponding page.

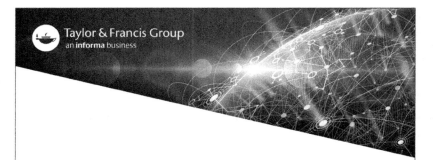